by

Donald Ernest Mather

While the author and publisher have researched extensively to ensure accuracy and completeness of the information within this book, we assume no responsibility for errors, inaccuracies, ommissions, inconsistencies or misunderstandings regarding this material. There is no intent to slight any people or organizations.

Published by Dogwood River Publishing, P. O. Box 5, Buffalo, Kentucky 42716-0005, (502) 325-3053.

ISBN 1-880471-04-3

Dedication

To my mother, Pearl Hornback Mather.

She taught me honesty and the love of the Lord. She showed me her love by keeping my clothes looking good and by cooking my favorite foods. But, I am most grateful to her becuase she made it possible for me to go to school by taking care of some of my farm chores while I was there.

To my loving and compassionate wife, LaHoma Deane.

She has shared my life, given me fine children and watched with me as they have grown. She has made our home and family life exciting. She has had confidence in me when things weren't going well, and been ready to celebrate when things were good. She has allowed me to be a little different from most other people, yet has continued to love me.

Acknowledgments

I would like to thank:

My former pastor, Isaac McDonald, who knew of my dream and offered to help in any way he could.

Cathy Harned for typing the original manuscript and for listening and encouraging me through our many long telephone conversations.

Judy Perry for being the first person to read and review my completed original manuscript. I value her opinion.

Helen Peace Hines, my school days friend and former LaRue County Public Library librarian, for helping produce copies to send to publishers. I value our long friendship, her opinion and her words of encouragement.

Jerome Crouch, Editor, University of Kentucky Press, who gave me some of his valuable time to advise and encourage. I am much indebted.

Diane Wires of Book Masters Publishing Company in Ohio who, through our conversations over the phone and through our letters, gave me the incentive to "press on".

Jeff M. Cohen, Coordinator, New Author Services, Dorrance Publishing Company. Though I have never met Jeff in person, through letters and the telephone, I have learned to trust him and his advice. He helped me see the "light at the end of the tunnel".

My wonderful wife, LaHoma Deane, for her support, ideas and advice. She spent many, many hours typing the original manuscript and listened to me from the beginning. In addition to our happy 32 year marriage, she had helped me unravel God's plan for me and our life together.

My five equally wonderful children and their families who had believed in me from the start.

My mother-in-law, Ruth Nichols who has accompanied, encouraged and shared so much over the years.

Mark Ridenour and Kelli Care from EXPRESSIONS PRINTING AND DUPLICATING for their expert guidance and quality workmanship.

June T. Bennett, Publisher, DOGWOOD RIVER PUBLISHING for her encouragement and skilled editing.

As a result of the help of all of these people I began to realize my book would become a reality.

My thanks to all of you fine people who gave me the push I needed to carry out my own life's motto, "A STEP AT A TIME, BUT ALWAYS FORWARD".

God Bless You,
Donald E. Mather
Author

Comments

Buddy Harpool
Seven Time Winner of the
RAILSPLITTER 10K

After 25 plus years of running, many of my fondest memories are of the Festival Weekend races held throughout Kentucky. At the top of this list would be the *Lincoln Days Railsplitter 10K*. I've been inspired by and have thoroughly enjoyed this race over the years. A major inspiration had been Mr. Don Mather who has been instrumental in the development and progress of this race. One can find what running is all about as well as relive a part of our state's heritage. Don Mather is one of the few people I have met over the years who has shared my enthusiasm for Festival Races which have become milestones to so many runners.

Sarah Bennett-Booker took my manuscript, my notes, my ideas and Ghost wrote RUN KENTUCKY RUN. We met weekly for three and one half months at which time she "drew" from me the humorous, the exciting, the touching and the love for other people which turned my "facts" into the story which became RUN KENTUCKY RUN.

Sarah is a psychologist, educator, newspaper columnist and author of TEENS AND STRAWBERRIES: TEEN SAFETY IN A DANGEROUS WORLD and other books published by Dogwood River Publishing.

Table of Contents

Foreword

Former Governor
Martha Layne Collins

When you finish RUN KENTUCKY RUN, many of you will think, “I ought to do that.” And, you’re right - you should! With this book, Donald Mather has shown us how to leave a special gift for the generations that follow. He put his life story in writing. He was able to tell many special people the joy they had brought to his life - the spirit of a life well-lived.

You can do the same for those you love; but as you write, be sure to give a special thanks to Mr. Mather for showing you how.

Introduction

RUN KENTUCKY RUN is more than the story of my life. It is the story of my life in Kentucky. It includes events, festivals, competitions and the wonderful, colorful, exciting people who have made my life the rich, satisfying process it has become.

I have built my story around competitive running for older runners, the Blue Grass Games and the Senior Olympics because I did not start running until I was fifty years old. Kentucky has many resources for older people if they know where to look for them.

Years have passed since I conceived the idea of writing this book. As I wrote, I realized this book represents the fulfillment of a dream.

Regardless of how skilled we are, writing a book is a challenging and time consuming task. In my case, I did not feel I had the technical skills to produce a finished manuscript.

I have never had an aptitude for English grammar, though my high school English teacher, Helen Hubbard, did her level best to help me.

God gave me other gifts which kept me from feeling too bad about my questionable grammar skills until I faced those empty yellow pads which eventually were filled with the first draft of this book.

Without the help of God, much prayer and the support of my family and many friends, I would have shredded the manuscript and told myself that I couldn't do it. You will find, as you read this book, that I love to win and I love a challenge.

I believe all of us humans are consistent. By this I mean that each of us learns to handle our problems in a certain way and tend to stick with that approach regardless of the situation. If we are content with failure, we seem to allow failure to happen to us. If we love to win, we will find some way to win even if winning requires much hard work and determination.

Of course, there are some people who will cheat to win, but a cheater is not a winner. A cheater is just a loser with an attitude regardless of whether he wins or loses.

If I had known just how much effort reaching the printing stage of this book would require, I might never have started, but God was there helping, giving me the interest and commitment and bringing to me the people I needed to help me along the way.

While I am not aware of God speaking to me directly about writing this book, He sent many people across my path who constantly said the same thing, "You ought to write a book."

Another such inspiration came through my daughter, Diana Lynn, and her son, Nathan. They gave me a book called, THE DREAM NOTHING BOOK. The book contained about 160 perfectly blank pages. The note inside read: "Daddy, thought you might find this useful. You can use it to record your races and the interesting people you met and the places you've been. Just maybe, you can write that book yet! Love, Diana and Nathan."

Their gift seemed to be the final step in the process which nudged me into writing and compiling the data I had collected over the years.

I did my writing propped up on pillows in bed with my yellow pad braced across my knees. I wrote the same way I ran - as fast as I could. Slowly, the pages of the yellow pads began to fill with the stories of dear friends, experiences, happy occasions, fun, family times and the story of a runner who never ran a step before he was fifty years old.

Eventually, the yellow pages of the first draft became the neatly typed white pages of the second draft. My wife, Lahoma Deane, spent many, many hours patiently typing pages of a less than perfect long hand script.

Even after the months, weeks, and hours of hard work, I knew RUN KENTUCKY RUN was not ready for the publisher. I felt I needed someone to craft the manuscript into a more readable form.

I wrote various publishers, printers and editors. I talked with many people who had the necessary technical skills, but they seemed as intimidated as I was by the amount of effort required and the very size of the project.

Another drawback was that some of the people I was contacting were from other states, but my book was about running in Kentucky and a Kentucky runner. Kentucky is a very special place. Kentuckians are very special people.

Capturing the breath, the life and the color of this wonderful place called, Kentucky, would require a skill beyond knowledge. I felt it would be necessary to work with someone who understood the traditions, the humor, the work ethic and the heart of Kentuckians.

To put it simply, I needed a professional writer who loved Kentucky as much as I did if my book were to be the finished work I intended. Again, God came through for me. He knew just what I needed, when I needed it.

In September of 1991, I read a news release in the LaRUE COUNTY HERALD NEWS about LaRue Countian, Sarah Bennett-Booker, whose book, TEENS AND STRAWBERRIES: TEEN SAFETY IN A DANGEROUS WORLD had just been published. She dedicated the book to a long time neighbor and fellow LaRue countian, Gilbert Raikes.

Of course, my interest was captured. I knew Gilbert and while I did not know Sarah well, I had known her parents, Albert and June Bennett, all of my life. Her niece, Robin Wilcox, was my daughter, Diana Lynn's, best friend all through high school.

The news release said the book was printed by EXPRESSIONS PRINTING AND DUPLICATING in Elizabethtown, Kentucky. EXPRESSIONS is owned by Kelli Care and Mark Ridenour, two young, progressive workaholics whom I liked on sight.

While Mark and Kelli could handle all aspects of layout, cover design and the printing, they were not publishers, nor could they provide the expertise to whip my manuscript into shape. They referred me to DOGWOOD RIVER PUBLISHING, the LaRue County based firm which had published Sarah's books.

Sarah eventually received the manuscript. She read it, said she liked it and seemed totally unimpressed with the amount of work the project would require. I found out she had written TEENS AND STRAWBERRIES: TEEN SAFETY IN A DANGEROUS WORLD and the Christian and Secular versions of the companion Leader's Guides, all in excess of two hundred pages each, in less than four and a half months. Now that was a work ethic I could relate to.

I asked Sarah why she had to write three books in such a short period of time. She said, "I'm dyslexic. I do my best work when my back is to the wall. Sometimes, I have to build a wall and back up to it."

I knew God had led me to the people I needed. He had provided me a Kentucky printer, a Kentucky publisher and a Kentucky writer. There are many advantages to working with people who are close enough to keep the communication channels open. There are so many details to consider in writing, publishing and printing a book that accessibility may be the key to producing the best product.

At this point, I felt certain that writing this book was the will and design of God for my life. Even now, I don't know exactly what God has in mind, but I am comfortable and conformed to however He wishes to use this book.

A race, a job, a book or a life on earth must have a purpose. Without God in our lives, it is impossible to find that purpose. While I feel God has used many things in my life, I believe that RUN KENTUCKY RUN is an important part of His plan for me.

If I can encourage one "couch potatoe" with clogged arteries and a two-pack-a-day cigarette habit to get off the couch and run for health and quality of life, all the effort will be well worth it. If my witness as a Christian man who loves God, family, country and Kentucky can help one lonely, hurting person find his way, I would gladly do it all over again.

My mother taught me to pray and showed me through her life how to walk in faith trusting God to lead, guide and protect.

At one time in my life I referred to myself as a "lucky" person. Now that I am past middle age, I know "luck" had nothing to do with what happened in my life. My life has been blessed of the Lord.

The Lord was with me every step of the way. God is the source of the courage, strength and all the good things in my life.

He led me to the woman who would become my wife. He helped us cope with the losses, victories, sorrows and happinesses of our lives together. He helped us as we faced parenthood for the first time and continues to guide us as we try to help the little ones he has entrusted to our care.

In every race that I run, every step that I take and every day I live, God is the source of my confidence, courage and strength.

I have prayed to find what God would have me do. I pray before I undertake anything. I pray for others because I care what happens to other people, even those I don't know.

As you read through the pages of my life, I will try to explain how my faith in God has helped me face dark days and how He has helped me achieve the days full of victory and good times.

What He has done for me, He will do for you. All God asks of us is that we witness for Him wherever we are and in whatever we do. With God, failures become successes and the victories become so much sweeter.

CHAPTER ONE

RUNNING IN MY SUNDAY SHOES

I have always been active. I played basketball in high school and have farmed on a part-time basis, if there is such a thing as farming part-time, most of my adult life.

My career as a mail carrier forced me to walk miles every weekday. The walking, the farming and a few other activities had kept me in good physical shape. I had never given running a second thought except as a means of catching wayward cattle or meeting some other crisis.

If I had thought about running as a hobby or in any other way, I would not have been running around the track at LaRue County High School one late summer evening in my Sunday shoes.

In 1979, running had become a national fad. Books on running were popping up on the newsstands faster than you could read them. Clothes were being designed for running, jogging, walking and for wearing while watching other people run, jog or walk.

Every celebration, contest or community event in Kentucky was beginning to include "foot races" in the schedule of events. LaRue County was no exception.

Each year the second weekend in October is reserved for our county-wide celebration of the birth, life and contributions of our most famous son, Abraham Lincoln. This celebration is called, cleverly, Lincoln Days.

I have a special feeling about the Lincoln Days celebration. Abraham Lincoln and I have, at least, one thing in common - we were both born in a log cabin. Mine had been covered with weather boarding, however.

There is also another connection. My great-great-great grandfather, Richard Mather, may have been instrumental in changing the direction of Abraham Lincoln's life.

I believe God has a plan for each of our lives. If we will listen, or simply take the opportunities which are offered us, God will guide us toward the completion of His plan for our lives.

Great-great-great grandfather, Richard Mather, was the first Mather to move to LaRue County, Kentucky. He was a wealthy man and owned many acres of land including the parcel of land which is now called The Sinking Springs Farm.

The farm takes its name from the spring where the Lincoln family obtained their drinking water. In addition to the fact that the main spring becomes deeper and deeper with each passing year, it emerges then disappears into the ground then re-emerges only to disappear again; thus, the name "Sinking Spring".

Richard Mather sold the farm to Isaac Bush, who resold the property to Tom Lincoln. Mather received no payment from either Bush or Lincoln; therefore, he was finally forced to take Tom Lincoln to court where Mather regained possession of the property.

After leaving Sinking Springs farm, Tom Lincoln moved his family "over the hill" to the Knob Creek farm a few miles away.

It is entirely possible that God used this incident to ensure that young Abraham would not remain a railsplitter all of his life, but would turn his attention to the law and the Presidency.

It is impossible to know what turn history would have taken if young Abraham had not been living in the little cabin on Knob Creek when the long line of slaves Lincoln referred to during his presidency passed by on their way to market in Bardstown or Louisville. History records that Lincoln mentioned the incident and credited it with making an indelible impression on his future thinking.

God's thoughts are not our thoughts, which makes it impossible to know for certain what He had in mind. Lincoln was known as a man of faith and godly ways who felt strongly about finding God's will and purpose in all things.

It is a matter of record that the move to Knob Creek effected the course of this nation. Believing that my grandfather's decisions were in God's plan is a much happier thought than thinking he turned a tiny Abe Lincoln out homeless into the wilderness, regardless of how justified he may have been.

Suppositions aside, the fall of 1979 would be the first time a foot race, called *The Railsplitter Run*, was to be included as part of the Lincoln Days celebration. Our eight year old son, Donnie, had entered the event.

Donnie was a gifted runner. In spite of his age, he had won many first prizes running in the fifty and one hundred yard dashes at the LaRue County fair each year.

Because *The Railsplitter Run* would be more challenging than anything he had faced before, we were preparing for the competition by "working out" every day.

One Sunday evening after church, I took Donnie to the LaRue County High School quarter-mile track for his workout. Donnie took off around the track like the little lightning bolt he was.

My wife, LaHoma Deane, and I are tremendously proud of all five of our children. We have always wanted to be involved in those things which are important to them. We have tried to stand back far enough to allow them to grow and find the plan God has for each of them, yet stay close enough to allow them to feel they have our support, respect and attention.

In order to demonstrate my support and involvement in Donnie's running, I decided to jog along with him as he worked out which is how I happened to be running around that little track on a late summer evening in my Sunday shoes.

The shoes performed better than I did!

I finished two laps gasping for breath with my heart trying to jump out of my chest by way of my mouth. Donnie continued to run steady, speedy laps.

There I stood in the gathering twilight with the scent of honeysuckle making magic of a Sunday evening, a fifty year old man bested by his eight year old son.

Psychologists tell us that men who have one or more older brothers and sisters grow up one of two ways. They either buckle under and feel like failures all of their lives or they develop tremendously competitive approaches to life. I don't know if that is true, but I am the youngest of five children and I do love a challenge.

I love competition. I love to compete and I love watching my children compete. In addition to the love of competition, I hate to lose. In fact, the feeling is so strong, I might avoid people who kept beating me at something after several attempts.

It is obvious that I have a competitive spirit regardless of the reason for it. As I gasped for breath while watching Donnie zip around the track as if he had wings on his feet, I remember thinking, "This is ridiculous. I can do better than this."

I made a quality decision then and there to whip myself into shape. Even as I made that decision, I knew there would be hours of daily training and something even more intimidating - if I were to be my best, I would have to quit smoking!

As with everything else in my life, I took my smoking seriously. I was not a heavy smoker, but I was a happy smoker. I smoked only about three-quarters of a pack of cigarettes each day, but I enjoyed every one of them. I started smoking when I was fourteen.

I attended Magnolia School in Southern LaRue County. My friends and I rode the bus as far as the Tanner store then walked the remaining mile home.

During that short walk, we had plenty of time to fellowship, play and lead each other into various kinds of mischief.

When my friends began smoking, I guess I thought they needed my help. Maybe, I began smoking to keep them from feeling lonely or - maybe not.

At first, we smoked the dried leaves of a weed we called "balsam". We rolled the leaves into shapes approximating cigarettes by hand. Balsam is also known as "fragrant cud weed" and "rabbit tobacco". It smells something like soy sauce and has a surprisingly good flavor.

We graduated to "bought" cigarettes. As World War II was in progress, the only brands available were unfiltered and strong enough to require some dedication on our parts to keep at it.

I didn't want my mother to know I was smoking at first, so I looked for clever hiding places for my cigarettes on the way home from school.

One such hiding place was in an old rabbit box which sat in a neighbor's field I passed through on my way home each evening. I would smoke a cigarette, put the rest of the pack in the rabbit box and retrieve it the next morning.

One night the heavens opened up and rained cats and dogs. The next morning, I discovered my cigarettes swollen and floating in the rabbit box. I found a new hiding place thereafter.

As I stood there that Sunday evening watching my son run with my middle-aged heart thumping in my chest, I knew I had a long road ahead of me.

It took a year to quit smoking, but I kicked the habit. It did not take so long to begin to improve as a runner.

On Tuesday evening of the same week, I went back to the high school track. This time I was determined to do better. By pushing myself, I was able to run a slow, laborious, painful two miles. Two miles, regardless of how slow or painful, was an impressive feat for someone who had never run before. It was enough encouragement to keep me going.

I began to run every night and was soon able to run anywhere from two to five miles during each training session. I have to admit I was feeling good about what I was accomplishing.

I was not running alone. Many of my friend were also running for health, fun and to prepare for competitions.

I frequently passed Bobby Haynes, who instigated and developed The Railsplitter Run, and his wife, Carol, training for the race as I drove to the track for my workout.

Several of us - Marv Dawson, Billy Druen, James Howell, Homer Nicholas, George Trumbo, Rick Linder and I - gathered with a few others early each Sunday morning to train on the Lincoln Days course before time for church.

My son, as many gifted people do, trained haphazardly. Talent had gotten him thus far without the hard work I was having to exert, so he saw little reason to tamper with a good thing. His mother was lukewarm on the idea of his running because he was so young; however, he joined my training sessions from time to time.

His apparent lack of commitment disturbed me a little. I still had not learned that a kid will only do well at what a kid wants to do.

There was tremendous excitement in LaRue County about the upcoming *Railsplitter Run.* People were talking about it at church, in the grocery, just about anywhere people came together. Runners stopped by the Post Office where I worked to talk about the race and ask who was planning to run and what their best times had been.

I felt I needed a little experience in running before attempting *The Railsplitter Run.* It is one thing to fall on your face and quite another to do it in front of everyone you know.

I spent my lunch hours reading the sports sections of other people's home county newspapers to find notices of up-coming racing events. Soon friends began giving me their newspapers or alerting me to advertised events as I delivered their mail.

It was in this manner that I discovered the racing event in Radcliff, Kentucky. Radcliff is a growing city just outside the gates of Fort Knox, Kentucky. Radcliff is highly supportive of its military neighbors and holds an annual celebration called the *Golden Armor Festival* which, in part, honors the armored military units stationed at Fort Knox and in part provides an excuse for people to come together to have fun.

The Golden Armor Festival was to be held in early September. I thought this would be a good place for Donnie and me to sharpen our running skills. We both entered the race.

We arrived in Radcliff to find the lOK run had been shortened to 4.8 miles to avoid flooding along the race route left over from the torrential downpour of the night before. Not knowing what to expect anyway, I didn't know whether to be relieved at the shortening of the race or disappointed.

As with all festivals which include racing events there was noise, excitement and activity everywhere I looked. When I view a scene such as the one we saw in Radcliff that day, I can't help wondering, "Where did all these people come from?"

Donnie and I took our places among the 412 runners who were registered for the event. Because there were so many runners, it was impossible to assess the competition. In fact, it was so crowded, I couldn't see most of my competitors.

Though all runners entered in such events run in a group at the same time, each runner actually competes on two levels; 1) one's own age group, and 2) for the overall winner of the race. This break-down allows many winners and encourages a larger participation in running events in general.

While I was thinking with my head that I had entered this race to gain experience, my heart had a mind of its own. I have never done anything in my life in which I did not intend to do my level best. I kept reminding myself I was here to learn, but my competitive spirit rose up on the inside of me and I realized as I stood there waiting for the race to start that I wanted to win.

When the gun sounded to begin the race, I came out fast.

Though a few young athletes ran ahead of me, I was confident I was making a good showing for my first race. I felt good. My body had responded to the regular workouts. The humidity was high from the rains of the night before, but I was accustomed to being outside in the weather. I don't rememher exactly, but I feel certain I was smiling a little in self-appreciation - until I came to the first hill.

It wasn't a big hill. It certainly wasn't as steep as the hill which stretches from the bank of the Nolin River through the center of Hodgenville all the way to the First Baptist Church on the very top which I walked every day delivering the mail.

At the beginning of the climb, my brain was registering - hill, slight rise in the roll and pitch of the land. After surprisingly few strides, my brain was searching the memory banks for another evaluation -

Mount St. Helen's? Kilimanjaro? Pike's Peak? Before I was half way up, I was panting, wheezing and gasping for air.

I might have become deeply discouraged if I had not been able to hear someone behind me who seemed to be having more difficulty breathing and making more noise doing it than I was. It was a great relief.

In spite of the noise and heavy breathing, I realized the runner behind me was running strongly, continuing to gain on me. Soon, he was even with me and began to pull ahead. As he passed, I saw that my competition was a huge, strong looking dog. In his excitement, he was pulling so hard on his leash that he was actually pulling his owner up the hill at a rapid pace.

I had to laugh at my mistake, but I kept going.

Finally, I was forced to slow down to a walk. For a while, I continued to walk, then run, then walk again. At last, it dawned on me that if I did not try to run so fast, I could keep running more steadily. This lesson proved to help me a great deal in future running events.

Suddenly, the finish line was before me. All at once, I forgot about being tired, winded or that I was not the overall winner. I was elated that I could "finish" in my first competitive race.

As soon as I crossed the finish line I began looking for my son. He was not far behind and soon finished the race.

Shortly after the end of the race, the awards were presented for the various age groups.

Paul Ennis, who was a vital, healthy sixty at the time, was awarded a rocking chair for being the oldest runner to finish the race. Of course, he tried the rocker on the spot drawing approving cheers from the audience.

Our son, Donnie, won as the youngest runner to finish.

He was awarded a skate board and matching helmet, a tank-shaped trophy, coupons for fast food, a tee-shirt and free soft drinks. I don't know how much he enjoyed the running, but he loved the prizes.

After the award ceremony was completed, we runners milled around in order to get acquainted with each other. We had shared an experience and this seemed to make us feel closer.

Runners tend to be highly competitive people. All of us run to win, but before and after the race, we are friends. We care about each other and are willing to help each other. This causes us to develop strong bonds of friendship.

I made some friends that day that would become stronger and stronger as I entered more running events around Kentucky. One of these new friends was Joe Uhlig.

Joe was about 45 years old and reminded me of one of the Three Stooges with his small frame, balding head and the long fringe of hair around the sides and in back. Here the comparison ends.

Joe is a competitor. He was probably the best runner in the 45 to 49 age group that I would ever see.

Joe was retired from the army and was known in racing circles as the "Little Tanker". When Joe entered a race, it was not to win his age group. Joe entered each and every race intending to win the whole event!

The competition had to be very stiff indeed to keep him from placing first or tying for first. Such was the case on this sunny September afternoon. The tough competition from the young soldiers from nearby Fort Knox kept him from winning the *Golden Armor Run* that year, however.

I made it a point to meet Paul Ennis, who is known as the "Jolly Jogger" from Green County. Paul and I would run many races together over the years. We also became very good friends.

As we left the festival, I knew I had accomplished a lot. I had finished in my first race. I had made friends who would continue to be valuable to me for the rest of my life. I had learned I could not compete against a runner being pulled by a big, strong dog. And, I learned an important lesson in competitive racing. I learned to pace myself to enable me to keep going the distance. Finally, I knew I had become "hooked" on running.

Though I had months and months of hard work to do to become what I wanted to be as a runner, the seed was planted and I knew I could do it.

With God's help, I was willing to work as hard as I had to in order to be the best I could be.

CHAPTER TWO

HILLY ROUTES AND CRUNCHY BROWN BISCUITS

The next week was a full one. Donnie and I practiced everyday. I was doing well on the flat track at the high school, but the memory of that hill in the *Golden Armor Run* was still fresh in my mind.

In Kentucky, we call any elevation in the lay of the land a "hill". The rolls in the fields of Western Kentucky are called "hills". The steep little knobs of central Kentucky are called "hills" and the mountains of Eastern Kentucky are called "hills".

It is very difficult for someone who is new to the area to know what we are talking about. If a stranger to Kentucky were to stop along the road and ask for directions to his destination, he might receive a response such as, "It's just over the hill a piece." Kentuckians would know what "over the hill a piece" meant by knowing where they were at the time they asked for directions.

For example, if you are in Hodgenville and ask for directions to a friend's house around the Magnolia area of LaRue county, "over the hill a piece" would mean a gradual rise in the road followed by a gradual descent.

If you were to ask for the same directions in the Roanoke section of LaRue county, "over the hill a piece" could mean some slow going over a steep knob with shaly cliffs and deep gorges.

For a stranger who did not know Kentucky "over the hill a piece" could mean anything from a barely noticeable incline to finishing the trip with a rope and climbing gear.

If you are going to become a committed runner in the Commonwealth of Kentucky, you cannot avoid some hilly race routes. In fact, I can't think of any in which there is not a hill or, at least, a sizable knob. A few of the routes could be considered mountainous.

Since our next race would be the 10K *Cow Days Festival* run in Green County, I knew we should expect a definitely "hilly" race route.

The only consolation I could think of was that the competition would be running up and down the same hills I was running up and down.

In spite of the hills, I was looking forward to running in Green County. In addition to the new friends I would see again and the competition, there was a restaurant, the Kozy Korner, which was then owned by a fine lady who served the best country ham and brown biscuits you can imagine.

LaRue Countians drove over to Greensburg after church on Sunday in droves to eat the "country ham" dinners at the Kozy Korner.

Kentuckians know there is as much art as skill in cooking country ham the way it should be cooked. It has to be taken out of the skillet when it is "just done". Over-cooking country ham makes it hard and tasteless.

Mrs. Edwards could fry country ham just right, but it was the crunchy brown biscuits she served with it that made me smile every time I thought of our coming trip to Green county.

As all ham is not created equal, not all biscuits are created equal. Her biscuits were light, warm brown and gave a satisfying crunch when you bit into them.

My love of crunchy, brown biscuits started early.

The year I started to school, my family and I lived near the farm of Add and Mac Burba. Miss Add, as I called her, made the most mouth watering blackberry jam and these wonderful little brown biscuits which crunched on the outside before your teeth sank into the fluffy light insides.

Mom knew how I loved those biscuits with the blackberry jam, but she also wanted me to grow up with acceptable manners. One day as we walked across the fields to Miss Add's house, Mom said, "Donnie, please, don't ask for any food. That would be rude."

I didn't want to be rude because, even at five years old, I suspected "rude" was a terrible thing to be. But, all the way across the fields I could see visions of brown biscuits with sweet, fresh blackberry jam oozing between the layers. I could see the steam rising in little curls from the tops of those biscuits. I could smell the warm, friendly odor of the fruit. Long before we reached Miss Add's front door I was wondering which was worse, being rude or starving.

I tried. I listened as Mom and Miss Add talked and talked. Finally, I could stand it no longer, "Miss Add," I said hoping Mom would forgive me. "I want a brown biscuit and blackberry jam, but Mom told me not to ask for it."

Soon, I was seated at the kitchen table gobbling down all the brown biscuits and jam I could eat.

It was with the same anticipation that I looked forward to the trip to Green County and the prospects of a meal at the Kozy Korner.

We arrived in Greensburg long before the *Cow Days Run* was to begin. This allowed Donnie time to enjoy the other events and allowed LaHoma Deane and me to talk with friends.

Community festivals are such fun and Cow Days was no exception.

The center of town was full of people. Children ran this way and that holding the strings of colorful balloons blown up by the *Band Booster Club*, munching cotton candy made by the *Rotary Club* or some other men's club. The workers in the community food and craft booths laughed and called back and forth to one another having fun in spite of the hard work.

The warm, friendly smells of meat roasting, burgers frying, bread warming, candy apples being dunked in hot, sticky syrup at the food booths caught the breeze and drew the crowd irresistibly to see what was for sale.

The sound of laughter, carnival rides and Bluegrass music blended to increase the excitement while everywhere you looked, colorful crafts and art work lined the streets.

Donnie was having a wonderful time sampling all the sights and sounds. All while we were walking around the booths and exhibits, I kept a watchful eye out for people who might be running in the fifty and over category in the upcoming race. I wanted to size up the competition before the race began after my experience with the dog in the *Golden Armor Run.*

Green Countian Paul Ennis came over to me and asked if I were running. I assured him that I was. He thanked me for coming and we discussed the race for a while.

I identified four or five runners who appeared to be my age or older. One of them looked familiar. I must have looked familiar to him as well because he came over to me. We recognized each other at about the same time.

He was Wallace Bright, who had grown up in the same community where I was born and grew up. His wife, Imogene, and I rode the same school bus to Magnolia school. We caught up on the years which had passed since we last saw each other.

We happened to see LaHoma Deane's uncle, Charlie Nichols, and his wife Edna. Miss Edna was an amateur historian. Community festivals are excellent sources of the history and legend which makes Kentucky the perfect subject for a lifetime of study and research. She was there pursuing her hobby and enjoying the activities.

I discovered that I was enjoying myself very, very much.

One of the history rich sites in Green County is the old *Green County Courthouse*. The race was to begin in front of the courthouse, follow a prescribed 1OK distance then end at the finish line at the same place in front of the courthouse.

When the race was called, we lined up in the street in front of the courthouse.

As with all runs, there is a period of preparation in which runners check their entry numbers, find their starting positions, begin their stretching and warm up exercises and focus their mental "sets" for the race ahead. The tension at this time is like a current slicing through the very air around you.

If a runner learns to use this short period of time to allow him/herself to become "energized", it can be beneficial and useful in giving the runner an "edge". If a runner allows all of the excitement to make him/her nervous, it can be a disadvantage.

As before every run, I prayed that God would help me to do my best and use me to His glory, then I turned the outcome of the race over to Him. I was ready.

The gun sounded.

We started off going down the hill which leads to the outskirts of Greensburg. It was the last time we were to run "downhill".

It seems reasonable to assume if you run "up" a hill, you must, at some time or other, run "down" that same hill. In competitive running, it appears that you are always running "up" a hill. The best you can hope for is to find a spot of level running, but there seem to be very few incidents of "down" hill running.

The *Cow Days Run* has a good course which makes for a good race, but it has its fair share of hills.

I passed Wally Bright who is ten years older than I am. He called out, "Looking good, Don!" I appreciated his encouragement more than he can know.

I started a little slower for this race and could see the positive effect it was having. I was running well.

We were to run to the Green River, cross the bridge, run a flat course for a while then up a slight incline. When we reached the top, we were to turn around and retrace part of the course. I was doing well until I got back to the Green County High School where I began to "fade" a little. I had to stop and walk a couple of times, but I knew the race was about over.

When I realized I was facing the last hill of the course, I leaned forward and went up it, made the last left turn then "poured it on" going down the main drag.

I guess there were a lot of people from LaRue County in Greensburg that day because I got a big round of applause as I crossed the finish line.

While I was still catching my breath, Donnie came rushing to me. "Look what I found!"

He had bought some heavy rubber balloons with pictures of the Beatles painted on the side. We were to learn later that these balloons are extremely rare and can be sold at a fine profit. I don't think Donnie was motivated to buy the balloons for profit as he still has them fourteen years later.

When the awards were given out I discovered that I had won third place in my age group. I was given a nice trophy.

There is just something about a trophy which makes a ten kilometer run, uphill all the way, in the heat or the cold, seem as if it were worth all the effort.

I have had a long standing love for trophies which began in 1941 when I joined the Barren Run 4-H Club. Edith Routt was president of the club at that time and had won many first prizes for her projects. My project was tobacco.

In 1942 the judging was held in the "Old Court House". I finished in fourth place. In 1943, however, I won first place for tobacco in 4-H and B.F. Brown won for the Future Farmers of America. We were given tickets to see a movie which B.F. and I went to see together, but the best part were the trophies. We were allowed to keep our trophies for one year and our names were engraved on the trophy for all time. It was my first trophy and I was thrilled beyond description.

Was I more delighted with that first trophy than the one I won in the *Cow Days Run*? I doubt it.

As I stood there with my trophy in my hand trying not to look too pleased with myself, I thought, "I like this running business." In fact, I liked it a lot.

Hey, bring on some more races!

CHAPTER THREE

THE DISASTER OF POLYESTER AND LONG AWAITED RACES

The long awaited *Railsplitter Run* was upon us.

Lincoln Days in 1979 was to be held in October for the first time.

As everyone knows, Abraham Lincoln's birthday is February 12. In the beginning, our *Lincoln Days* celebration was held on Lincoln's birthday which seemed a logical choice until you found yourself standing on a street corner in the middle of an erratic Kentucky winter waiting for a parade to pass by you.

It was so cold that Otis and Rita Smith parked a car on the parade route overnight so their children could sit in the car where it was warm to watch the parade the next day.

The LaRue County Historical Society held a pageant in those early years which was performed on the bed of a wagon in the public square. Marilles Terry owned a horse and knew how to ride, so she played the part of the mid-wife who delivered Abraham Lincoln.

She was to ride her horse at a dead run from the banks of the Nolin River up Lincoln Blvd to the Baptist Church at the top of the hill, turn around, come back down the hill then leap onto the bed of the wagon to deliver little Abraham. Of course, she did this wearing a long dress, authentic petticoats and a shawl. (As the youngest member of the Society, she may have been the only one who could safely leap from a horse on a flat run to the bed of a wagon wearing a long dress and petticoats.)

Obviously, this costume left something to be desired in the warmth department. Marilles said she added long underwear and blue jeans under the costume.

It is difficult for me to understand how a woman, even with Marilles' athletic ability, could manage all that riding and leaping wearing such a costume in the cold. To my knowledge, she never missed the wagon, however.

Some LaRue Countians had special outfits they reserved only to wear at Lincoln Days. Elizabeth Vittitow had an old fur coat which had been magnificent in its day. Each year, Elizabeth drug out the old fur and wore it during the festival.

Rita Smith, partially because the coat looked warm and partially because Rita is such a "cut-up" (What Rita and Peggy Hawkins can't think of to get into probably can't be done.) asked Elizabeth, "If you die before I do, will you leave me that coat in your will?"

Of course, Elizabeth said she would. A few years later Elizabeth moved to Louisville and gave Rita the coat. Then the festival was changed to October so Rita never got to wear the coat at *Lincoln Days*.

Lorena Russell made her husband, Adrian, a Confederate Officer's Uniform for his part in the festival. Because it was so cold, she made if of heavy wool. Lorena did a wonderful job on the uniform. It was authentic in every detail. Of course, his friends couldn't just say, "Adrian, you are wearing a great looking uniform." They had to find some way to tease him. Since it was made of wool, they said they couldn't "tell which was more moth-eaten - the uniform or Adrian."

It was all in fun. The great thing about *Lincoln Days*, whether the weather is cold or hot, it has always been great fun.

I have attended nearly every major celebration in the Commonwealth of Kentucky at one time or another. I have run in 60 of Kentucky's 120 counties and participated in many festivals on a yearly basis.

In my opinion, the *Lincoln Days* celebration is probably the best festival in Kentucky.

All native Kentuckians believe their area of the Commonwealth is the best. We are a fiercely loyal bunch of people who, if forced to leave the state for any reason, work diligently to come back home to Kentucky.

Most of us can't imagine why anyone would want to live anywhere else. Many of us believe, if all else fails, we can find us a little hill somewhere, stand on it and just look at Kentucky.

Being able to see the beauty, smell the green trees and grass, feel the breeze and hear the birds chirping is enough to make life seem worth living. Of course, if we happen to have a country ham and brown biscuit sandwich in our backpack, we can also "taste" Kentucky!

I have a strong loyalty to the Lincoln Days celebration because it represents "home" to me. Aside from my personal biases, the Lincoln Days festival has a little something for everyone which is what makes it so special.

We have a railsplitting competition which has drawn railsplitters from all over the nation. In fact, one of our home town boys, Ralph "Mac" Trumbo, has been National Railsplitting champion three times. His brother, George Trumbo, won the National title once as well.

The *National Railsplitting Championship* is held in Lincoln, Illinois. Mac has been competing for nineteen years and has finished first, second or third every year.

The Lincoln Days committee provides a trophy for railsplitting called the *Golden Ax.* The Golden Ax is a "traveling" trophy which means a team of railsplitters must win the trophy three times in a row to be allowed to keep it.

Our local team made up of Mac Trumbo, Tennessee Dishman, The Edlin brothers, the Coffee brothers, George and Homer Trumbo won the award three times in a row. The trophy is now on display at the Lincoln Museum on Lincoln Square in Hodgenville.

Colonel Harlan Sanders was greatly impressed by our LaRue County railsplitters. Each year, he invited them to attend his birthday party. He invited them for the whole week-end as his guests, then they would do a railsplitting demonstration at the party.

Mac is forty-nine years old now and is having back trouble, but he is working hard to get into shape to win the National Title *one more time*! I know just how he feels.

We also offer the Tomahawk Throw, the Frontier Games, the Rolling Pin and Skillet throwing competition for ladies, Lincoln look-a-like contests, Frontier-type cooking contest which is done at the "Creekfront" on the bank of the Nolin River over open fires. A little frontier village is built for the occasion and contestants wear frontier dress. We also offer the Lincoln breakfast, a parade, arts and crafts and Blue Grass music played by expert local musicians.

In 1978, George Trumbo and I won the cross-cut saw competition. We sawed our log in 50 seconds which George says is a "World's Record", but then George has been known to stretch the truth just a little bit.

There are Gospel Singing contests, story telling at the LaRue County Library and at one time there was the Lincoln Ball with live music and dancing. Our local cloggers are as good, or better than any in the state while our Homemakers groups and men's clubs cook some fine food for hungry visitors.

There is a marvelous quilt show, art show and competitions, window decoration judging and many other events.

Joel Ray Sprowles hosts a pig roast and talent contest on the site of the Lincoln Jamboree.

There are contests for children in the Little Abe and Little Sarah costume area and many other competitions and events for little ones.

In short, the Chamber of Commerce, Lincoln Days committee and many other LaRue County residents work themselves to the point of exhaustion to provide entertainment, food and fellowship enough to satisfy any interest or personal taste for three days and two nights in October. The hard work continues all year.

Of course, the area in which I am most interested is the racing competitions. I was looking forward with many others to the 1979, 1OK *Railsplitter Run.*

October weather is unpredictable in Kentucky. The *Railsplitter Run* has been held when it was as hot as 93 degrees and so cold you could hardly breathe.

This first race in 1979 was held on an extremely cold Saturday morning. The temperature had been in the thirties the night before then warmed up as the sun rose. This warming trend had not begun, however, as we prepared for the race at 8:00 AM that Saturday morning.

When the weather is hot, dressing for competitive racing is fairly simple - you just get down to the bare essentials and hope you don't become dehydrated. In the cold weather, it is almost impossible to decide how to dress.

The last thing a competitive runner wants to do is allow him or herself to become overheated. Excessive body heat in combination with too many layers of clothing acts something akin to a sauna cabinet. The heat cannot escape because of the clothing which then increases the heat of the body. Once a runner becomes overheated, the loss of water through sweating can cause serious dehydration resulting in the loss of the race at best or dangerous physical symptoms at the worst.

After two or three miles of competitive running, runners' body temperatures are so high it is impossible to tell how cold the outside air is, anyway.

On the other hand, a competitive runner must never start a race with cold muscles. Forcing cold muscles into rapid activity can cause muscle tears and painful cramps.

As I gained experience in cold weather racing I found that if I would run about a mile to "warm-up" before a race, my body temperature would reach a satisfactory level to help me decide what I needed to wear and what I needed to leave behind.

Long before my warm-up was over, I realized I was wearing too many clothes. At the last minute I took off my sweat suit and gave it to LaHoma.

Though inexperienced at the time, as the first *Railsplitter Run* progressed, I found I had made a wise decision in leaving my heavy clothing with LaHoma, but I was to find I had not made a wise decision in my choice of running shorts.

I chose to wear the orange uniform I had worn when I was coaching a community league men's softball team. The uniform had a jersey top and shorts which were made of a jersey fabric with a polyester blend.

I chose this outfit because it was orange, one of my high school colors which I had not worn since my basketball playing days at Magnolia High school. I had been forced to make some hard choices in order to earn the privilege of wearing the orange and black colors of Magnolia, so I was proud to wear my old school colors even if no one else noticed.

I began school at the two-room Barren Run school near our farm.

I loved Barren Run school and my teachers Eula Wilcox, Edith Hall and Sara Ellen Howard.

I was especially fond of Sara Ellen Howard who was my fifth and sixth grade teacher. She helped me a lot in arithmetic and geography. She tried to help me break my bad habit of laughing too much. I think she whipped me every day of the fifth and sixth grade, but I loved her and still do. We attended the same church for years and I often noticed her looking up to the balcony to see if my family and I were in our usual seats.

In spite of my love for the Barren Run school, I had discovered sports .

The summer before I was to enter the seventh grade, I found out I could attend Magnolia which was a bigger, consolidated school with a high school. Magnolia had a very impressive, for the time, sports program. The thought of attending high school and playing basketball was irresistible.

My cousin Johnny Catlett and I obtained permission from our parents then set off to leave our mark on Magnolia High School (which I think we did).

Another "Tanner" boy who went to Magnolia that year was Gay Hazle.

Gay liked to play marbles. We played a game called "Keeps" which meant, if you won, you got to keep the other player's marbles.

I won a lot of Gay's marbles.

Gay's daddy, Walker Hazle, put up a peach basket on the eave of the chicken house for us. Gay had an old basketball with no air in it. (It was stuffed with something.) It was here that we Tanner boys were first exposed to basketball.

The following summer, Albert Hazle built a basketball court. There were enough of us to form two teams from the neighborhood. This was the roughest, roughhouse basketball I would ever play.

Gay moved to Hodgenville that summer, so Johnny and I returned to Magnolia alone.

This year, Coach McGee formed an eighth grade basketball team called the "midget team". I made the team along with Smitty Gardner, Ken Bell, Junior Hines and Bomar Chaudoin.

There was a midget league and a tournament which included teams from Munfordville, Hodgenville, Upton and Magnolia.

We drew Hodgenville in the tournament and beat them 20 to 11 points. I scored 14 of our 20 points.

The following summer the Hodgenville coach, Ernest Broady and the president of the Lincoln National Bank, Walter Cole, came to our farm and talked to Daddy about sending me to the high school in Hodgenville. I guess that was recruiting.

Daddy allowed me to make up my own mind. It was not an easy decision. Kentuckians take their basketball seriously and the compliment of being "recruited" as an eighth grader was a heady experience. In the end I chose to go back to Magnolia to wear the orange and black. I guess I had fallen in love with Magnolia and the basketball program there.

As the 87 runners who were entered in the first *Railsplitter Run* lined up in front of the Lincoln National Bank on Lincoln Boulevard, our breath sending smoke signals in the cold morning air, I felt very proud to be wearing my old colors once again.

Fred Howard was to start the Railsplitter Run. He had two black powder pistols which he fired into the air to start the race. Firing one of those pistols into the air could have awaken the dead, but with both of them going off simultaneously, I thought the fillings in my teeth had fused.

With this unforgettable beginning, we raced to the Baptist Church at the top of the first hill, the only hill of consequence any where near Hodgenville. By the time we reached the top, many of us were wondering if we had been totally sane when we decided to enter the event. We also found we were no longer concerned with the cold weather.

The course leveled off thereafter and I found all my hard work was beginning to show dividends. I passed some runners who were younger than I before the race was over.

We ran out of town on highway 84, cut across past W.L. Patterson's farm to the Old Sonora/Hodgenville road and started back toward town. It was about this point I noticed there was a cut or burn on the back of each of my legs. Each step I took caused a very unpleasant sensation. I was determined to finish this race so I tried to ignore the puzzling condition.

Just before we reentered the city limits, we had to run up the second steepest hill in the Hodgenville area. By the time I made it to the top of the hill the backs of my legs felt as if they were on fire. I made it, finishing second in my age group and 51st over all.

We had a long wait to find out the winners of the various age groups. I spent some of the time trying to figure out what happened to the backs of my legs.

I discovered that the problem was polyester.

The combination of sweat, salt, friction and synthetic fibers resulted in a very painful burn on my skin. I was to discover later, that the same combination with nylon mesh shirts can cause a painful burn on the chest.

Clothing for running must be chosen very carefully of soft, non-irritating fabrics to avoid distraction and disaster.

Eventually, the data was collected and the awards ceremony began. Jean and Earl Hatcher presented the awards at the ceremony which was disappointingly brief.

There were only two awards given, the over all winner which went to Buddy Harpool of Elizabethtown and the youngest runner to finish.

A little girl received the award as the youngest runner, though she was only one month younger than our son, Donnie, who had finished twelve minutes ahead of her.

I do not believe anyone has a right to complain about anything unless he is willing to become involved and work, at least, as hard as the ones whom he is complaining about. For this reason, I resolved to become involved in the planning of the race and offer my assistance as well as my suggestions.

I did as I planned and in a couple of years was elected to the *Lincoln Days* festival board and served on the race committee. I was able to help instigate a run-walk competition, a one mile run, many additional awards, and a wheelchair run among other things.

The primary reason for my racing activities had ended at the end of the *Railsplitter Run*, but my enthusiasm for running was just beginning.

My next race was to be in November around Thanksgiving, the *Elizabethtown Turkey Trot*. Again, Buddy Harpool of Elizabethtown won the over-all race, but Bruce Hacker of Hodgenville finished an impressive second. I finished 31st over-all and 1st in my age group. It was a first and it made me feel wonderful.

CHAPTER FOUR

A BIG RACE AND A GREAT SORROW

I immediately began to prepare for the *River Bank Run* which would start on the Louisville side of the Ohio river, cross the bridge to Jeffersonville, continue over the flood wall and on to New Albany.

To avoid the polyester disaster of the *Railsplitter Run*, I had purchased standard racing shorts and felt I was as ready as I could be for the competition.

One of the first people we met that crisp December day, was Wally Bright. As soon as LaHoma and I saw him, we knew something was troubling him.

Runners very quickly become like members of your own family. We develop intense friendships in which we care what happens to each other. We seem to rejoice over our friends' successes and happinesses as if they are our own, but we also grieve with each other when one of us hurts with a genuine and shared grief that only true friends can experience.

Wally is a baker by trade and makes the best Hummingbird cake you ever ate. He is friendly and pleasant and makes friends where ever he goes. Wally also chews tobacco and can be seen chewing away as he runs. I don't know if the tobacco helps or hinders, but Wally has a train load of racing trophies to his credit.

On this particular day, Wally looked near tears. We discovered that he had come from the hospital where he had spent the past week at the bedside of his wife, Imogene, who had suffered an aneurysm. His children insisted that he run in the race as they were hoping the running would help him deal with his grief and because Imogene had always been so proud of Wally's skill as a runner.

The *River Bank Run* was my first big race. There were about 1,600 runners participating in the event.

The race began and we were soon on the bridge over the Ohio. I saw Wally on the walkway running all by himself and my heart went out to him. I remember praying a lot for Imogene and him in the next few days, but to no avail. Imogene died a few days later.

As Christian people, I believe we have a right to expect to be privileged to enjoy the years after rearing our children and retiring from our careers with the love of our youth.

God's word says in Isaiah 65:22 (KJV) "... for as the days of a tree are the days of my people, and mine elect shall long enjoy the work of their hands."

While God also says in Isaiah 55:8 (KJV) "For my thoughts are not your thoughts, neither are your ways my ways, saith the Lord.", I believe "Every good gift and every perfect gift is from above, and cometh down from the Father of lights, with whom is no variableness, neither shadow of turning." as we are told in James 1:17 (KJV).

I do not pretend to have all of the answers, but I believe we blame God for a lot of things God doesn't do. Until Jesus comes for His bride, the world will remain an evil place with conditions and situations God did not intend his people to suffer.

While I know our prayers for Imogene did not appear to be answered, I know God heard us and did remain, has remained and will always remain as close to us as our own breath.

When we lose someone as close as a wife or husband, we need to take time to grieve before we can reaffirm God's plan for our lives. At that time and later at Imogene's funeral, I probably had not settled in my own mind just how I felt about God and death and life. As Wally's friend, all I could do was continue to pray for him and believe God would help him through that awful time.

I finished sixth in my age group at the River Bank Run and began to prepare for the Cherokee Road Runners Club's first *Life Begins at Forty Run.*

I think the *Life Begins at Forty Run* is the absolute best run for older runners. The name itself attracts the best of the older runners. We have more in common, more shared experiences and a similar attitude about running and many other things.

I competed in this race over and over through the years to come.

It was here that LaHoma and I met Bill and Joy Peterson of Louisville. Bill was a healthy, competitive sixty year old runner with a room full of trophies and his wife, Joy, also ran competitively. They hosted a party for the runners and their families after the race.

We were not able to attend the party that first year, but did so the following year and subsequent years. The party allows runners to talk, share information and enjoy being together.

There were sixty-five runners entered in this event in 1979. The Courier-Journal sent a photographer to take pictures and do a feature for the paper. When we formed a group for one of the pictures, I was in the third row next to Wally Bright.

Isn't it amazing that when older Americans do something physical it is a news-worthy event?

I think we, older Americans, do ourselves a disservice by not becoming involved in more of what takes place around us. Age is a relative thing at best. If we feel and think "old", we are going to grow old. If we think in terms of using the gifts God gave us with some modifications for the physical decline of advancing years, we can do anything we want as long as life lasts.

This is one of the positive things about competitive running for older people. Most competitions are designed to allow each age group to compete with its own; therefore, each competitor can enjoy the challenge, the excitement and the fellowship with an equal chance to take home an award.

While I am glad that the public is becoming interested in what older Americans are doing and what we want, I look forward to the day when many more of us are determined to stay active and involved. It is the activity and involvement which guarantees the quality of life.

If we think of ourselves in a positive deserving light, we will be much less likely to accept second best or tolerate the attitude of some of the country's "youth culture".

Regardless, when the picture came out in the paper the next day, we were all pleased with the interest.

My final race of the 1979 season was the New Albany, Indiana *VFW Run.*

This was an odd length race of about six and one half miles. I finished fourth in my age category. Each of the runners was given a warm hood with VFW inscribed on it.

I was to use that hood many, many times in the cold weather running I would do in the future.

In addition to the gift of the hood, I learned a method of race recording which would help in my work with the *Railsplitter Run* in the future.

The organizers of the race had painted two huge plywood boards which they had braced against the side of the building. As each runner crossed the finish line they went to the officials who wrote the runners name, age, time and order of finish. When the last runner crossed the line the recording was finished and they were ready to proceed with the awards ceremony.

While the process tended to bog down from time to time if a large number of runners crossed the line about the same time, it proved to be a far more efficient way of managing the awards than I had seen in many other races

The *VFW Run* finished my first running season. I had improved physically, learned things about myself and become a racing enthusiast. I had won some awards and was beginning to place or make a respectable showing in just about every race I ran.

Of course the most important part of the whole process, were the friends we made and the challenge of working to get into the physical shape necessary to be a competitor.

I was looking forward to the 1980 season.

CHAPTER FIVE

SWEET POTATOES, PHEIDIPPIDES, AND A STREAMLINED RUNNER

Staying in shape for competitive running requires a consistent commitment to working out. It is impossible to improve as a runner unless one is willing to go out everyday or several times a week and run.

I had a consistent workout of thirty-five and a half miles of walking every week to deliver the mail. By adding two to four miles of running several times each week, I was able to stay in shape and continue to improve in gradual stages.

Since runners have to be outside running all year, it seems there is no actual "season" for competitive racing. While most of the races cluster around the spring to fall months in Kentucky, there is plenty of racing activity all year long.

My first races of the 1980 season were a couple of training races at Iroquois Park in Louisville during January and February. I was able to win a couple of satisfying awards.

By March of 1980 I had been running less than eight months, had won some awards, a trophy or two and thought I had this running thing on a downhill pull. More out of cockiness than preparation, therefore, I entered the *Pheidippides Marathon* in Lexington, Kentucky.

The *Pheidippides* takes its name from the Battle of Marathon and an ancient Greek soldier who, during the heat of battle, was charged with running a message to the Athenians who were fighting some distance away. Pheidippides ran the message to the commander who gave an answer back to him.

Pheidippides ran back to his unit, delivered the message and dropped dead on the spot. The distance he ran was 26.2 miles which, in his honor, is the traditional distance of all marathons. A mini-marathon is half the distance, or 13.1 miles.

My greatest distance running without stopping at this time had been eighteen miles in a practice run. I started at my house, ran through Hodgenville, out of town past the Nationwide Sewing Factory and on to Bob Vance's farm where I turned around and started back toward home.

After a few miles of this practice run, I kept debating with myself whether I should try to make it all the way back home or if I should give up because I was having a little trouble with the muscles of my legs trying to cramp. At Druther's Restaurant, as I ran back on highway 210, I thought I could make it all the way home. At the Convenient store a little further on, I called LaHoma to come pick me up in the car. I decided I had run far enough for one day.

That was the extent of my preparation for the race. Perhaps I should have considered the fate of poor old Pheidippides, but I confidently drove to Lexington, signed up for the race and returned to *Rupp Arena* where the race was to start.

The *Pheidippides Marathon* was sponsored by John's Running Store, which is still in business today. To my knowledge this was the one and only marathon ever held in Lexington, Kentucky.

In 1980, the Pheidippides was to be held in conjunction with the *NCAA Basketball Tournament* in which the University of Kentucky was competing.

As every Kentuckian knows, about half the state loses its collective mind for a few months during basketball season every year. During a tournament as large as the NCAA in which a favorite Kentucky team is playing, a special excitement grips the city hosting the event. Of course, there was tremendous excitement on the day of the race. Though there were around ninety runners at the starting point of the *Pheidippides*, many who were registered did not run because they were at home watching the University of Kentucky basketball team on television.

As is my habit, I looked around for runners in my age group. I saw four people I thought I would be competing against. From the looks of them, I didn't think my chances were very promising.

One of them, Roland Anspagh from Ohio, helped me pin on my racing number. Roland was a fine runner who showed no signs of the rheumatic fever he had suffered as a child. He was in great shape and for all practical purposes, Roland was a "contender". I would run with Roland many times after the *Pheidippides* and he always did well.

The race started. We ran through town, then out the Richmond Road. The first sixteen miles went fine, but as we were running up a hill, the runner in front of me stopped. When he stopped, I stopped.

My strategy had been to run slowly, but to keep running. Once I stopped I had to stop every two miles and walk a while before I could run some more.

There were a few times when I thought I could not finish, but it was a beautiful day so I kept going.

Upon returning to Lexington, I turned down a street and ran steadily along knowing my first marathon was nearly over. I gained confidence and looked around. I was running alone. There were few people on the street and those who were out were looking at me strangely.

Sure enough, I was lost. Luckily, I was able to get back in the race after losing only a couple of blocks.

When we reached the Lexington city limits the sun was going down and there was a nice breeze blowing. It seemed to revive me, so I cranked up and finished looking pretty good.

I received a nice hug from one of the pretty girls who was working with the race committee. She said I "looked good to have run a marathon" which didn't hurt my feelings one bit.

I finished 63rd and third in my age group behind Roland Anspagh from Ohio and Robert Graves of Lexington.

There was a great party at *John's Running Store* after the race. As always, I was campaigning for the *Railsplitter Run*. Everywhere I went I took entry forms for the Railsplitter and signed up runners on the spot.

I sometimes wondered if they signed up because they were too tired to argue, but it wouldn't have mattered much to me either way. The *Railsplitter* is a good race and we are all proud of it.

I met Mike and Angela Murphy from Lancaster. Mike is a lawyer in Lancaster. He and Angela both run. They entered the *Railsplitter Run* one year and Angela was the over-all women's winner.

Many circumstances determine the outcome of a race. A runner can beat everyone in sight in one race only to find those same people running off and leaving him in the next.

Some runners run best in cold weather, others in the summer races while some are consistently winners. Paul Ennis was one of those consistent runners.

Though Paul was ten years older than I, one of my goals was to beat him in a fair race.

In the next race, *My Old Kentucky Home Classic*, on a very cold day in late March I finished second to Paul. I felt I was making progress. In the same race Bruce and Brian Hacker of Hodgenville both won beautiful plaques. More LaRue countians were becoming interested in running and were entering and winning more of the races across the state.

It just proves there is a wealth of talent in LaRue County. There isn't much some LaRue countian can't do better than everyone else if she/he gets half a chance.

At the Next race in Shelbyville, Kentucky, I happened to see John Snaden, Gene Priddy and Joe Connelly. I had seen John Snaden many times, but this was the first time I had an opportunity to talk with him.

Gene Priddy was on the committee for the 15K *Moonshiner's Run* which would be held in Springfield. He said it was the "hilliest course in the state of Kentucky with thirty-seven hills."

I asked him how he knew. He said he had counted everyone of them.

I did not win in the Shelbyville race, but I was close to those in front and my running time was coming down.

In April I was to run in the Saint Catherine College *Spring Fling*. The Spring Fling is the prettiest race in Kentucky and may be the prettiest race anywhere.

Ray Parella, Gene Priddy, Marilyn Scott, Cathy Fetters, Buddy Harpool and Joe Uhlig were all entered in the race.

The race began at a bridge over a creek, then continued along the country roads in a rough circle which ended in a short run up the little road to the main college building through trees covered with cherry blossoms. It is the most beautiful sight imaginable.

The earth smells fresh and green in April. The trees have that tender, fluffy green look of early spring while running through those cherry blossoms is like running through pink tinted clouds.

Even if one does not enter the racing event, it would be worth the time and effort to go to the *Spring Fling* to see Kentucky dressed in her spring wardrobe. Art, crafts and fun among the cherry blossoms is an experience never to be forgotten.

Buddy Harpool and Joe Uhlig tied for the first place overall. Buddy Harpool gave the 1st place award to Joe because Buddy is a thoroughly nice guy, but also because Joe was almost sixteen years older than Buddy. I finished third and my time dropped a little more. The winners received little medallions.

I broke 50 minutes in a lOK run for the first time in the *Cherokee Road Runners' Run* at North Hardin High School in Elizabethtown, Kentucky, in May of 1980. It was a big race of about 1000 runners which was chaired by Tom Gill. Five awards were given for each age group which increases participation and anticipation among the runners. I finished sixth and received no award.

Though awardless, I was pleased about reducing my time, yet again. I made a mental note, however, of the fact that two of the runners who won awards passed me in the final mile.

While I was running for the fun of it, I have to admit that I just loved to win an award.

It is interesting to note that God has created all of us with a place in this world. If we look for it, each of us can find a sport which matches our body type perfectly. The problem is that many times we fall in love with a sport that is not perfectly suited to the natural equipment God gave us.

Unfortunately, I am not physically well suited to running. I'm too tall, too big boned and tend to develop muscles too quickly. This would be a definite advantage if I were playing football or lifting weights, but this has been a liability in running. Small, thinly built people make much more capable runners.

In order to become more competitive, I had trimmed my weight from 184 to 170 which I felt helped me improve my running time. Considering the amount of running I was doing it had not been hard to do, but it represented a change of life-style for me.

I had never had to worry about my weight because I was so active. I could eat just about anything and everything I wanted without worrying about the effect.

There were only two times in my life when eating had caused me any serious trouble.

The first time occurred when I was very young and attending an "ice cream supper" at school. The proceeds from these suppers provided income for books, maps or other things for school use which the very meager budgets did not allow.

On this evening I had my ice cream money in my pocket. I may have had as much as thirty cents, but I felt very rich because I could buy a huge cone of ice cream for a nickel back then.

Things were going just fine until I ran into Calvin Thurman. Calvin was Barren Run's answer to Huckleberry Finn. What Calvin couldn't think of to get into wasn't worth mentioning.

Maybe I was a little suspicious, but remember I was just a little boy at the time and Calvin was up to no good, for sure.

He was holding this vegetable in his hand that looked something like a turnip. "You want some Indian turnip, Donald?" he asked.

"Sure, if it's good," I said, innocently.

"I'll cut you off a slice so you can see if you like it," Calvin said, smiling sweetly.

I put the slice of whatever it was in my mouth and began to chew. In less than three seconds I knew I had made a big mistake. My tongue and the inside of my mouth felt as if there were a thousand needles sticking out of them.

I looked at Calvin who was laughing as hard as he could. He bent over and slapped his leg he was laughing so hard. I sincerely wished I was big enough to slap more than his leg. I wanted to whip him right then and there. He was entirely too big for me to take on, especially in my condition, but I wanted to - oh, how I wanted to.

I spent all of my money on ice cream that evening partially because I loved ice cream and partially because I hoped it would help the burning in my mouth. It didn't. My mouth was on fire all night long.

Did I ever forgive Calvin for his prank?

Well, I'm not sure. I'm not mad at him any more, but I still have some vivid memories.

The only other time I ran into trouble with something I ate I didn't have Calvin around to blame it on. I had no one to blame, but myself.

I came home from work at the Post Office one day, rested a few minutes, then went out to bale hay. I worked all afternoon in the hot sun with the dust from the hay blowing over me and sticking in my throat.

It was as if the heat reached inside one's body and pulled the life and energy right out. To make matters worse, the humidity was so high it was difficult to breathe. I kept baling and the heat waves kept rising out of the field in front of me.

As I finished up, hot, thirsty and tired, I walked by our watermelon patch on the way to the house. I looked at the melons hiding in the shade of their own vines and knew the insides would be cool, fresh and wet. I broke open one of those big green watermelons and scooped out the insides with my hands. I ate *all* of it. At the time, I was certain that melon saved my life.

When I got home, LaHoma had baked sweet potatoes for supper. LaHoma cooks the best sweet potatoes in the world. I like them right out of the oven, with the jackets split, piled with butter and a little sugar. While I don't remember exactly how many of them I ate, it must have been about eight of them.

At 2:00 o'clock in the morning, I woke up in the most horrible pain imaginable. I thought I was dying. Not wanting to die alone, I woke LaHoma and scared her half out of her wits.

LaHoma was pregnant with our son, Donnie. By the time I finished expressing my extreme discomfort and the tragedy of being cut down in the prime of life by a nameless but dread disease, she was firmly convinced she was going to end up a pregnant widow.

Sandra, our oldest daughter, heard the commotion and came in about the time I fainted and stopped breathing (LaHoma said I also turned dark.).

Sandra said later, "All I could think about was, how is Mama going to raise this baby alone?"

LaHoma called Bennett-Bertram Funeral Home, not to pick up the remains, but to take me to the hospital. In those days, funeral homes did the ambulance work as well as the work they were designed to do.

By the time George Bertram and Albert Bennett reached our house, I had begun to throw up and was feeling better. After listening to the symptoms and seeing the chaos we were in, they encouraged me to go on to the hospital because it could have been my heart (I don't think they knew about the watermelon and sweet potatoes at the time.)

Albert and George put me in the ambulance. Sandra would stay to take care of Donna, Diana, and Jo while LaHoma would ride with me in the ambulance.

We started toward Elizabethtown and the hospital. Riding backwards in the ambulance just about finished me off.
I got sick all over again.

By the time we reached the hospital, I was a little better. I had a few unpleasant physical symptoms for a few days thereafter, but managed to live to be teased about the situation for a long time to come (Bob Vance has never let me forget about eating all those sweet potatoes.).

At the same time I was in the hospital, LaHoma's father and aunt were also critically ill in various hospitals. As an only child, LaHoma was forced to be everybody's support system, take care of our children, worry about me and deal with a pregnancy. Sometimes I think the wrong people are given the big shiny trophies in this life.

While I was in the hospital, the doctors discovered I had an ulcer. For the next year I had to take medicine and follow a strict diet which included no chocolate pie and definitely - no sweet potatoes!

I realized that if I were reasonable about my eating and continued to run as I was, I would have no trouble keeping my weight at a competitive level. I worked at it slowly and had no real problem keeping it down as long as I was running regularly.

CHAPTER SIX

HOT WEATHER, HOME COMING AND A DOWNHILL FINISH

In 1980 Magnolia, Kentucky, celebrated its 125th year as a town. The celebration committee had asked George Trumbo of the LaRue County Parks and Recreation Department to develop and chair the race which would be part of the celebration.

Magnolia has always figured prominently into the history of LaRue County. At the time I was in high school it was also a force in high school basketball among other things.

Mr. H.W. Puckett was principal in 1944 when I entered high school. Our basketball coach was Brother McGee. Brother McGee coached our team all the way to the regional tournament where we lost to Elizabethtown.

In my sophomore year, James "Pud" McClain from Buffalo came to Magnolia as coach. We really loved Coach McClain. He was one of those wonderful teachers who not only know the subject they teach, but understand the needs and emotions of the children they are teaching. It was a great tragedy that he was forced to leave teaching to make a living.

I made the starting team on the Junior Varsity along with Herbert Peace, Stuart Pepper, Charles Akin and Ken Bell.

Coach McClain's younger brother "Doodle" played for Buffalo and Buffalo was one of our arch rivals. Doodle was a great basketball player who liked to take long shots from outside though they were only two points back then. Coach McClain had me guard him. I finally learned to stay close and in front of him so I could knock down those long shots.

Coach McClain paid our way to the state tournament that year. He paid for our hotel and the tickets to all the games. All we had to do was pay for our food.

For some little country boys who thought a trip to Hodgenville was a big deal, the trip to the State Basketball Tournament was a dream come true. You can understand why we loved him and will never forget him.

My junior year began the fall of 1946. We lost some of our basketball starters through graduation, Charles Waggoner and Harold Jackson, but we had some veteran players returning as well - Bill Lemons, Stuart Pepper, Charles Reed, Coleman Miller, Hobart Bowen, Ken Bell and me. Darnall McCubbin transferred from Horse Cave and J.D. Avery came to us from Upton. We also had a new principal, Tommy Houk, and a new coach, W. L. Reed. Charles Ward was home from the Army and returned to school.

We won 47 of our games that year. We won the county tournament, Greensburg Invitational, the district tournament and the regional tournament. In December of 1964 the Lithenhouse ratings in the Courier- Journal placed Magnolia's basketball team fifth in the 444 basketball teams in the state. I believe this was the most memorable moment of all the things that happened during my school years.

Going to the state tournament that year was Magnolia's finest hour.

There were only 42 boys in the entire high school. All of Magnolia went to the state tournament to see us play.

Some of our big fans were "Biggie" Miller, Sheriff of LaRue Co., D.G. Meers, the three Richardson men, Shorty Owens, Maupin Parker, Adrian Russell and Curt McCubbin to name a few. Maupin Parker often sat in the stands keeping his own boxed scores and player's individual scores. He was a tremendous source of inspiration.

At that time the state tournament was played in the old Armory in Louisville. Louisville and its hotels were a sea of fans, players and cheerleaders for a week.

Our fans and cheerleaders, Mary Elizabeth Salt, Mary Rose Corum, Helen Puckett and Charlene Lawson, were on the opposite end of the Armory from where our team was located, but we could see them. Just being able to see our fans and cheerleaders helped to make us more comfortable, but I think they were about as scared as we were when we came out on the floor.

We were too short to dunk, as players do now, but some of us could touch the rim of the goal. We had drilled on defense all year allowing only about 29 points per game. The second team allowed only 16 points per game.

Bill Lemons had a sweet soft jump shot, quick hands and all these head fakes that could cause an opponent to misjudge what he was going to do and jump into the air at the wrong time. Charles Reed was a clever ball handler and Stuart Pepper was a great scorer as well.

We won the first game against Dixie Heights of Covington, 45 to 43 in an overtime, with balanced scoring - Lemons with eight, Miller with twelve, Reed with six, Avery with nine, Pepper with 9 and Ward with two.

We lost our next game against Maysville in the last three minutes. Maysville eventually won the tournament. Their coach, Earle Jones, gave Magnolia the compliment of being the hardest game his team had played.

My cousin Johnny and I had come a long way since those peach basket goals and the ball without air and Magnolia had left its mark on Kentucky basketball forever.

Mr. Reed was very sad as he, Johnny, Kenneth and I walked back to the hotel that night, but he said, "You know, we could have a pretty good team next year." And we did, too.

Returning to Magnolia in any type of competition was a great treat for me. The race was to begin in front of the oldest Church in LaRue County, The South Fork Church. We would run along the highway and cross the finish line in front of the Magnolia Bank.

There were about fifty runners entered. I was in the fifty-one and up age group. As usual, I looked around for people who would be competing in my age group. I saw only one, so I turned my attention to doing as well as I could.

I was running well and had not seen my age group competitor since the start of the race. When we reached David Peace's house where we were to make the turn to go into town I saw a grey haired fellow just ahead of me who I had not seen at the beginning of the race.

I sprinted and pulled around him. After that I just held on, but I had to work hard to keep my scant lead. I managed to cross the finish line just ahead of him.

After the race, I learned he was Roy Brill and was only forty years old. We were not even running in the same class. I learned not to try to judge age by the color of a person's hair or the lack of it, for that matter.

There was a nice picture of me crossing the finish line with Roy close behind in *THE LARUE COUNTY HERALD NEWS* the next week. It was the last time I ever beat Roy.

I won my age group, but was so engrossed in talking with some of the Magnolia people who had returned for the festival that I missed the awards ceremony. LaHoma had to receive the award for me.

I'm sorry Magnolia did not continue holding a festival every year or, at least, every five years. The planners and organizers put on a fantastic festival and it would be nice to continue to celebrate together.

In late April, The *Louisville Run for Health* was held at Seneca Park with 700 to 800 runners in which I finished fourth in my age group. This race was followed by the Gold Rush at Fort Knox, Kentucky.

In time for the *Gold Rush*, we had formed a group of local runners made up of Bruce Hacker, Brian Hacker, David Otis and Danny Owens who had played on my softball team at church. We all won awards. I think we impressed some of those city boys before the day was over.

From here the team went to Hardinsburg to the Mayfest. Again, Brian, Bruce and I won our age groups. The winners were being given "running flats" by a store owner. A running flat is a low quarter shoe which is very light in weight. Bruce talked the store owner into giving us John Walker Brooks shoes which had to be especially ordered. They were very expensive, but in about six weeks we received our shoes in the mail.

It was now time for the 1980 Campbellsville race where I won my age group. Donnie was no longer racing because he got too hot in the Campbellsville race the year before. He did not wish to race, but he still enjoyed going with me to the races.

The *Cherokee Club Championship* which followed was so hot it came down to the survival of the fittest. I was extremely proud of finishing third behind Lou Sneidner and Al Wagner.

Shortly thereafter was the Kentucky Derby Mini which was a 13.1 mile race. I finished twenty-second in my age group and ran the whole way. Paul Ennis caught me at the 10 mile marker, then ran off and left me. I stood beside him as he was awarded second place in the 60-64 age group. I was really happy for him. We shared a Coke after the awards were handed out.

While studying the results I was to find I had beaten most of those twenty one people at some time or other in the past. I realized I was not at my best.

LaHoma and I were extremely concerned about our daughter, Diana, who was planning to get married that summer.

We had hoped she would go to college after high school because she was so bright and was so talented musically. She was certain she knew just what she wanted to do, so there came a time when we just had to let go.

All of us needed a break so Donnie, our youngest daughter Melissa Jo, LaHoma and I went to London for the *Wilderness Road Run* in June.

The *Wilderness Road Run* is a great race. Donnie decided to come out of retirement to run in this one. I placed third in my age group and was given two awards. What I remember most about this race were the pretty legs on some equally pretty girls who had come from all over the state.

After the race was over, some one said, "They're having a race in Corbin at 3:00p.m. called the *Pepsi Challenge*." Several of us jumped in cars and drove over to Corbin to sign up for the afternoon race. It was a two mile run, and I won my age group.

I don't think I was running from my concerns over Diana, but the running helped me feel better.

I had to remind myself that our oldest daughter, Sandra, had been conscientious and practical about her career. After she and her future husband, Kenny Devore, became engaged, she took advantage of her scholarship and attended Elizabethtown Community College graduating as a nurse.

I hoped Diana would be equally practical.

After returning from Corbin, we went to the park to the stage there and listened to some excellent country musicians. The following morning Jo, Donnie, LaHoma and I drove to Cumberland Falls State Park where LaHoma and I had honeymooned many years before.

It is difficult to say which of Kentucky's state parks is the most beautiful, but Cumberland Falls has to be near the top. I am glad to see that more and more Kentuckians are taking advantage of the facilities offered in the State Park system which offers a little something for everyone at affordable family prices.

The falls were beautiful, tucked into its valley of green trees and boulders smoothed by eons of rushing water. We waded in the ankle-deep water at the top of the falls. LaHoma lost her footing on the slippery moss covered rocks and fell, hitting her head. Fortunately, she was not seriously injured, but she had headaches for weeks afterward.

In September, after placing third in the *Golden Armor Run* in the morning, I ran third in the *Cow Days Run* in Greensburg the same afternoon. Things were definitely looking up.

While I don't pretend that running in two races a day is not taxing, if one is in good physical shape, accustomed to running long distances and motivated it can be a great challenge.

In October the 1980 *Railsplitter Run* was held on an extremely hot day. The previous year the weather had been miserably cold, but in 1980 the weather was more like August than October - hot, humid and oppressive.

About 150 runners were entered in the event. Paul Ennis had entered and there was a man from Louisville, Eugene Barker, who had just turned fifty. I could tell by looking at him there was no way I could beat him.

I was running ahead of Paul until we reached Donald and Jean McCubbin's house, where Paul pulled up beside me. We began to talk as we ran. I said, "Paul, did you see Eugene Barker? He's in our age group but we can't beat him."

"I know that," Paul said.

I suggested that we just run steadily and work for a tie to avoid wearing ourselves out trying to beat each other when neither of us had a chance to win.

Paul agreed, but said, "Don't you sprint on me at the end." Paul had been beating me steadily over the long run, but was not a sprinter.

I promised I would not sprint and we ran comfortably along, talking as we went. We had both worked hard and were in great shape even for the terrible humidity and heat. This was not the case for many of the other runners. In fact, the 1980 Railsplitter turned out to be a near disaster.

We saw Lori Douglas overcome by the heat and have to be taken to the hospital. When we reached the third mile marker, another runner was lying in the road with a "charlie horse". At the four mile marker, a Japanese exchange student was lying in a ditch with his feet sticking straight up in the air. Paul asked him if he were all right.

"Yes, just resting," he said in broken English.

At some distance ahead of us, an ambulance was picking up another runner who had become overheated.

When runners enter races sporadically rather than on a regular basis, their tendency is to practice at a specific time of day which is most convenient for them. This allows the runner to build running muscles and to develop strength, but does not prepare him/her for running under a variety of temperature conditions.

If the runner has been practicing regularly in the early morning or late afternoon, then enters a race which begins at 1:00 o'clock in the afternoon, he/she could be in big trouble before he/she realizes it.

Knowing his/her distance and time abilities, he/she fails to take into account the toll sun position, temperature and other conditions take on the body. Before he/she realizes what has happen he/she is in serious trouble.

When Paul and I crossed the finish line, we touched hands to signal a "draw" or a "tie", then we found out Eugene Barker was not running in our age group after all. The committee had changed the group arrangement to 46-50 years of age and 51 and older; therefore, Paul and I had tied for first place in our division and both received first place trophies.

Donnie's last race was the *Green River Lake Run*, a beautiful race along the banks of the *Green River Lake* in Campbellsville the following weekend. The weather was still unbelievably hot, but there was also a drying wind blowing which made it very difficult to run.

Heat and humidity makes running unpleasant, but adding a drying wind to excessive heat can be dangerous for even experienced runners.

There were many runners having to stop running to walk and cool down from time to time. As I was nearing the finish line, I saw a man lying on the side of the road. Emergency workers were preparing to put him in an ambulance. I was doubly concerned because I thought I recognized Paul Ennis as the runner down.

I finished the race, second in my age group; Donnie won youngest runner. I began trying to find out about Paul. Sure enough, the race officials said Paul had been taken to the hospital. I called later to find he was fine. He had become dehydrated and passed out, but after a night in the hospital he was okay.

All runners should be very careful about weather conditions because even the best can fail to consider all the factors which could cause them to get hurt.

After finishing second to Eugene Barker of Louisville in the *Turkey Trot Run* in Elizabethtown in November, I entered the first *Wendy's Classic* at Bowling Green.

There were over 2,000 runners entered in the race. I have a picture of the line-up for the start of the race. I can see LaHoma and Donnie in the photograph, but I couldn't identify any of the runners.

John Snaden, Charlie Fetters and I had a great race. I beat Charlie, but John beat me. I ran my fastest race to date, 45:29 for the 1OK race, but Buster Tankersley from Tennessee ran 36 minutes in our age group and was given a standing ovation as he crossed the finish line. Nick Rose, a small Englishman who had gone to school at Western, won the race over-all.

Wendy's provided breakfast and lunch for the runners and gave each a medallion. The party after the race allowed us to meet and talk with runners from other states as well as the best from Kentucky.

The *Wendy's Classic* is rated in the top twenty-five races in America. David Mason, who chairs the race, is a fine person and handles the details and planning of the race expertly.

Two of the details which stick out in my mind which makes the race so special are the finish and the college students. The race ends on a downhill run to the finish line with a crowd lined up on each side of the road which helps you "pump up" for the end. The college students help with the race and are such fun, so helpful and make everyone feel welcome in Bowling Green.

The *Wendy's Classic* was a wonderful way to end the 1980 racing year.

CHAPTER SEVEN

OPPORTUNITIES, BABY BIRDS AND A LOST HERO

During the entire time I was training, traveling to races and making new friends, I was working daily at my job as a mail carrier. LaHoma and I were rearing the children who were still at home, Jo and Donnie, while trying to provide a safety net for those who were already on their own - Sandra, Donna Gail and Diana.

When I look back to those years, I am utterly amazed at how LaHoma was able to do all she did.

Even if our children had been quiet, ordinary children and her husband a quiet, ordinary husband, she would have had her hands full. Our five children, however, are active, creative, involved children who offer all the complex needs and problems of the artistically inclined.

To complicate things further, LaHoma's husband had leaped with both feet into a hobby which required as much work as a career at a time in life when most men are settling down and taking life more slowly.

She worked her job, was there for the children, took care of our home and supported me in all my efforts. Perhaps, at the time, I took what she contributed a little for granted. Looking back I can only imagine the effort it took to do all she did, yet stand in the shadows and cheer me on from one race to the next and one interest to another.

As do most couples, we have had our share of sadnesses, challenges and hard work, but we may have had a shade more fun doing it. At the very least, we have never been bored.

I was never bored with my job as a mail carrier, either.

I had worked for civil service at Fort Knox for two years when Mr. Russell Parker, the postmaster in Hodgenville, chose my name from the Postal Register and helped me transfer from civil service to postal service.

I liked the change. I had only three miles to drive to work which would give me more time to farm.

I did a variety of jobs with the Post office. Sometimes I received the mail when it came in. Sometimes I would carry the parcel post, special deliveries or do the relays. Sometimes I worked the windows selling stamps, certifying letters - "work flat mail" as we called it. I sometimes posted and put the mail out for delivery. Every Saturday I carried one of the city routes or substituted for the regular carriers when they were sick or on vacation.

When I went to work at the Post Office in Hodgenville, Mr. Howard Gardner was still delivering the mail. I idolized Mr. Gardner.

As a little boy, my job was to go down to the end of our driveway, take the mail out of the box then bring it to the house. Back in those days, people did not hop in the car and "run to town" like we do now. Any automobile traffic at all was cause for excitement.

Mr. Gardner delivered the mail in a Model A Ford, which was a fascination to me. I couldn't wait until it was time to go down to the main road to watch him pass our farm.

I learned to watch the shadow the sun cast on the porch to know when I could run down the long driveway where I hid behind a tree to wait because I was too shy to let him see me.

I would watch him appear down the road coming closer and closer. Then he would stop at our mailbox to put the mail inside, close the box and drive on to the next house. I watched until he was out of sight, then dashed from hiding to get the mail and run to the house as fast as I could.

Mr. Gardner had been a Rotarian for many years. When I received the Rotarian Award at my high school graduation, Mr. Gardner presented the medal to me with my parents and friends in the audience. I thought it was the grandest thing to have Mr. Gardner, the man I idolized, present that award to me.

Howard Gardner could sort mail faster than anyone I ever saw. He had an ulterior motive, however. Once he sorted the newspapers and magazines, he had time to go over to the corner drugstore for a cup of coffee with his friends before coming back to the Post Office to sort the first class mail and run his route. Of course, the faster he sorted, the more time he had for coffee.

In later years, my sister married Theo Terry, Howard's brother-in-law which gave us a family connection. I got to know him as a personal friend after that. It was a privilege to work with and learn from someone I admired so much.

Early in my career as a mail carrier, I made a very embarrassing mistake which rather took the wind out of my sails.

One fine spring morning I was delivering packages to local businesses. I worked my way down to Water Street to Bennett-Bertram Funeral Home. One of the owners, George Bertram, was sitting in the swing on the front porch of the funeral home when I drove up.

I parked in front of the funeral home, took a nine by seven inch box which had been sent "registered mail" out of the delivery vehicle and started up the walk with it. The box was light in weight and there was no rattle or shift suggesting the contents were either very well packed or made of a material which would not be damaged in shipping.

I felt great. The weather was warm. The air was clean, fresh and smelled of springtime flowers while the whole world was beautiful, as only a Kentucky spring can be. In my enthusiasm and sense of well-being, I tossed the box in the air and caught it, turning it a little each time it came down.

A strange expression came over George's face as I came up the walk. As soon as I was close enough, he said quietly, "Do you know what you have in that box?"

"No," I said puzzled.

"That is a delivery from the Crematory in Louisville," he said, a pained look on his face.

I guess my mouth fell open for it dawned on me that I had been gleefully tossing the remains of someone's "Dearly Departed" into the air. I quickly handed George the box and backed up a few steps.

After that experience, whenever I had a nine-by-seven inch box to deliver to any of the county funeral homes, I handled them with the utmost respect and tenderness, just in case.

As the years passed I moved up to a regular mail route delivering the mail daily until I retired in 1989.

My route was seven and one-half miles from start to finish. As the old saying goes, "in the rain, sleet, snow, hot sun and storms". If you are interested in a career which promotes good health, walking a mail route keeps you in great shape.

In December of 1988, I received an award from the Post Office because I had amassed over 2,700 hours of unused sick leave throughout my career which included my Air Force duty and the time I worked for the Army. I received a tie pin with a blue stone and an eagle on it. It was called a "Pin of Significance". Ray McDowell, Hodgenville Postmaster, presented the pin to me with a letter of appreciation from G.F. Van Fleet, Bowling Green Sectional Manager/Postmaster.

It is a unique aspect of being a mail carrier that you are often on the scene at times when other people are not. Your work is woven through the fabric of a community in such a way you are delivering the mail to a business owner one minute and walking by his home and talking with his/her family members the next. Taken as a whole, this provides a solid sense of what is happening around town. This "connectedness" allows mail carriers to develop a sensitivity to the life of a community which few people enjoy.

There are times when you can walk for a long time without seeing anyone. At other times, people are out doing things and want to exchange a few words.

Hodgenville is a small town and everybody knows everybody else. Most of us went to school together, or our parents knew each other or we may even be related somewhere along the line. The closeness encourages some lively discussions.

Some of the people I met wanted to ask about their mail, postal services or Social Security checks. Sometimes they had a bit of gossip to pass along in whispered tones or they went to the same church as I did and wanted to discuss something that had happened or was going to happen at church. Many times the people on my route just wanted to express concern for people who were sick or having some bad luck.

There were times when people were waiting for me as I made my rounds to offer congratulations when my family or I did something of significance. These nice, thoughtful people will always hold a special place in my memory.

Since the mail carrier is out in the community at a time when most people are away from home or busy with house work, we are often the first to realize something or someone is in trouble.

I was delivering the mail on Kirkpatrick Avenue one morning when I discovered Sister Marie Swails, pastor of the Full Gospel Assembly Church at the corner of Kirkpatrick and Maple, had fallen in her garage and broken her arm. I helped her to her feet and rushed across the street to enlist the aid of Mrs. C.E. Shoffner in getting her to the hospital.

On another day, while delivering the mail to the home of an elderly resident, I saw him get out of his car leaving the motor running to go back into the house for something. He, apparently, left the car in neutral because as soon as he left the car, it began rolling down the hill behind his house. I ran after it, catching it just before it crashed through a fence and into the ditch beyond.

I was more than aware of the dangers of leaving a car running unattended because I had done the same thing. When the Post Office leased two new Pinto vehicles to be used by city carriers to deliver packages, I left my vehicle running one day to make a quick delivery of a package.

As I dashed to the porch of the house, I must have sensed something was wrong, for I looked behind me in time to see the Pinto rolling down the street. I chased it, catching it fifteen feet from a culvert with a very deep ditch behind it. After that incident, I exercised extreme caution in the care and safety of unattended vehicles.

While delivering the mail in the area behind what is now Bell's Grocery, I walked up minutes after a little boy accidentally shot his playmate through the leg. The two boys had been playing with a rifle and a near tragedy had occurred; fortunately, it was a clean wound which missed the major blood vessels and arteries. I encouraged the father of the child to take him to the hospital which he did. The boy healed nicely and without complications.

No occupation is without its hazards, I suppose. One of the greatest hazards to mail carriers is dogs.

Many pet owners are responsible, safety-minded people who keep their dogs behind enclosed fences or on chains for their protection and the safety of friends, neighbors and mail carriers. Some are not.

Even in cases where pet owners have done everything in their power to keep their pet safe from people and people safe from the pet, things can go wrong. A dog can leap a fence, break his chain or jump through a screen door.

It seems there is a special animosity between mail carriers and the whole canine species. Dogs who bark for no other reason on earth, bark at the mail carrier. Dogs who would lead a burglar to the family silver and wave a friendly tail as he hauls everything off, will lie in wait for hours just to snarl and snap viciously at the innocent mail carrier.

The dogs that disturbed me most were the ones which hid quietly under parked cars until I turned my back to them; then they rushed out to try to bite me before I knew they were there. Many dogs simply bark and warn you away from their property, but others will walk a mile just to try to make an opportunity to bite.

One nasty tempered little dog on my route would follow me down the street every day trying his best to get an opening to chomp on me. One day, he managed to give me a painful bite on the leg. It made me so mad, I counter attacked.

I grabbed a stick and charged after him. He ran under his porch, but I managed to get a couple of good licks in before he disappeared.

Generally, I am not afraid of dogs, even after they have bitten me, but there was one exception. Virgie Shacklett owned a huge, healthy looking German Shepherd about which there was no bluff. He took himself seriously and seemed to expect the world and everything in it to do likewise.

One of the things which made him so impressive was that he was exceptionally well trained. Virgie's front yard is bordered by a low stone fence with no gate. The Shepherd was trained to stay in his own yard whether his owner was at home or not.

The fact that he never broke training regardless of how angry he appeared caused him to seem more dangerous. He was deliberate about everything he did. When he came rushing off the porch, teeth flashing to tell me I had better stay away from his property, I had a tendency to believe he meant it.

Fortunately, I did not deliver Virgie's mail to her home, but at her beauty shop "up-town" in order to avoid a possible altercation between me and the dog.

When I walked by the yard on my route, the dog would rush out to the stone fence which surrounded his yard and bark viciously, but would go no farther than the fence. He knew where his property ended and would go no farther.

One day as I walked by the fence, I must have gotten too close because he came charging out of the yard, teeth bared, snarling and growling low in his throat. I thought I had carried my last letter.

I put my mail bag between me and the dog which began ripping the mail out of the bag and tossing it over his head. Each time he realized he had mail in his mouth and not mailman he attacked again.

I began backing slowly away, thinking that if I could get away from his territory, he might feel he had done his job and stop the attack. Eventually, I backed completely across the street in front of Albert and June Bennett's house, but he showed no signs of giving up. I was beginning to feel desperate.

Suddenly, I lost my footing. I had backed into a muddy place in the yard and fallen backward. I was sure I was already "the late Donald Mather".

Everything happened so fast, I have no idea what I was thinking at the time. I feel certain I was preparing for an ignoble end;

however, as soon as I hit the ground the dog stopped attacking, turned and walked sedately back to his own yard. There he sat watching me gather up the abused mail before limping unsteadily down the street.

Because we can be counted on to appear at people's homes at about the same time every day, sometimes mail carriers are asked to do a simple kindness. One such incident occurred after a terrible storm which uprooted about three hundred trees in the city of Hodgenville in the summer of 1987.

I reached the Gaines residence the morning after the storm to find a note from Lisa:

> Dear Mr. Mailman:
> I need your help! There is a baby bird in the flower basket under my mail box. It needs to be fed while I am at work. Would you give it several eyedroppers of the mixture there in the basket (green beans, squash) and some water out of the glass? Will you feed and water? Usually it will stop when its full. Just drop the eyedropper in the cup of water when you get done.
> Thanks, Lisa
> P.S. It's a victim of the storm and its name is "Stormy".

I replied:

> Dear Lisa:
> I did just as you said. I enjoyed doing it. D.M.

The next day Lisa left me this note:

> Dear D.M.;
> Thanks for your help! When I came home yesterday, "Stormy" was nowhere to be found. We tried.
> Thanks, Lisa

I replied:

> Dear Lisa;
> Let's hope he made it. D.M.

There is nothing more rewarding to me than when I find God has chosen to put me in a particular place at just the right time to do His work. There was at least one time in my career when I know without a doubt God chose me to do something for another of His children and I remain grateful and awed by the experience.

On the first route delivery of a terribly cold February morning in 1988, I was delivering the mail on North Lincoln Boulevard. I was about halfway through my first loop when I went to the back porch of the Sam and Jay Walters home where I always delivered the mail.

Much to my amazement, I found Mrs. Jay Walters lying on the back sidewalk. I knew instantly something was terribly wrong.

I rushed to Jay, who calmly told me she had fallen and thought she had broken her kneecap. She was holding her house key in her hand and asked me to open the backdoor, go in and tell her daughter, Cokey, who was visiting from Ohio, what had happened.

I quickly opened the backdoor and began calling to Cokey. I wanted to get her attention, but did not want to alarm her. She answered from a bedroom somewhere upstairs. I said, "This is Donald Mather, your mailman. Your mother has fallen and we need to help her."

I moved a comfortable chair near the door, then went back to Jay. I told her that as cold as it was, she needed to be taken into the house as quickly as possible. I am certain the prospect of moving even a little bit with a broken kneecap was terrifying, but Jay is a fighter. Without complaint, she let me help her.

Once she was on her feet and leaning on me for support, she was able to hop on one foot. I can only imagine how much pain each one of those hops caused her, but we finally made it into the house and into that comfortable chair.

Cokey and I wrapped her in a warm blanket then gave her some aspirin and hot coffee.

Jay's husband, Sam, was out running errands and we weren't sure where to find him. We called their son, David, who was at the First Baptist Church where he was Minister of Youth. In about two minutes, he came flying into the house. Luckily, Sam arrived soon afterwards and called the ambulance service.

The entire family was most appreciative of what I was able to do for Jay. Judy Florence, another of Sam and Jay's daughters, wrote the President of the United States, Ronald Reagan, to tell him about "a helpful city carrier". He sent the letter to the Postal Service.

A few weeks later, a framed "Certificate of Appreciation" was presented to me by the Hodgenville Postmaster, Ray McDowell. The editor of *THE LARUE COUNTY HERALD NEWS*, Celia McDonald, sent a photographer to take pictures and a nice article appeared in the paper.

In this incident I was able to help, but in another there was nothing I could do.

In the years which had passed after I began to work for the Postal Service, Mr. Howard Gardner had retired from the Post Office. After his retirement I became his mail carrier and each day delivered his mail to his door.

I was delivering the mail on Forrest Avenue one warm day. Howard was in the yard talking to a woman about some wedding pictures he had taken. I had just delivered the mail to Edna and Charlie Nichols' house when I glanced in his direction to see him crumple to the ground.

I knew something terrible was happening. I ran toward him, but the minister of the Christian Church in Hodgenville, Will Wallace, had been in his own yard across the street from Howard and was able to reach him a step before I did. The Reverend Wallace began to administer mouth to mouth resuscitation, but it was too late. There was nothing we could do.

With Howard's passing went a fine man, a dear friend and a little boy's hero.

CHAPTER EIGHT

BANANA PUDDING AND THE HILLIEST RACE IN KENTUCKY

In the spring of 1981, my first race was in Springfield, Kentucky, for the *Moonshiner 15K*. My old friend John Snaden was chairman of the race. Gene Priddy and I went to the race together.

Gene and I agree that this must have been our hardest race of all the races we have run. Gene said he had counted every hill in the course and there were thirty-seven. By the time I finished the 9.3 mile course, which included one hill after another, I was willing to admit he was probably right about the number of hills. I finished third to Bill Long of Louisville and James Waldorf of Bardstown.

The next race of 1981 was one of my favorites, the *Banana Festival Run* in Fulton, Kentucky.

Because we had such a long trip to reach Fulton, LaHoma, Donnie and I went down the night before the race. The crowds had begun to gather for the festival which made if difficult finding a motel with vacancies, but we found one and settled in for the night.

The next morning we drove over to the race headquarters and found everyone joking, laughing and having a great time. I knew nearly everyone by now and felt right at home.

Buster Tankersley from Waverly, Tennessee, who had run the 36:00 at the *Wendy's Classic* in Bowling Green, Kentucky, was there. The race committee was offering only two awards in each age group so I knew if I wanted an award I would have to finish somewhere close to Buster because he was sure to win first.

I was right. Buster won and I held on for second. The awards were a very unusual, large medallion. I have never seen another one like it which made me doubly glad I was able to win second place.

A very special runner competed with us that day, John Glisson. John was blind. He ran with a friend, Howard Moran, who rode along on a bicycle holding a long cane to John. John used the cane as a guide and did very well in the race. He received thunderous applause as he crossed the finish line.

LaHoma and Donnie and I went back to the motel after the race where I showered and changed then we returned to the park to enjoy the festival.

Martha Layne Collins, who was Lt. Governor of Kentucky at the time, was there. We were able to talk with her for a few minutes and found her to be a lovely lady who loves Kentucky and its people.

One of the highlights of the *Banana Festival* is a two ton banana pudding which was brought to the festival on a wagon pulled by a tractor. Though there were five or six thousand people waiting, there was enough for all of us to have big servings of pudding. It was undoubtedly the best banana pudding I have ever eaten.

Later we were entertained by paratroopers from Ft. Campbell, which is near Hopkinsville, Kentucky.

They had drawn a six foot circle on the ground. As each man jumped from the plane and floated downward on his parachute, he landed closer and closer to the circle until the last one landed squarely in the center of the circle. Colored smoke bombs were exploding in the air as the men jumped which added to the spectacle. Donnie caught the action in the air with his camera.

On the trip back the following night, we stayed at a motel in Nortonville, Kentucky, where I went jogging and found a new knife along the way. At times, things just go your way, regardless.

There are probably as many reasons why people take up competitive racing as there are people racing. At my next race in Glasgow, I met two runners who were prime examples of running to improve one's health and ensure a longer life.

Fleetwood Fesmire retired from the Airforce. At sixty years of age he weighed 190 pounds and needed a back operation. He had never run before, but decided running and eating healthy foods might be a way of getting his back and general health in shape.

At sixty-five years of age, he still had not had that back surgery and he ran a 40:03 lOK race. I saw him beat the famous Dr. George Sheehan, who writes articles on running for the Rodale Press and who has published several books on running, including running for older adults.

The year Fleetwood beat him, Dr. Sheehan was entered in the 60 to 64 age category. Fleetwood was in the 65 and up. Dr. Sheehan was 64 when he sent in his entry form, but turned 65 on the day of the race. Fleetwood finished first, but both Dr. Sheehan and Fleetwood won in their own age groups because they were not competing with each other.

Earl Moriz was also competing. He began running to recover from open heart surgery. I finished third to Fleetwood and Earl.

Glasgow, Kentucky, always has such a nice race. They give competitors running magazines and coupons for free meals, but the thing which makes the races in Glasgow so special is the response from the local newspaper.

The newspaper sends photographers and reporters to the races to cover all of the events. All of the winners pictures are taken and published in the paper the next week along with a nice article which includes as much interesting information as possible. Nearly all of the runners try to get their hands on a copy of the newspaper when it comes out.

We went from Glasgow to Marengo, Indiana, then on to the *Dick Lugar Fitness Run* in New Albany, Indiana.

The *Dick Lugar Fitness Run* was held on a very hot day, but I still think of it as one of my favorite races. I have always admired Dick Lugar. I finished second to Jim Flynn, a priest from Louisville, who is an avid runner. There was only one award given, but they announced that Dick Lugar would give some special prizes. I received a fountain pen of which I am very proud.

Because some of us had been doing some hard work promoting the *Railsplitter Run* in 1981 there were about 250 runners who began the race. I finished second to Paul Ennis in our age group, but it was a great race.

I was "shut out" of the *Turkey Trot* in Elizabethtown, Kentucky, in 1981. I had been running very well all year and had not finished so low in the last seven races. Oh, well, that's competitive racing. Sometimes everything goes your way and sometimes nothing does.

I placed third and received an award in the second *Life Begins at Forty* in Louisville, so I was beginning to come back. This year, when Bill and Joy Peterson invited us to their home for the party at the end of the race, we were able to attend. Bill and Joy have a beautiful home that also includes a trophy room.

Bill and Joy had been serious running competitors for several years and were the best in their special categories. Bill had even been into "ultra-running". He had run the *Western States 100 Miler*, winning his age group. Their interest and enthusiasm for running has added a lot to the sport in Kentucky.

The party was great fun. Bill and Joy served every imaginable Christmas goodie. I remember thinking it was a good thing Bill was putting so much effort into running or he would never stay so thin.

By the end of 1981, I had been running only a few months longer than two years. I was gaining skill and experience and my enthusiasm for the sport was steadily increasing.

There is a phenomena in running which all serious runners experience. It may be part biological and part emotional, but, for whatever reason, once you reach a certain point, which appears to be different for each runner, you feel as if you have to run.

I had reached that point. If I did not run regularly, even for a day or two, I found I became very uncomfortable.

While I liked to think I was in control of my running, my running may have been controlling me - at least, to some extent. In any case, it was an expensive, time-consuming sport which had provided me with fascinating experiences and wonderful friends. The idea of slowing down never crossed my mind.

I was looking forward to the 1982 season with high expectations.

CHAPTER NINE

A KINDER, GENTLER MAIL CARRIER

Every man and woman on the face of the earth has a "philosophy of life". They may not realize it or want to admit it, but their philosophy is the force motivating what they do, what they don't do and the choices they make. It may not be easy to distill one's life to one single word which describes the motivating force behind it, but it can be done if one gives the matter enough thought.

Beyond what we choose to believe in or in whom and in what we choose to place our faith, there is something we believe which causes us to become who we are. P.T. Barnam believed there was a "sucker born every minute". Abraham Lincoln believed "people are just about as happy as they make up their minds to be". The founding fathers of this nation believed, "All men are created equal...".

I suppose, my motivating force is the "philosophy of kindness".

The Bible tells us, "God is love" and that we Christians are "known by our love". I strongly suspect this is not the image the world has of us, however.

Instead of loving people into wanting to be like us, too often we try to force our feelings, thoughts and beliefs down other people's throats denying them their human dignity and God given free will. There is much evidence to indicate that the world sees our efforts as self-righteous, rigid and anything but loving.

What is kindness, but another word for love?

Kindness includes recognizing the basic value of all people and the willingness to take the time to help someone else if the need arises. Kindness also means that we must have a deep and abiding respect and appreciation for others.

I love to win, but not to the extent that I do not appreciate the skill, dedication and, sometimes, sheer luck involved when someone else wins and I don't. My philosophy of kindness requires that I cheer louder when my friends stand in the winner's circle than when I am there myself.

Of course, this does not preclude the "winner's circle" from being my favorite place to stand. It just means I enjoy winning and I enjoy the success of others, also.

Kindness also includes "fairness". Fairness is a simple matter of "doing unto others as you would have them do unto you".

Perhaps, kindness is easier to live with than fairness. Kindness requires simple acts of decency which one performs when the occasion presents itself. We are kind when we take the opportunity to do something for someone which helps them in some way. This usually means we are reaching out to someone we know, already love, or someone in our communities whom we will come to know as time goes on. Kindness radiates from our circle of acquaintances.

Fairness, on the other hand, requires that we put our personal needs and selfishness aside to do the "right thing", whether we want to or not. Behaving fairly, might mean that we do not always win or have the advantage. In order to be fair, we might be called upon to give the other fellow the advantage.

As I have already said, I wanted to beat Paul Ennis, the expert older runner from Green County, in a fair race. When Paul was overcome by heat and dehydration in the *Green River Lake Run* at Campbellsville, I finished the race. Technically, I suppose, I beat Paul; however, there was no joy in beating him that way.

It was not Paul Ennis, the man, I wanted to beat. I wanted to pit my skill, conditioning, training and strength against Paul's. I wanted to grow into Paul's league.

I had to work extremely hard to compete with Paul even though he is ten years older than I am. There was no joy in beating Paul in a race unless he was at his best and I at mine.

Fairness means we take no pleasure in an unfair advantage.

There is no way we can be fair unless we are honest, responsible and self-confident. I believe most of the unfairness I have seen in this life has been motivated by fear. When a person chooses to be unfair, he is usually reacting in some way to something he fears. It may be as simple as the person being afraid he/she will never be good enough to beat another runner fairly or an umpire fearing the team he favors is not skilled enough to win without his help.

It could be argued that unfairness is a result of greed, but what is greed except another form of fear? Greedy people seem to me to be fearful people. They are afraid they will not have enough, or will lose something they already have. Life must be horrible for greedy people.

My philosophy of kindness and fairness leaves no room for prejudice. Of course, prejudice is another type of fear.

I have been privileged in my lifetime that God trusted me enough to force me to address this type of fear in myself. God gave me the opportunity to grow beyond my surface satisfaction with my life as it was and to get to know myself better so I could "grow up in the likeness of His Son".

While we are going through one of God's "growth opportunities", I don't think any of us actually likes what is happening. I didn't. I suffered, agonized, got depressed and wondered where I had failed.

Finally, I faced myself and my thinking, just as God had planned all along, and grew past my fear. Once I put my fear aside, I was able to see that race, color, creed or what church a man attends has nothing to do with how God sees that man. He looks into the heart of each of us and measures the amount of love the heart contains, but he sees all of us as having equal value. If we as Christians do less, we are not following the example of His Son, Jesus.

Now, it distresses me greatly if I hear someone speaking about others in a prejudicial way. I do not want to hear prejudicial slurs, jokes or anyone putting anyone else down.

I have heard someone say that a church should be a hospital for sick souls. If this is true, it may account for why there seems to be so much bickering, back stabbing and unfairness in churches.

Many, many times we church members, and even ministers, select people for offices and committees based not upon prayerful consideration of the skills, abilities and the special calling from God they have on their lives, but because of their social influence and other political factors.

It often seems members of churches and pastors spend more time babying spoiled spiritual brats who can't get along with anyone else in a church than they spend winning souls and helping members who want to grow into closeness with God. This saddens me.

I believe each one of us has a purpose and we should keep busy doing whatever God created us to do. When we spend our time trying to keep people happy who refuse to be happy, we are wasting our God ordained purpose, wasting the resources of the church and wasting God's time.

I believe children should be regarded as a "holy trust" from God. The Bible tells us "children are a blessing". There are a lot of jokes about praying God will help us "endure our blessings", but most Christian parents feel as LaHoma and I feel - genuinely blessed.

We feel tremendously blessed by each of our five children. We also feel a responsibility to treat each of our children and grandchildren as equally as possible. Herein lies the difficulty.

Equal is not always fair.

I suppose the process of rearing children is another of God's "growth opportunities". None of our five children need or want the same things from life or from us. While they each require equal love, none of the five need our love demonstrated in the same way.

Some children have more needs than others. Some children want more attention, more support or more independence than others. It is easy to temporarily overlook the quiet ones while one is desperately trying to grease the squeaky wheels.

Sometimes parents and parents-in-law are tempted to push their ideals and beliefs on their children. When this happens, it is very difficult to avoid trouble.

Children need time and space to learn, grow and make their own mistakes. It is hard for a parent to watch his/her child headed in a direction he/she feels will result in the child being hurt without trying to offer advice.

Parents who genuinely love and trust their children, however, have to try to stand back far enough to allow children, especially adult children, to learn and grow at their own pace. Many times, this means that parents have to learn to mind their own business.

My philosophy on parenting is to do the best you can and spend a lot of time in prayer. You'll need it.

If someone were to ask me what I thought the major social problem facing us today was, I would have to say jealousy. Jealousy seems to motivate so many of the mean things people do to each other.

Again, jealousy is another form of fear. When people feel insecure or threatened in some way the jealousy translates into in petty meanness which does more damage to the jealous person than to the person of whom they are jealous.

There are many things I would like to see changed in this world.

First, I would like to see newspapers give more space to people when they do something good, achieve something or succeed rather than make such a big issue of the crooks, criminals and thieves. Newspapers are meant to inform the public. Most newspapers have more influence over the thinking of their readers than they realize.

Along with influence comes responsibility. If they are given the power to influence, they must learn to assume the responsibility for presenting their findings as fairly as possible. Fairness and responsibility would require the front page be filled with success, kindness and achievement. Mayhem and destruction could then be relegated to the inside pages where it would cause less damage.

I would like to see people learning to be themselves rather than trying to be something they are not. Most of us are just fine the way we are. Besides, I've never seen anyone successfully fool people for very long anyway.

I would like to see people who judge contests, referee or umpire sporting events take their positions seriously. These people should see their position as the honor it is and do everything in their power to judge fairly and honestly.

I would like to see politicians running for office on their own merits, achievements and platforms rather than trying to discredit their opponents. I cannot trust someone who constantly degrades his opponent and I don't think others do either.

Probably my strongest code to live by involves minding my own business. I love to help others, when I can. I love to share whatever I have to share; but if you need me, you will have to ask because I do not believe in butting into someone else's business unless invited to do so.

CHAPTER TEN

A MAJOR FALL AND A MAJOR GOAL REACHED

1982 was a busy year.

I entered several new races and I served on the Lincoln Days committee for the second time. With our jobs, family responsibilities and church activities, I sometimes thought LaHoma and I would meet ourselves coming and going. Somehow we managed to keep everything together and move on through a very challenging year.

The first race of the year was the *Tumbleweed Restaurant Race* held along the Ohio River in February. It was bitterly cold, but turned out to be a good race, anyway.

I finished 2nd to Ed Bridgewater from Sellersburg, Indiana. Ed and I raced against each other many, many times. I think we are nearly even in the number of times we have beaten or been beaten by each other. I like this kind of balanced relationship and it added excitement to the races because we never knew which one of us would win each time we met.

After the race, the Tumbleweed Restaurant provided a meal and presented the awards. The beer was flowing. I've noticed a lot of racers drink beer after their efforts.

I won my age group at the *Ft. Knox Gold Rush Run* shortly after the *Tumbleweed Restaurant Run.* I always enjoyed winning this race because many of the post commanders were fifty or older which put them in my age group at the time. I enjoyed beating these military leaders who were always in fine physical shape and were highly competitive.

I only ran in *Louisville's City Run* one time and that was in 1982. Even though Louisville was only sixty miles away, we decided to go up the night before the race and stay in a hotel.

That evening, after dinner, we went to listen to the Sleepy Marlin Family Band. Sleepy Marlin had been the "World Champion Fiddler" at one time. We enjoyed hearing his band play and seeing the famous "Sleepy Marlin".

I have often told people that I think Louisville, Kentucky, must be the sports capital of the world for a city of its size. Louisville hosts the *Kentucky Derby*, the greatest horse race in the world. The University of Louisville has a great winning record in all its sports programs including basketball, while their football team is coming on strong. Johnny Unitas, one of the greatest professional quarterbacks of all time attended college at the University of Louisville.

During the *Kentucky Derby*, Louisville provides a super riverboat race between the *Belle of Louisville* and the *Delta Queen*, which is owned by Jeffersonville across the river in Indiana. Three world heavyweight champions trace their roots to Louisville. A group of runners from Louisville won the World Championship Cross-Country Run.

The Kentucky Colonels baseball team won several Little World Series while the Redbirds set a national attendance record which will probably never be broken. Finally, Peewee Reese may never be equaled as a shortstop in the field of baseball.

The next morning the race started at the dock where the *Belvedere* is berthed. The *Belvedere* is a steam powered paddle boat which is reminiscent of the old Mississippi River boats of the Civil War era; colorful and easy to locate if you are from out of town.

After leaving the *Belvedere* the runners were to follow River Road to a specific point, then turn around and return to the Belvedere for the finish of the race.

At the half mile marker, there were still about 2,000 runners, bunched up and running close. As a race progresses, runners begin to spread out along the race route as some tire and some begin to pull ahead. As early as the half mile marker the spreading out had not occurred.

I was running along in about the middle of the group innocently minding my own business when I stepped on the back of my own heel and fell flat in the street. I jumped up as quickly as I could and did not get hit by any of the other runners. I thought I was all right and continued the race.

There is not a great deal of difference between the amount of danger involved when a human falls during a race and when a horse falls in a horse race. Neither a horse nor the humans running behind expect to find a body sprawled out in front of them; therefore, they find it difficult to adjust to the change. A fall can cause a "pile up", where runners trip over each other adding to the confusion. Serious injury can occur.

Fortunately, disaster was averted and no one was hurt.

There was heavy competition that day from the likes of Wally Dawkins and Bob Crow. I finished the race in 46:42, but still came in sixth in my age group. I crossed the finish line, then discovered I had sprained my ankle and skinned a knee and an elbow rather badly in the fall at the half mile point.

The *Cherokee Road Runners Club* is a fine organization for anyone interested in running. I had joined this group and enjoyed receiving my magazine and the newsletters and announcements of upcoming races.

In 1982, Frankie Crume, a fine master's runner, was president of the *Cherokee Road Runners Club.* The club sponsored a four mile run at Moore High School in the late winter.

I ran the four miles in 28:33 and placed 2nd to Frank Robinson in the 45 and older group. Frank was several years younger than I so I wasn't too distressed to place 2nd to him, especially when my time was so good.

I was running about thirty miles a week in addition to the thirty-seven and one- half miles I was walking every week on my mail route. I had lost the fourteen pounds I wanted to lose and I looked like a runner.

I had, also, kicked the cigarette habit. It had been a struggle, but I finally made it. To be honest, the thing which finally stopped my smoking was when LaHoma quit; I didn't have anyone to swipe cigarettes from, so that ended that.

I was in great shape and felt "too good". Don't ask me how someone can feel "too good" because I don't know. I guess, I just hadn't expected to feel so great when I passed fifty.

In America, we have been taught that the only people of value are the "young and beautiful". I don't think there is a thing wrong with being "old and beautiful". In fact, a lot of us think young can not be beautiful. Young can be pretty, but it takes the depth, grace, and insight which can only come with the passing of time to develop true beauty.

We have a tendency to think, as the grey hairs begin to appear, that we should begin to slow down, that the best of life is over. If you will remember, I made a similar mistake when I saw Roy Brill's gray head ahead of me in the race at Magnolia's homecoming. I thought, since he had grey hair, he was my age and nearly killed myself edging him out of first place only to find he was twelve years younger.

Just think about the story of Caleb in the Bible. He stood up in the council of war and said someting like, "I am eighty-five years old today, yet my eyesight and hearing are as good as they were forty-five years ago, and my body is just as strong. Give me that mountain! I can lead my boys up that mountain, but the rest of you can go home. I can do it myself!"

As you know, Caleb did "take the mountain" and ended Israel's war over the Promised Land.

It didn't take a miracle to keep Caleb young and strong. It took faith. Because of his faith, God blessed Caleb and gave him his heart's desire.

That's all any older person needs - courage, faith and determination. None of us have to wither away and begin to act feeble at any age unless we want to do so.

A reasonable diet, a steady daily exercise and some common

sense will keep any of us in top physical shape. The operative words here are "common sense", however.

If you have spent the last ten years lying in front of the tube, wolfing down the gooey goodies while your mind went on vacation, don't think you are going to jump up and chop a cord of wood. You'll end up dead as a door nail.

Start small. Instead of lying there and yelling for your wife to bring you some cookies, get up and get them yourself. Next, start walking around the house every day for a few days, then around the block, then around two blocks. Keep slowly and gradually increasing your activity level until one morning you will wake up and realize, nothing hurts.

If you keep it up, soon you will wake up, jump up and start looking around for something fun to do. You will have crossed over from the "I'm not as young as I once was" to the "You kids had better hurry up if you want to go with me" syndrome.

If you can talk your sweet little wife into walking with you, it won't be long until you are considered an "awesome twosome". She'll be out buying new clothes to keep up with your new life-style.

Running isn't for everyone, but nearly everyone can walk by starting slowly and gradually building up. (A little secret for the wise - the more you exercise, the more you can eat without the effects showing up on the bathroom scales.)

I didn't run again until April when I had two major races scheduled for the same weekend.

On Saturday, I was entered for the second time in the run held in Bardstown, Kentucky. I ran along with Linda Waltman, a professional singer from Louisville, for a while.

The race committee in Bardstown doesn't give many awards so I knew I would have to win to receive the trophy. I just did the best I knew how.

My best was good enough to win my age group and to beat Paul Ennis for the first time in a fair race. There was only one trophy given for each age group, so I got the trophy and the thrill of beating "old Ennis". I was sky high. I had reached one of my major goals in running. Life was good!

The next day I was competing in the *Spring Fling Run* at St. Catherine's College in Springfield, Kentucky. I think this must have been the most beautiful day in my life.

Everything was in full bloom. The weather was perfect and everyone I met seemed to be in a happy, friendly mood.

I met several new runners including Emory Brewer from Richmond, Kentucky. In the *Spring Fling*, runners can run on a team as well as compete individually. I joined Emory's team. We won the *Master's Team Award* and I ran second in my age group to Bill Long.

When I lined up for my next race, the *Kentucky Derby Mini-Run* of 13.1 miles, I realized I would be starting with Jerry Miller from LaRue County, Louie Dampier, the ex-pro basketball player, and the mayor of Louisville, Mayor Harvey Sloane. We ran together for a while, but soon became separated.

Though I was feeling great, physically, the first mile was terribly slow. On the second mile, I was able to pick up speed. When I reached the tenth mile, I rejoined Jerry Miller. We tried to encourage each other and to assure ourselves that we would be able to finish the race.

Shortly thereafter, I passed Wayne Collier. Wayne must have been having a bad day because I was never able to beat him again and he has been a tough competitor in the *Bluegrass Games*.

I finished in 1:43:03 which put me 13th in my age group out of 76 older runners. I kept records of the twelve runners who beat me that day and at one time or another beat everyone of them except Bob Crow, Eugene Barker and Bill Long.

At the time, I planned to stay in running after I retired and continue to improve. I was planning to pick them off one by one as they aged and slowed down. Of course, I may yet.

I made a new racing friend in Salem, Indiana, at my next race, Jerry Greenlee. Jerry had gray hair which always makes me think a runner is in my age group. Jerry looked as if he were a real threat so I was concerned about running against him. Later, however, I found out he was much younger than I. That gray hair caused me a lot of needless worry, again!

I won my age group while Buddy Harpool won the race overall. We had time to visit with Buddy's wife and little boy, which was a lot of fun.

The race in Salem, Indiana, was quickly followed by the *Tank Trail Run* at Fort Knox, Kentucky. Several LaRue County runners competed in this race including the Hacker boys, David Otis and Danny Owens.

One would think that competing against the soldiers at Fort Knox would be a near impossibility because of their very active and physical life-styles. This is not the case, however.

The Fort Knox community is always receptive to their neighbors and seem happy to welcome us to participate with them in their games and competitions; however, they are much more interested in competing with each other than with the community at large.

The men ran in "companies" as there is a company trophy as well as individual awards. They run along together at a respectable speed until the company trophy is "locked up". At the very end of the race, they sprint and try to beat each other for individual awards. While this practice is effective for their "in-house" competition, it usually means they are not able to compete effectively against skilled "outside" runners.

The Hacker boys won trophies, but the competition was too stiff for me in my age group. I finished fifth which was not a good showing considering how well I had been doing all year.

CHAPTER ELEVEN

MY FAVORITE RUNNER AND A BIT OF UNPLEASANTNESS

As the 1982 running season progressed, a special treat was in store for me. I was invited to enter the *White Mills Run* in Hardin County.

White Mills, Kentucky, is a picturesque area in Hardin County which holds memories for me of visiting and swimming when I was a child.

White Mills once boasted a flour and feed mill from which the town got its name. An old bridge, which had been impressive in its time, spans a beautiful stretch of river which offers a little bit of everything nature lovers could want.

Under the bridge is a fairly shallow area strewn with huge boulders which have been worn smooth by the action of the water. Farther down stream is a deep quiet pool surrounded by high shale banks and an archway of green leafy trees bending over the river to shade young swimmers from sunburn. I had been swimming in that cool, shaded spot when I was very young.

From here the river follows the road for about a half mile. The upper bank is steep and overgrown but the lower bank is more gently sloped and closer to the water. Giant trees shade the roadway and provide a beautiful view for the houses which face the river from the opposite side of the road.

Farther up stream is a "hidden" spring which pours out of the side of the river bank over stacks of moss covered rocks and into the rushing current of the river. It is a beautiful area of Kentucky which tourist may miss because it is not on the guide maps, but it is well worth a side trip to enjoy a quiet picnic along another of Kentucky's wonderful rivers.

During the 1940's, my dear friend Howard Jaggers from Magnolia, Kentucky, was a coach at Lynnvale High School, which was located near White Mills. As he was from Magnolia, he invited the Magnolia team down to Lynnvale for a practice game before the regular basketball season opened.

The Jr. Varsity and the Varsity teams would play each other. After the ball games were over, there would be field events. It was great fun and gave us country kids a chance to meet new people and have new experiences.

It is hard for young people now-a-days to understand the degree of isolation boys and girls experienced while living on farms in the forties and fifties. By the early sixties, television and affordable automobiles were helping to close the gaps between city, town and country, but when I was in high school, being allowed to travel to another school district to visit, play and compete was a great treat.

In 1982, Bobby Williams was the track and cross country coach at West Hardin High School. Mr. Williams was chairman of a race called the *White Mills Run.* I was delighted to get the chance to run in the race and jog old memories of an earlier time in my life.

I finished first in my age group. Since White Mills does not hold an award ceremony, they handed me my trophy as I crossed the finish line. I guess this is an example of immediate gratification. Since you know how I love to win trophies, you know I was immediately gratified.

The *White Mills Run* was held on a Friday night. The next morning we traveled to Lexington for the *Bluegrass Run.* When I arrived I was told the race was closed for registration, but I could run "unofficially". Those in charge gave me a tee shirt and I decided I would run for the fun of it.

The *Bluegrass Run* in Lexington is one of the best races in Kentucky, but the day was extremely hot which is not a good day to run. Mary Witt won the women's race. Even if I had been running as a legal runner, I wouldn't have received an award because the competition was so fierce. I was also at a disadvantage because I had run so hard the evening before.

I ran 3rd in the 1982 *Run With The Stars* in Bowling Green, Kentucky, and moved on to the race in Upton, Kentucky, which was sponsored by Upton's Ruritan Club.

Upton is a unique small town. The LaRue/Hardin County line runs right down the center of the town. Residents on the east side of the main street live in LaRue County while the residents on the West Side of the main street live in Hardin County. While such a situation might cause split personalities in lesser folk, the citizens of Upton handle it quite well.

Though Upton is a small town, its race offered superior competition. Much of the credit must go to Gary and Sharon Cruse who had planned the race and encouraged so many of the runners to take part. Gary was still interested in racing in 1982 though he had hurt his knee a few years before in a marathon and had given up the sport.

I finished 2nd to Ed Bridgewater in the *Jeffersonville Four, 5K's*, then on to Harrodsburg, Kentucky, and the *Pioneer Day Race.*

LaHoma always enjoyed going to Harrodsburg because one of her close friends from her college days at Campbellsville College, Barbara Jo Young, lives there.

The first time we went to Harrodsburg for a race we stopped at the Stone Court Restaurant for a meal. As we went into the restaurant, the manager and owner was standing by the cash register. LaHoma and Barbara recognized each other immediately though it had been twenty-five or more years since they had seen each other. They were so thrilled to see each other and get the chance to re-hash old college days. Barbara Jo introduced us to her parents and husband while we were there. Now we make it a point to eat at the Stone Court Restaurant when we are in the area.

I finished 4th to Bob Graves, Tom Radden and Gordon Bell. A year later, I beat Bell and Radden, but was never able to beat Graves.

By the end of the summer, it was time for the *Steamboat Festival* in Jeffersonville, Indiana. The *Steamboat Festival* hosts a huge race which is well chaired and masterfully managed. The awards were ten-deep in each age group which attracts large numbers of runners, but the age groups cover a ten year span instead of the usual five.

In those days the Steamboat Festival competed with the *Kentucky Derby Run* or the *Run for the Roses* in Louisville. Runners came from everywhere for both races, but a lot of the older guys competed in the *Steamboat Run.*

The *Steamboat Run* has a lot of character and interest from the organizers and local people. The finish line was on Spring Street on the river. Arts and crafts were scattered throughout the town and clustered around the finish line.

I won an eighth place trophy and was thrilled. I placed first before Al Vogel, a man I had never beaten before; I was pleased.
In September, it was time for the Green County Festival, *Cow Days*. *Cow Days* is unique in many ways. For one thing the committee gives away a live cow. There is a plastic cow you can milk but gives Kool-Aid rather than milk, which would spoil in the hot sun.

I won 1st place in my age group. Paul Ennis was up to no good at the awards ceremony and wanted to kiss all the lady winners. Everybody loves Paul so he gets away with a lot more than he should.

After the race, Gene Priddy and his family joined me and mine at our beloved Cozy Corner restaurant where we ate all the ham, "red eye" gravy, homemade preserves and little brown biscuits we could eat. Mrs. Edwards was such a good cook.

Our daughter and her husband, Kenny Devore, were living in Louisville where Kenny was working as a Naval recruiter. As part of his duties, Kenny was also on the race committee for the *Military Challenge Run* to be held in the neighborhood of Standiford Field in Louisville.

Kenny insisted I enter the race and promised that it would be a flat running course because he knew all the trouble hills had caused me during various races. Jimmy Howell, James Sallee and I entered the race.

Of course, Kenny had told his comrades that his father-in-law would be running in the race. It caused a bit of a stir and I got more attention than I was used to getting in other places.

There was a huge turn out for the race from both civilians and the military. The competition was stiff as a well attended race always is. For a long way, Ed Bridgewater, Art Rousseau and I ran side by side. We three had some very good races that year.

I ran a 44:18, but was only able to place 4th behind Jerry Ruff, Ed Bridgewater and Art Rousseau.

Our next race was Spencer County's *Spencer Homecoming Run* which was sponsored by Ken Combs' Running Store on a day when the Kentucky weather played one of its nasty little tricks. Though it was only early October, the weather was unseasonably cold for a day or two.

James Sallee, Danny Owens and I drove to Spencer County together. We parked in the Post Office's parking lot and warmed up. Afterwards, we took our clothes off down to our running suits at the starting line. Before the race began, we turned blue and started to shake. However, once we began running, we were all right.

I finished 3rd to Bill Long and a guy named Spangers. It was a good race and I had a trophy in my hands, so I was pleased.

After the race, we had to hurry to get into our warm-up suits to avoid a chill and muscle cramps. As I was getting into the car to go home, I accidentally sat on my trophy and broke the little man off of the top. Later I had to glue him back together.

The weather returned to high temperatures and high humidity in time for the *Lincoln Days Railsplitter Run*. It was terribly hot which makes for a very tough race.

This was my second year on the *Railsplitter Run* committee and all of us had worked hard to keep attendance up. In spite of the heat, around 151 runners started the race.

I consider this "my race". I have worked hard over the years to help make it a success and feel strongly about it. It is always fun to run "at home", but I think it is a little harder to do well. For some reason, most of us feel a little more pressure to do well in front of family and friends with poor results for the most part.

Joe Kim, a bank auditor from Franklin, Kentucky, was there and Ray Parella from Jeffersonville, Indiana. I had seen Joe often and run with Ray several times before.

Ray owns Parella's Italian Restaurant in Jeffersonville, which serves delicious Italian food. Ray is always concerned about the runner's comfort and safety at the end of races everywhere he goes. If a race committee fails to provide water, or enough water, they have to deal with Ray. After he finishes his own race, Ray stays and brings water to each racer as he/she crosses the finish line.

Ray has his trophies in a case at his restaurant. His Railsplitter trophy is right in front, which says a lot about the value he puts on it.

I finished 2nd behind Paul Ennis. A Butler man from Versailles finished 3rd and Joe Kim finished 4th. Buddy Harpool won the "overall", again. Angela Murphy won the women's division with Sue Boone of Howardstown, Kentucky, 2nd.

The LaRue County trophies went to Jimmy Howell as the first runner in the men's division and Sue Nichols in the women's division. Bryan Perkins, aged nine, was the youngest runner.

The following weekend we went back to the *Green River Lake Run* at Campbellsville where I was beaten by Bob Maclin and Owen Comer in a close race.

This was the first time I met Bob Maclin, but we became good friends as time went on. I ran into Bob at the *Bluegrass Games* and was disturbed to find he had suffered some serious injuries. I hope he has recovered fully as Bob loves to run.

My mother-in-law, Ruth Nichols, and her cousin, Howard Cessna, went with us to Campbellsville where Howard treated us to dinner at The Catfish House.

Howard was an interesting fellow of 88 years who seemed much younger. He retired from the Detroit Police Department nearly thirty years earlier and had a passel of police stories to tell. He knew the famous Joe Lewis who owned a farm near where Howard lived. He sold Joe a registered fine harness mare once. Howard said Joe was an exceptionally nice person.

Howard and Ruth went with us to New Albany, Indiana, for the *River Banks Run.* It was a good race, but with the ten year age group, I didn't place. After the race we went to Ray Parella's restaurant for dinner.

Next we went to Columbia, Kentucky, where the Christian Churches sponsor a race which is now called the *Bell Pepper Race.* I got off to a slow start, but finished strong just ahead of my old friend, Owen Comer and a Burden fellow from Louisville.

My friend Roy Ingram lives in the Columbia area. Roy is unusual in that he is one of the few farmers who has gotten involved in running as a hobby. I guess, most farmers think they have too much to do to run when they don't have to. I know I felt that way when I was farming.

Roy ran well. He usually finished close to the leaders or won himself.

This was the only time I raced in Columbia, but it was a good race and a nice memory.

One of the highlights of 1982 was the "Stan Cottrill Run" in Munfordville, Kentucky.

Stan Cottrill is one of my favorite runners. He grew up in the Cub Run district near Munfordsville, Kentucky. He is listed in *Who's Who of Ultra-Running*.

Stan has run across the U.S.A., but says one of his most difficult feats was running across Kentucky. He made three tries at running across Kentucky before he was successful, but Stan is one of those dedicated, determined people who will make every effort to succeed.

Stan is the only person to succeed in running across Kentucky; however, I had wanted to try for some time. I thought it would be a great challenge for an older runner.

Munfordsville honored Stan by naming the race after him, which was such a loving, supportive thing to do. Regardless of who we are, or what we do, there is no feeling in the world which equals being recognized by the people you know and love, and who have shared the early years of one's life.

Too many communities, especially small communities, fail to recognize the accomplishments of their noteworthy citizens. The very people among them who are recognized in other places are ignored at home. Perhaps there is some jealousy involved or insensitivity, but it seems a fairly common failing.

The *Stan Cottrill Run* was only held twice and I won my age group the second time.

The day of the first *Stan Cottrill Run* was the hottest day I ever ran. I ran 3rd behind Earl Moriz and Theron Kessinger. We were all sweating profusely and there is no telling how much weight some of us lost during the race.

The course was excellent except for the finish, which was terrible. After crossing the Green River bridge, we had to run straight up hill for about 1,000 feet where the awards were given by the courthouse. About the best a runner can hope for is to survive.

There aren't too many Hart countians who race, but two notable exceptions were J.D.Craddock, a local lawyer and Jerry Ralston, a principal in the Hart County School System.

After the race Donnie had his picture taken with Stan Cottrill.

I was looking forward to running in Glasgow because they treat their runners so well. I've made some great friends in Glasgow: Don Minor, Lisa Witty, Steve Metzer, Terry Reed, Ernest Cassidy, Ernest Neel, Oliver Bush and Billy Hall Baxter to name a few.

There seems to be an occasional unpleasantness in nearly all activities that involve people. There was one which had been bothering me for several races.

An older runner and his younger friend had worked out a system which I felt was unsportsman like. The younger man ran his own race, finished, then came back and "paced" the older runner to the finish line.

At the end of a long race, if another runner "paces" a runner, it gives the runner a decided advantage. This older runner had managed to beat me a few times with this method. I decided if this man ran the *Metro Marathon* in Louisville, he would be in trouble.

I practiced three long runs and headed for the 26.2 mile race in Louisville in late November. It was bitterly cold and we would be running along the Ohio River for at least part of the race.

Sure enough the older runner was there with his young friend.

It was so cold, I ran with my warm-up jacket and gloves on, though I had gotten rid of the warm-up pants. I had made up my mind to beat this man come cold, sleet or frigid winds off the Ohio.

There were 1,200 or more entered in the race. I started slowly with the man I was determined to beat. He must have noticed something different about my attitude because he said, "You are going to beat me today," and I did.

The wind coming off the river was terrible, but when I got to the turn-around at Rose Island I was feeling fine. I did not stop for water until after the first 23 miles. I drank two full cups then began running again. I was determined to break four hours for the 26.2 miles.

I was on schedule after the stop for water. I caught up with a wheelchair runner and fell in behind him and coasted to the finish line at 3:55:39.

LaHoma, Donnie, Jo and her boyfriend had come to the race with me. They took my picture just as I crossed the finish line. I looked good considering I had just run a marathon at my best time ever, but I finished 8th Kentuckian in my age group. I got a medal for this, my second marathon.

After the race, we went down to The Louisville Galleria to shop. My family shopped. I sat on the floor against a wall, watched people and tried to recover.

Mr. and Mrs. Kenneth Devore, our daughter's in-laws passed me as did our pastor's son, Paul McDonald. They stopped to talk with me. They said they were happy I had survived my run and hoped I would feel better the next day.

The following day I took a vacation day, soaked in the tub and went to the barber shop where I got to tell all about my race.

The next Thursday I went to New Albany to run in the *V.F.W. Run.* I was a little dull after the marathon, so I didn't do too well. I hoped I would be at my best the next week for the *Life Begins at Forty* in Louisville.

I finished 3rd to Wally Dawkins and a Swanson man I did not know well. From the race we went to a post race party and Christmas party at Bill and Joy Peterson's house.

The next race was a *Big Man Run* at Seneca Park on Sunday afternoon. I finished eighty-third over all and second in my age group.

In addition to age, there was a weight category. Even though I am a big person, I cannot compete with a big young man.

The *Southern Indiana Classic* was an eight mile race. My old friend, Marilyn Scott beat me then rooted for me to finish. I ran 2nd to Ed Goddin. I received a medallion.

I finished the year with the *Wendy's Classic*, finishing second to Eugene Barker at the *Elizabethtown Turkey Trot* and finishing 2nd to Eugene Barker at the *Life Begins at 40.*

This was the year that Bill Peterson and Eugene Barker ran in the *Kentucky 50 Miler* between Louisville and Frankfort. They had run together and finished only a couple of minutes apart.

I was beginning to think more seriously about the possibility of running across Kentucky. Older people were running long distances successfully and remaining competitive even into their retirement years. It was beginning to sound more and more as if I might have a chance.

CHAPTER TWELVE

PIGS IN THE OVEN AND A GRUMPY BELL

I have always felt the important thing in this life is not so much what you do as with whom you do it.

I love to compete when I know my family will be at the finish line at the end of a race. I could win every award the world has to offer, but it would not mean as much to me as knowing my wife and children believe in me and are on my side.

As I have said before, I feel God led me to be in the right place at the right time and to do the things He wanted me to do throughout my life. Certainly in the choice of a wife, He had the perfect life's partner picked out for me, maybe since the world began. I dated a lot over the years, but when God led me to LaHoma, it didn't take me long to understand what He had in mind.

After my four year tour of duty in the Air Force ended, I came home to LaRue County, bought a four door, 1956 Chevy, got a job at Fort Knox and began to adjust to life as a civilian. This would have been a fairly uneventful period in my life if it had not been for Aileen Skaggs.

Aileen and I worked in the same office and rode to work in the same car pool. One Saturday, we had to work overtime. I probably mentioned that I had a "big date" Saturday night as we were driving home. Aileen offered me a stick of chewing gum which I innocently accepted.

It tasted and behaved strangely for chewing gum, but I didn't think much about it until I realized Aileen was laughing. You guessed it - she had given me a laxative gum. I barely made it back to town in time to avoid public humiliation that evening. I told Aileen I would never forgive her; I have, of course.

Thomas Wolfe wrote that "you can never go home again". Perhaps from his standpoint one can't go home. It has been my observation that some things never change and home is always home. There can be a deep sense of homecoming even when we must cope with a few changes. These changes can be welcome or not so welcome.

Most of my friends had married and/or moved away. Bobby Thomas had just been discharged from the army and was in the same boat I was. We began to run around together.

One Sunday afternoon, Bobby and I were "cruisin'" in the car. It was 1958 when "cruisin'" was the "in" thing for young people to do. As we had planned, we happened to see some girls "cruisin'". They began talking to us.

One of those girls was a beautiful blond fifth grade school teacher named LaHoma Nichols. I made a date for the same evening.

LaHoma and I double dated with Bobby Thomas and Phyllis Blakeman after church that evening. I met her parents who were exceptionally fine people and her three year old daughter, Sandra LaHoma. Sandra was a little blond haired doll who seemed to think I was really special.

I celebrated Christmas with LaHoma's family and it turned out to be a wonderful time full of Christian fun and fellowship. I gave Sandra a big doll which she seemed to love.

By Valentine's day, LaHoma and I went to Louisville to pick out her engagement ring. LaHoma wore a black pants suit and like most blonds, she looked great in it. I just love black, especially if LaHoma wears it.

We were married the 28th of June, 1959, at her parent's home, by the Reverend Peter Ginn, Pastor of the First Baptist Church in Hodgenville. Bobby Thomas was my "best man" while Jane Nyhlom was LaHoma's matron of honor. We honeymooned at Cumberland Falls, Kentucky.

I bought a house from Phyllis Blakeman's father on Maple Avenue in Hodgenville where we began establishing our home. In July of 1960, our second daughter, Donna Gail, was born. Eighteen months later Diana Lynn made her appearance. We had bought a farm by this time and I was just beginning to work for the Postal Service. Life was good.

When we got our three little girls dressed for church on Sunday morning, I thought they had to be the cutest, sweetest little girls God ever created.

Four years later Melissa Jo was born and we thought our family was complete. A few years later, Donnie took us completely by surprise and has been amazing us ever since.

Our five children are so uniquely and delightfully different. I cannot tell you that every minute of their growing up has been easy, but I can attest to the fact that we have never been bored for one single minute of our married life.

Sandra, our oldest, seemed to be the outdoor type. She was always willing to help me with the farm work, especially, with the animals. In fact, she became our resident veterinarian.

Sandra turned her room and every available space into hospital facilities for her ailing animals. It was nothing for Sandra to have a sick calf reclining over the heat register in her bedroom while tending a cat having kittens in a closet.

During one of her pediatric efforts, a kitten she had just delivered began to show signs of respiratory distress. Deciding the kitten needed mouth to mouth resuscitation but not wanting to put the kitten's head in her mouth, our quick thinking Sandra improvised some type of equipment from things she found in her mother's makeup drawer. She successfully revived the kitten. He died a few days later, but not because his little doctor had not given the effort everything she had to give.

I relied on Sandra to help out with the animals because she was not only responsible and trustworthy, but because she was good at it. One day one of the sows gave birth to a litter of pigs. I helped her deliver twelve, but had to leave for work. I showed Sandra how to take care of the little pigs and the mother, thinking the process was about over. After I went to work, Sandra delivered five or six more pigs.

Of course the sow could not take care of all of them. When LaHoma and I got home from work, we found a nest of blankets on the open oven door with the little pigs nestled inside. Sandra had a feeding schedule going and was tending her little charges.

She was able to raise one of the pigs to adulthood. He slept in a basket by the bed and thought he was a dog.

A friend of LaHoma came to visit one afternoon. The pig came rushing out to greet her by rubbing against her leg. Thinking he was a dog, she leaned over to pet him then discovered she had been rubbed by a pig. She screamed and threw a pure fit in our front yard because she had been rubbed by a pig.

I really can't understand how a dog and a pig are terribly different in the rubbing department. He was a very clean pig, after all.

The pig grew up. We sold him to a family who ate him, unfortunately.

Even with Sandra's expertise in managing animals, it was impossible not to have at least one scary accident (it was mostly scary to her mother and me, of course).

When LaHoma was a little girl, her parents gave her a pony. Every so often she would ride her pony over to Jack Thompson's farm and have it bred to Jack's famous "fine harness" horse, Noble Kalarama, or one of his descendants.

By the time our girls were old enough to ride, their grandparents had presented them a granddaughter of Noble Kalarama and a daughter of LaHoma's pony. This particular union must have been a fiery mix because she was one of the feistiest little horses I ever saw.

As the oldest and most proficient with animals, Sandra did most of the riding. One afternoon as Sandra was riding, the horse went racing toward a barbed wire fence then came to a sudden stop. Sandra, unfortunately, did not.

Sandra eventually came to rest entangled in the barbed wire fence with a badly scratched leg. While this episode nearly gave her mother and me heart failure, Sandra took the whole thing in stride.

Donna Gail, with her olive complexion and brown eyes, seems to look more like my side of the family than any of our children. She has a quiet, pensive quality which always made her appear serious. She has also tended to be quite practical and domestic.

She cut teeth at three months and was walking at nine months. LaHoma says there is an old proverb that when a child is so far ahead of their age group, they are "getting up and out of the way for the next one". In Donna's case it proved true since Diana was born so soon after her.

One of Donna's outstanding features was a magnificent mane of hair. It was thick, shiny and had a naturally "frosted" look to it. We kept it long enough to sit on until she found balancing marriage, motherhood and college too great a challenge to give her time to take care of all that hair.

One day when Donna was quite small, she got mad at her mother and me. She announced she was going to "run away from home". LaHoma said, "I'm sorry you feel that way, Donna. But if you have to, you'll just have to go."

Donna stomped out of the house and slammed the screen door. LaHoma and I rushed to the windows where we could watch her, but she could not see us.

When she left the house, her little feet were flying and she was tossing her head so that the late afternoon sun glinted in her long hair like spun silver. By the time she reached the edge of the front yard she was walking a few steps then glancing back at the house over her shoulder. The farther she went, the slower she went until, at the top of the hill on the road in front of our house, she stopped. She stood there for a minute then turned around and came slowly back. We watched her until she was close enough so we knew she was not going to turn around and go back then hurried about our business so she would not know we had been hovering over her the whole time.

She came back into the house and never mentioned a word about the incident again.

Donna also had her share of scrapes. When she was quiet small she was playing around a barberry hedge during the season when the little red berries were on the bushes. For some reason, she stuffed one of the little berries up her nose.

Of course, this was very upsetting to her. When she found she could not get the berry out of her nose, she ceased to be a quiet, practical child. By the time we reached Doctor Handley's office, she was howling, crying and making her extreme displeasure known to the world. Just as Dr. Handley took her in his lap, she sneezed, coughed or something. Whatever it was that happened, the berry came out on its own.

Donna was also the only one of our children to sustain a serious injury. LaHoma went to the Lincoln National Bank one Saturday morning taking Donna with her. As they entered the bank, LaHoma, who was holding Donna's hand, realized Donna had stopped moving. Looking back she saw that Donna's finger was caught in the heavy doors.

LaHoma thought Donna's finger had been cut completely off. She got sick and weak in the knees looking at our baby who was apparently in shock.

Shelby Howard grabbed a handkerchief from a lady in the bank, wrapped the finger and carried Donna across Lincoln Blvd., through Morgan Marcum's store, out the back door to Hogdenville's clinic. Dr. Handley took one look at the finger and told them to take her to Hardin Memorial Hospital.

Shelby drove LaHoma and Donna home to get me, then we rushed to the hospital. Dr. Aaron was in the emergency room that morning. They injected pain killers into the mangled finger, but Donna was hysterical from the pain and everything that had happened to her. It took five adults to hold her steady to allow the doctor to sew her finger back on.

Dr. Aaron was famous for a lot of things, one of which was his tobacco chewing. He would work on Donna's finger then turn and spit, sew and spit, sew and spit.

He saved her finger, but she carries the scars to this day.

Though she was athletic and played baseball, Donna was the "domestic goddess" of the family. She seemed to enjoy anything about homemaking. It was not unusual for LaHoma to come home from work to find Donna calmly sorting toys, cleaning and straightening the house.

All of our children were active in 4-H, but the activities of this club seemed to be one of Donna's favorites, along with her high school home economic classes. Both Sandra and Donna sewed their own clothes throughout high school.

Diana Lynn was born the third of January, 1962, though she was supposed to be born in December.

Diana would prove to be the family musician. LaHoma and I spent twenty plus years in the band as four of our five children played in the LaRue County Band. Sandra was also a majorette and was on the team that won the State Majorette Championship. Diana was exceptionally talented in music as was her brother, Donnie.

She began taking piano lessons from Ann Gibson when she was quite young. Soon, she was playing very, very well. She competed in a county wide 4-H talent contest in 1972 playing "The Long Haired Lover from Liverpool"; she brought the house down! She won first place and went on to the regional competition in Bardstown.

The night Diana was to compete in the regional contest, I was so sick I could barely move. I laid in abject misery in the back seat of the car until it was time for Diana to perform then went in and watched her. As soon as she finished, I rushed back to the car to lie down again.

Diana won 2nd place that evening. LaHoma took the girls to eat dinner in a restaurant in Bardstown to celebrate. They left me lying in the back seat of the car, alone.

When Diana was twelve or thirteen, Mrs. Burress from the Wesley Meadow Methodist Church heard Diana play in a piano recital and asked her to become the organist for the church. The church members paid her a little salary and picked her up at our church after Sunday School as both LaHoma and I taught Sunday School and could not transport her. Diana continued as organist at Wesley Meadows Methodist until she graduated from high school.

Diana, like Sandra and Donna before her, was in "everything". She played on the softball team and participated in everything the school and our church had to offer.

Diana did not make it through childhood without her own little mishap, however.

About a half mile from the house on the farm we bought when the girls were small, a creek wound through the property. I taught the children to swim in that creek which was strictly off limits unless LaHoma or I was with them.

It could be possible the children slipped away to go swimming and we haven't heard about it yet, but they were not supposed to go to the creek alone. Each time one of the children got out of our sight for any length of time our hearts would sink into our shoes as we immediately thought of the creek.

Diana disappeared one day. After some frantic searching around the house and barns, I got on the tractor and started for the creek.

I found my bedraggled daughter just emerging from the creek dripping wet in her clothes without her glasses. Diana had been walking along the creek bank when she slipped and fell in, losing her glasses in the process. Of course, it was hopeless to try to find them so we decided that one day someone would catch a catfish out of the creek and he would be wearing Diana's glasses.

When the girls were little, we had the world's best babysitter in Christie Jewel. The girls loved her, she was dependable and we trusted her completely. However, one summer day, we nearly lost her.

Sandra, Donna and Diana got into a fuss, fight or World War III, we were never sure. After fighting for a while, they separated and hid. They were not hiding from Christie. They were hiding from each other, but the results were the same.

Christie looked everywhere for them. After a while, she became frantic and thought of the creek. She called LaHoma at work nearly hysterical with fear. A short while later, the girls emerged from their hiding places in the chicken coop totally unaware of the chaos they had created. Christie called LaHoma and turned in her resignation.

LaHoma called me and we pleaded with Christie not to leave us. We promised we would talk with the girls that very night and we did.

She stayed. It never happened again and the children grew to adulthood.

In 1966, our last little girl was born. Because we had three girls already, we had hoped for a boy. As soon as we saw our baby girl's sweet little face we could not remember why we thought we wanted a boy. We named her Melissa Jo.

One thing I can say for my children is that they have always been delighted when they found out a new baby was coming. Sandra, Donna and Diana were delighted with Jo, played with her, helped take care of her and seemed to think she was the grandest child.

Jo was a good baby. She was quiet and had the sweetest disposition and manner.

Jo may have gotten into her share of mischief, but the other girls must have covered for her and kept us from knowing about it. She seemed as if she were an unusually well-behaved child.

When Jo was very small, she quietly disappeared one Saturday afternoon. We searched everywhere we could think of that a small child could possibly have gone, but we could not find her.

We eventually progressed from concern to panic. Our first thoughts were of the creek, of course. At the exact point we were beginning to dissolve into disorganized chaos, someone spied a little tuft of blond hair protruding from a circle of car tires I had stacked on the car port.

Jo had crawled into the stack of tires and either couldn't or didn't want to get out. She had fallen asleep and the tires had blocked the sound of our voices as we called to her. She heard nothing, therefore, she continued to sleep through the whole episode.

About the same time Jo, who never complained, began to complain of her ear hurting. When LaHoma combed her hair, she screamed if the comb gently touched her ear.

We took her immediately to Dr. Handley.

Dr. Handley was an important part of our lives, as small town doctors often are. He delivered LaHoma and our daughters, Donna and Diana Lynn. He was our first line of defense against the evils of disease and tragedy.

Dr. Handley looked into Jo's ear and said, "Hum."
A few seconds later, he said, "Hum, hum."

After a few more "hums" and a little head-scratching, he told us the ear drum looked "strange" suggesting we take her to an ear, nose and throat specialist in Glasgow.

The specialist was a nice man who seemed to be especially skilled in working with children. He showed the instruments he was using to Jo and explained what he was doing and how each instrument was used. Jo sat quietly showing no signs of stress or fear.

He explained that there appeared to be something on the ear drum and ran a tiny vacuum tube into Jo's ear, removed the material, sniffed it and said, "It is hard to tell at this point, but it is either Dentyne or Juicy Fruit."

Jo had apparently gone to sleep with chewing gum in her mouth and somehow it became lodged on her eardrum. Jo had no more trouble with her ear.

While Jo is quiet, she has the most expressive eyes of anyone I have ever met. Jo can say more with her eyes than most people can say with words.

Jo was a scholar and an athlete. Her favorite school subject was math; she was an honor student and played both softball and basketball in high school.

She played softball on the Charlie's Angels team which won 27 games in a row and went to the State Championship games. LaHoma and I helped with the car washes which raised money for the trip.

We also accompanied the team on the eventful trip to the Championship games.

After Jo was born, we again thought our family was complete, but surprise, surprise, four and one half years later Donnie was born in 1971.

The night Donnie was born Ellen Ann Terry Brown was the nurse on duty. Ellen had been a lifelong friend and was a sister of my brother-in-law, Theo Terry.

The birth took a long time and Ellen was off duty, but she

stayed because she said she, "Wanted to be the one to tell you that you have a son."

After the baby was born and Ellen was sure LaHoma and the baby were all right she came out to the waiting room. "Donald, you have a son," she said.

"You're kidding," I said.

"No, I'm not," Ellen said. I could tell she was telling the truth so I jumped as high as I could. She said later she would never forget the expression on my face when I finally believed her. She tells this story over and over to our children when she sees them.

After a lot of deliberation, we finally named the new baby Donald E. Mather II.

We brought him home and everybody helped raise him. In fact, we may have been too involved with him for he went through a stage of being quite spoiled and hyperactive. Fortunately, he did not suffer permanent damage, but grew into a loving and giving child who adored his sisters and loved being at home.

I referred to Donnie as "hyperactive", but that may not be correct. He may have been unusually busy. Donnie could entertain himself with his projects and activities without any help from the outside world.

Donnie was and remains a bundle of physical energy whose mind is constantly working at something. Fortunately, Donnie is not the least bit fragmented. He is a steady, dependable type of gifted person who sees projects through to their completion. If Donnie says he is going to do something, you might just as well stand back out of his way because he is going to do it, regardless.

Early in his life Donnie showed signs of being extremely gifted in many areas. In music, art, speech, running and in his school work.

In the first grade, Donnie won the Lincoln Day Art Show in his age group for a drawing he had done of his principal, Mr. Harvey. The same year he won the fifty yard dash at the LaRue County Fair and the watermelon seed spitting contest.

From art to spit, Donnie is ready to compete in any event and has inherited the family love for winning.

When he was very small, Donnie was to perform in a talent competition at the Hodgenville Elementary School. He was to perform a little number which included a song beginning with "My name is Grumpy Bell ...". He wore a little bell costume and looked cute as a button.

Donnie did his little number, but only won 2nd place. He was so distraught over failing to win1st place he would not talk, nor could we console him. He turned out to be the world's grumpiest little Grumpy Bell.

In spite of his distress, something about the situation must have impressed Donnie because he came away from this situation with a love of performing which would lead him to more auspicious performances and, eventually, a trip to Hollywood to perform on national television before he graduated from high school.

CHAPTER THIRTEEN

A WINNING YEAR AND BLISTERS ON A COUNTRY BOY'S FEET

The first race of 1983 was the annual *Hangover Classic* in Louisville on New Years Day. The winners received bottles of champagne. I suppose I didn't need any champagne for I finished 4th to Clyde Keeler, Bill Long and another runner.

I was fairly pleased with myself. I finished in 79 minutes though I had experienced some serious "Christmas Goodie Overloads" during the holidays.

The Tumbleweed Classic in Louisville has always been a successful race because it is held in February, which tends to open the season for running. In 1983, we arrived for the race to find ice covering the streets and the race committee debating about calling the race off.

The streets were beginning to clear and LaHoma talked them out of canceling the race because her "husband has traveled sixty miles to run in this race". The race was held and I finished third to Jack Bradford and Ed Bridgewater.

I won Fort Knox's *Gold Rush* for the third straight year, again beating General Ballantine, the Post Commander.

In 1983 I had one of my busiest racing years. I was in excellent shape, felt good and suffered few injuries; therefore, I ran in more races than I could mention in the space of this chapter. A few of the spring runs included the *Little River Run* in Hopkinsville, the beautiful *Scott-*

Bourbon Classic between Paris and Georgetown, Kentucky, and a race in Brandenburg sponsored by the *Christians Against Drugs and Alcohol* where I finished first and received the trophy for oldest runner. Winning two awards helped to make up for some of the races where I placed and did not receive an award - a little anyway.

One of the most scenic races is the *Scott-Bourbon Classic 30K* (18.6 miles). The race is run on the Paris Pike between Paris and Georgetown, Kentucky. The race route runs directly through some of the horse farms in the Lexington area of Kentucky. As I ran along I could look around and see rolling green fields and sleek horses who twitched their aristocratic ears in our direction as we passed.

Half the runners seemed to come from Ohio for this race. The Ohio runners bring down several buses for the runners and their families.

I was beaten in my age Group by Caton Meburg and Ernest Southworth from Stamping Ground. Ernest is a farmer and a skilled tobacco cutter. At 61 years old, he cut 1,536 sticks of tobacco in 8 hours. That is probably a world's record.

Ernest said once that his ambition was to run a marathon then cut tobacco for eight hours to see how many sticks he could cut. Amazing; utterly amazing.

The race ended at Georgetown College with Don Coffman the overall winner. Don is one of the best runners in the country for his age. He is extremely confident, and nice to talk with at races. He has even had his elderly father competing in the Bluegrass games' race-walk.

The *Tank Trail Run* at Fort Knox was the next race where I finished second to Bob Crow for the second time. The race director was Stephen Swan from Victory, N.C. who was a Captain in the Army. He came to the Railsplitter at the Lincoln Days Festival and won our one mile race later in the year.

It is extremely difficult to group races for convenience sake when each one is so unique and involves such unique and delightful people. No exception is *Down Home Days* at Big Springs. Big Springs is a tiny little community located in both Hardin and Meade counties.

Big Springs figured strongly into the history and color of Kentucky by serving as a stage coach stop. I went into the little country store which doubled as a post office and talked with the post mistress.

Big Springs held a nice festival in 1983. Mary Carman was in charge of everything: the road race, the arts and crafts, the baby contest, the King and Queen competition, and the rooster catching contest. She carried a clipboard around with her and managed everything efficiently. There are any number of organizations and governments which could have benefited by asking this lady for help in management.

I finished 1st in my age group and 11th over all in this race.

I finished 45th and 1st in my age group in the *Sports Shop Run* in Campbellsville then went on to the *Sonora Days Festival* where school principal, Carl Henry Ford, gave the awards. I won my age group as did Marty Sutherland.

After the Ruritan Race in Upton, where I finished 3rd in my age group, we visited with Parson and Mrs. Money. I had worked with Parson at the commissary at Fort Knox. We have always enjoyed each other's company and have remained friends through the years.

I won my age group at the *Seneca Sunrise Race* at Seneca Park In Louisville in the late spring of 1983. Seneca park is a great place to run. The trees block the wind which can cause difficult conditions for runners.

Another of Louisville's successful races is the *Ford Ranger*. In 1983, over a thousand runners competed. I ran second in my age group until the last mile when Earl Moriz and Art Rousseau passed me by. The awards were great but I was disappointed at losing out by only one place.

At Scottsburg, Indiana, only one award was given. I ran second to Ed Goddin, but was able to beat their local "older fellow", Olan Blomguiest. Their plaques were shaped like the State of Indiana and I would have loved to win one that day, but I would return to Scottsburg at a later date.

I had a minor injury before the Bardstown race and was beaten by General Ballantine for the first time. After the race he told me he was leaving for assignment in Washington D.C. and we talked about having enjoyed running together over the past few years.

I was still troubled slightly by the injury for the 13.1 mile *Kentucky Derby Mini-Marathon*, but ran 1:46:40. By this time I knew at least half of the runners and was constantly saying hello as I ran along.

I had a lucky day at the *Southern Indiana Classic*. It was an 81/2 mile race which was not clearly marked. At the first turn there was no official to tell the runners which way to go. I chose the left turn which proved to be correct, finished seventh overall and won my age group. The age group was forty and up so I would have lost to Scott Davidson, but he made the wrong turn and ran two extra miles.

In the very hilly Salem, Indiana, run I finished 2nd to a Methodist preacher named Lyle Rasmusson.

In the *Fort Knox Run* I finished 2nd to Bob Crow. Bob Crow's daughter was a reporter for WHAS news at the time. I enjoyed this race because LaHoma, Diana and Nathan were all with me. I love to win when the family is with me.

I got beaten in Glasgow, mainly because of those bad age groups.

I didn't do too well in the Clarksville, Indiana, run out of more than 1000 runners either, but at the awards ceremony my name was drawn for a $25.00 gift certificate.

LaHoma, Diana and my grandson, Nathan, had gone with me to Clarksville for the race. I got the tee-shirt they gave in Nathan's size. It made me feel good because he was so proud of it. With eleven grand children it is hard to do all of the things for them I would like to do, but I try. All of my grandchildren have received shirts and souvenirs from other trips.

Elizabethtown organizes a fine mid-summer *Heartland Festival* every year. They have a large parade, arts, crafts, a country ham breakfast and a sensational balloon race. A two thousand dollar prize was offered to the balloonist who could descend upon Freeman Lake to pick up a floating object and without landing, ascend again. Several balloonist came close, but no one won the prize in 1983.

As well as Elizabethtown does with their festival, I know they could provide a better race. The course is terrible. It begins on grass, then follows a road, then cuts through a wooded area which is very rough, narrow and the footing is dangerous. By this time they had expanded their race groupings from 46 and over to 50 and over - big deal!

It is possible that such lack of sensitivity to the age differences and skill level changes past the age of forty reflects the prejudices of the people directing races toward older Americans in general and older athletes in particular. It is as if they are saying "everyone has value until you reach forty, then you are all alike. We'll lump you together in a worthless general category called "40 and over" or "46 and over" or "50 and over".

Of course, Elizabethtown is not the only festival which needs to upgrade their road race, but I tend to feel more strongly about Elizabethtown's poor race management because they have the resources and people available to do a race the way a race should be done.

Be that as it may, I survived the course and finished 2nd in my highly generalized 50 and over category.

In late August of 1983 I ran in what ranks close to my favorite race, the *Daniel Boone Run* in Winchester, Kentucky.

As we entered Winchester, the balloon race was in progress. We arrived just minutes before the race was to begin. LaHoma dropped me off in the area of the race's starting point where I finished getting into my race uniform in the street while she parked the car. I had just enough time to get my race packet and line up for the starting gun to sound.

As we raced along I began to see so many of my racing friends; the Powell family from Glendale; Curtsinger from Lexington; Mike and Angela Murphy from Lancaster; and many others.

Ahead of me as I ran, I saw Tom Radden and Joe MacCauley running ahead of me on opposite sides of the road. Tom has blond hair and does not look his age. I wondered if I could hold on and beat them in this race.

I put on a burst of energy and ran between them. I held my speed for a long time. They did not pass me after this surge.

I was eager to hear the results of the race as I was in a strange place and did not know exactly who I was competing with.

Joe MacCauley of Prestonsburg won the sixty and over class. Bob Maclin won the 55-59 age group and I won the 50-54 with Bob Elsa in second place and Jake Curtsinger in third.

My award was a trophy and a print of an open running bag with the contents clearly visible. The bag contained about everything a runner might carry in a running bag and made a nice award.

Later in the day we went to the Linville Puckett Restaurant out past the Daniel Boone Monument.

I had seen Linville play basketball in high school where he was coached by Clark County High School coach, Letcher Norton. After graduating from high school Linville had attended the University of Kentucky where he was coached by Adolph Rupp.

His restaurant is in a beautiful setting on the water. In a trophy case in the restaurant, Linville had on display a collection of mementos from his University of Kentucky playing days.

We were not fortunate enough to meet Linville, but his son was there and we talked with him for a while.

I ran the *Steamboat Race* for the last time winning a trophy by seconds in September.

I beat Earl Moriz for the first time at the *Run with the Stars* in Bowling Green, Kentucky. Fleetwood Fesmire and Theron Kessinger finished before me.

Earl had always beaten me in the final part of the race so this time I paced myself slower. When he came up on my shoulder at the last half mile marker, I poured it on and continued to the finish line. We finished with Earl only three or four steps behind me. Earl quit racing after his wife died. I miss him. He was such a nice fellow to race and talk with.

On Friday night I won my age group at White Mills. Duane Wolff from Elizabethtown, Kentucky, won the overall. We drove home, changed cars and drove to Butler County for the Morgantown *Catfish Festival Run* of five miles. We had some trouble finding a motel, but we slept well and I was ready to run again the next morning.

The *Catfish Festival* is fun. The organizers tag fish with numbers. If someone catches a tagged fish during the day, he receives a prize. One fish has a $10,000 bounty on him.

I ran 3rd to Vern Hayes from Evansville and a new friend I made that day from Dawson Springs, Glen Menser. Glen was a coal miner.

The race began in Morgantown and ended in the country. Glen's wife picked us up in the truck and brought us back to town. After the race we had planned to watch the mud pull, but a storm came up so we ate and came home.

The *Oldham County Festival* offered a five mile race. There were a lot of "oldies" entered in the event, so I didn't know how well I would do. I finished first in my age group ahead of Reed and Comer.

I ran poorly in Upton's annual *Ruritan Race* primarily because Theron Kessinger and Eugene Barker were there and I knew from experience I was no match for them. One of the worse things that can happen to a competitor is to run into someone who intimidates him/her. Theron and Eugene intimidated the daylights out of me.

Elizabethtown was having a race which I decided to avoid. They had a new chairmanship and were just learning about racing. They had decided to have only a forty and older group which I knew was utterly ridiculous. I have always felt Elizabethtown would be an ideal place for a big race if they would put someone in charge who understood what makes an attractive race.

I went to Harrodsburg for *Pioneer Days* instead.

After eating breakfast at the Stone Court Restaurant, I finished third to Bob Graves and Bob McCall. The finish line was just past the Mercer County courthouse which was a beautiful place to finish.

I made a new friend, John Fitch, who came to LaRue County for the *Railsplitter Run* later in the year. A few weeks after the race, my old buddy Jim Sharp sent me a picture his wife took of me passing the courthouse. That picture has a special place in my scrap book to this day.

My next race was the *Tobacco Festival* in Lancaster, Kentucky, where our old friends Mike and Angela Murphy lived. The tee-shirts given by the racing committee were exceptionally beautiful. I won my age group in Lancaster.

The summer was beginning to come to a close and it was back to Greensburg for *Cow Days*. I had run in all of the *Cow Days* runs and certainly did not want to miss this one. I ran a close second to Owen Comer. I caught him near the school, but spent myself in doing it. He came around me to win at the last minute. Paul Ennis didn't run in 1983 because of a recent injury.

Ed Bridgewater beat me in the *Golden Armor Run* in Radcliff, Kentucky, in spite of my 46:27 running time. I finished second in the 50 and over group but didn't receive a trophy. This is another race which could be improved by providing more trophies.

Ed received a trophy and a framed picture of the "Old Skeleton Running". I was happy for him.

In the fall of 1983, WHAS Radio held the *WHAS Run* for the Crusade for Children Fund at the Bluegrass Convention Center. I finished 6th in a ten year age group.

I finished 2nd to Ed Bridgewater at Brandenburg which was close to being the toughest course I have ever run.

I ran only once in the *Louisville Metro Parks and Recreation Run* where I finished first in my age group and fifteenth over all.

I finished fourth in the *Pepsi Challenge* in Louisville and the very next day we drove down to Clarksville, Tennessee, to run in the *Queen City Classic* which was chaired by Jerry Koch in 1983.

I had made friends with Jerry in the races at Glasgow, Kentucky. He seemed so pleased to see me and thanked me for coming. Chairing a race is an unbelievable amount of work and it is a pleasure when people support your efforts by coming to participate in the race. I knew how Jerry felt and was glad I could support his hard work by participating.

I had chosen the lOK of the three options open to us. The previous day of running probably cost me a trophy as I finished 4th and felt the effects of the earlier race every step of the way.

In Bardstown the following weekend, I finished 3rd to Owen Comer and Jake Curtsinger who sort of slipped by me in the late stages of the race.

In 1983 *THE LARUE COUNTY HERALD NEWS* was owned by Bob and Celia Creal McDonald. The paper had been in Celia's family for three generations. Under Bob and Celia's management the paper had taken on a whole new perspective. They were winning awards hand over fist for various aspects of the paper and our little hometown newspaper was taking on a professional look.

THE HERALD NEWS, as we called it, sponsored a race with the proceeds going to the Crippled Children's Fund in Louisville. George Trumbo was still Parks Director for LaRue County and was asked by the McDonalds to help in the planning. Judi Perry, a reporter for the Herald News, was to chair the event.

There was a lot of local interest in the race, which was held at Lincoln National Park, the only race ever held there.

The night before the race there was a rain storm which left water standing over the race route. George said we would just wade through the water.

I had my doubts about that as George was a football player and football players will slosh through snow, ice, mud or big puddles without jeopardizing the game. Running is a different type of sport and requires a tad more finesse.

There was a one mile *Fun Run* in which Ray Ingham and David Buckman tied for first. Donnie ran and finished 3rd in his age group.

In the main race, out of 96 runners, the first five runners were from Louisville: Buddy Harpool, Don Noe, Larry Strange, Harlan Logsdon, and Tom Gill. Leslie Richardson was the overall women's runner.

I easily won my age group, but I had failed to wear socks and the combination of wet shoes and wet feet resulted in some painful blisters. Country boys aren't supposed to get blisters on their feet.

The McDonalds provided some unique and interesting awards including drawings for additional awards. They are certainly to be congratulated for sponsoring a fine race.

My friend John Fitch turned out to be the oldest runner in the *Railsplitter Run* the second week of October. DeeDee Benthall, the pretty lady lawyer, beat me by 12 seconds the same day.

I had been to several races in Indiana in 1983. Since I always took a stack of entry forms with me to all of my races, we had a bunch of Indiana runners in the *Railsplitter Run* this year.

Ed Bridgewater and Al Thompson came down and made me 3rd in my own race; however, I still hold the distinction of never having been beaten in my age group by a Kentuckian in LaRue County.

Buddy Harpool won the overall and Rhonda Powell won in the women's division. Christie Jewell, our former baby sitter, was our oldest runner in the *Fun Run*. Brock Barnes, 2 years old, was the youngest.

Jimmy Howell, a local barber, was the first LaRue countian in the men's division and Sue Nichols was first in the women's.

Both races were highly successful. Bobby Haynes chaired our 1OK and Virginia Stewart chaired the *Fun Run*.

The third week of October, I ran in the *Foothill Run* held in Albany in Clinton County.

LaHoma, her mother Ruth, and Howard Cessna went to the race with me. We got caught in a traffic jam going into town which could have made me too late for the race. I asked someone where the race was to begin, got out of the car and ran to the starting line.

I ran the 5K in 21:30 and won my age group. I received a great big trophy, so you know my day was complete.

By the time I won my age group at Campbellsville I had begun keeping scrapbooks and picture albums which included the history and results of the races in which I was competing. In addition to providing the frame work for RUN KENTUCKY RUN, it has been fun to sit on cold winter nights running back through all the memorabilia I have collected over the years.

James Sallee went with me to the *Banker's 1OK* in Munfordville the first week of November where I won my age group and he placed second in his. I got a chance to visit with J.D. Craddock and Jerry Ralston while we were there.

Donna, Mike and Matt went with us to the *Wendy's Classic* in Bowling Green the following week. Mike and Matt are more interested in softball, baseball and basketball than they are in running, but we enjoyed the day and the atmosphere.

The Elizabethtown *Turkey Trot* was held at Freeman Lake in 1983. The lake is beautiful at sunrise with the sun sparkling across the water. In the few days remaining before Thanksgiving it was also chilly until the sun had been up for a while.

Paul Ennis ran 1st with me running second. The race committee announced that Paul had won every year, but that was a mistake for I had won in 1979 on a different course. On Thanksgiving Day I ran at Iroquois Park in Louisville finishing 3rd to Doug Medley and Eugene Barker.

Doug had been a boxer in his younger days. Part of his training had been a great deal of running. When the running craze came along, he just picked up where he left off.

The following weekend we came back to Iroquois Park for the *Canned Goods Run* sponsored by the Iroquois Hill Runners' Club. Our entry fee was canned goods to give to the needy at Christmas time. I ran second to Doug Medley.

Down the road from Iroquois Park is Swag Hartel's sports shop. Swag was an All-American at Western Kentucky University and is, probably, the most popular runner in Louisville. He and his wife are personal friends of mine. I truly enjoy going to his store and talking with him.

This combination of facts may be why Iroquois Park has become a "running heaven". The park makes a hard, hilly course, but with the trees blocking the wind, it helps build stamina and strength in runners.

Runners can work out, run on down to Swag's store and get sound coaching while they replace their worn out running gear.

It was now early December of 1983 and I had had a busy and productive year running in and around Kentucky. My list of friendships was growing ever longer as well as my list of wins. I was in the best physical condition I had been in for years and I was looking forward to the coming season.

CHAPTER FOURTEEN

ALL GOD'S CHILDREN GOT ROOTS

As I have mentioned before, I was born in a log cabin in the Barren Run section of LaRue County, Kentucky. Of course, I make no claims as to its similarity to the birth place of LaRue County's famous son, Abraham Lincoln.

It was, in actuality, a partial log cabin covered with weather-board and might have been considered quite elegant in the days of Lincoln if the same house had existed in its remodeled form at that time, but it didn't. At the time of my birth, it was not considered elegant, just comfortable. I considered it home.

Regardless what we call it, family history, heritage, pedigree or roots, all of us have it. Some of us take great pride in our roots. Some of us brag about being related to kings or political leaders or famous people. Occasionally, some of us discover our only ancestor of public notoriety was a horse thief.

It really doesn't matter. The only thing that matters is what we do with what the Good Lord gave us to work with.

I know of no kings or famous public figures in my family tree and, try as I might, I have not been able to unearth a single horse thief. Kings and public figures being what they sometimes are, I might prefer a horse thief, but I am blessed with neither.

I am infinitely grateful, however, that my roots reach down through the nourishing soil of an honest, God-fearing family who loved me. Better yet, I was blessed in that my family made their living farming good Kentucky soil.

When I think back remembering my parents, I remember their faith, their honesty and the fact that they loved me. Can anyone anywhere ask for better?

My life began on the 25th of July 1929 a good while before the doctor arrived. I don't know if I was in a hurry to get on with life, or the road conditions and inadequate communication systems delayed the doctor, but there I was, the fifth and last child born to Pearl and Ernest Mather.

I was welcomed to the family by two older brothers, Madison and Robert. I also had a very pretty older sister named, Leona.

A sister, Margie Estell, died before I was born. She must have been a special child from what I was told. Mother kept a vase full of odds and ends that were Margie's before she died.

Daddy raised tobacco, corn, milked cows and raised watermelons (somebody was always raiding his patch.). Mother raised chickens and sold the eggs. We milked the cows separating the whey from the cream.

We fed the whey to the hogs and took the cream to Tanner Store to sell it. The income from the cream and the eggs paid for our "store" needs.

One of the best farms in LaRue County was owned by John Routt. His son, Fred, did the farming. The Routts lived near us and Mr. Routt had some grandchildren about my age, Burton and Geleanne Cooke. I used to play with them when they visited their grandpa. I still have a picture of us together. Each of us is holding a little sheep. My mother dearly loved Mrs. Routt so we visited her often.

One of my earliest memories was being scolded for wetting a neighbor lady's lap. I also remember a serious accident my brother, Madison, whom we called "Mac", experienced.

Mac fell off the back of a truck while it was going down the road. He had a concussion which kept him unconscious from Sunday until the following Friday.

Dad had gone to Tanner Store which was operated by A.L. Hazle and his wife Ora, where he bought some candy for me. I was standing in the doorway looking at Madison while eating the candy. He began to stir and opened his eyes. He saw me standing there and began to make noises like he wanted some of the candy.

In a few days, he was up and around again. I guess it was a miracle he got well with no more medical attention than he received, but the Lord is the best healer, after all. I believe after we do all we can do, God takes over and does the rest.

My brother, Bob, was a big tease. He aggravated me every chance he got and sometimes it was about all a little boy could handle. One day he had teased me beyond what I was willing to take. I picked up a rock and threw it at him hitting him in the head.

Instead of getting mad and pounding me to within an inch of my life, he began to do acrobatics. Finally, he stood on his head, then toppled slowly over to lie still on the ground. I thought I had killed him.

Mother wore her hair long and rolled it into a knot on the back of her head. Dad wore overalls, sometimes with patches on them. We had a buggy for transportation. Dad farmed the land with a team of two horses.

Mother and Dad put out a big vegetable garden every year. We ate delicious fresh vegetables all summer long and Mother canned what was left for the winter months.

As everyone knows, raising a garden is tremendously hard work, but for us and most people back then, it was a necessity. When I was a very small child I wanted to help, but didn't really understand what was going on.

One evening my parents were in the garden planting a row of late vegetables when I spied the recently planted tomato plants which were just beginning to "take hold" and begin to flourish. I, systematically, pulled up each and everyone of the plants.

I was banished from the garden while my parents re-set the plants. The plants grew and grew in spite of their rough beginnings.

A few weeks later, after the green tomatoes began to appear Mother and Dad and I were in the garden. Dad was plowing. Mom was hoeing the rows of young vegetables. Again, I must have wanted to help because I began pulling the green tomatoes off the vines and stacking them in a neat pile.

When Dad noticed what I was doing, he yelled at me. When he yelled, I knew I had done something wrong so I began to run. Those little green tomatoes came flying after me like machine gun bullets. Dad had, obviously, reached his point of no return over the tomatoes that year.

When I was a boy, school started in July to enable farm children time off for tobacco cutting, stripping, corn picking and other necessary chores. That first July I still wore my hair in long curls which was not unusual, even for boys, until time to start to school.

Mother curled my hair around her fingers in six huge bouncy curls. I was out in the sun so much as a child the sun had burned those curls to brown and gold. They were beautiful, even if they were mine (I still have those curls in a box at home.).

The day came. Mother put me in a big chair and cut the curls while Leona and Bob peeked through the kitchen window snickering and teasing me.

When she finished, Mom said, "Go show your Daddy what you look like."

I trotted off to find Daddy who was plowing corn in the back field. When he saw me, he got off the plow seat and hid behind the horses pretending to be afraid of me. I was really upset until he assured me he was only teasing and that I was "now a nice looking boy".

My brother Bob walked the mile with me on the first day of school. My first teacher at Barren Run was Eula Wilcox. Some of my classmates were "Doc" Rock, Buddy Gusler, Nataline Wells and the Catlett twins, Doris and Donald.

That first day, two of the older boys, Calvin Thurman(Remember him from the turnip incident?) and William Routt told me you were supposed to jump our of the window the first day of school. I did and they did. We all got a whipping. It was an interesting introduction to the educational process.

I only attended three months the first year so had to repeat first grade with my cousin, Johnny Catlett, who was a year younger. Johnny and I stayed together the rest of our school years and graduated from high school at the same time. Johnny's older brother, Lloyd, sort of looked out for us.

Below the Barren Run church and school there is a beautiful creek. When I was growing up, there was a wonderful place to swim. One summer day, the boys from the neighborhood made a plan to dam up the creek to deepen our "swimming hole".

We worked long and hard filling sacks with sand and placing them across the creek. Eventually, we had a six foot dam across the creek holding the water back.

About a quarter of a mile down stream from us Alta Meers came to the creek to water his mule. He must have been puzzled by what he saw for he told Lee Routt he had never seen the creek so low.

We enjoyed the fruits of our labor for a while, but our make shift dam did not hold long. The water soon broke through the dam. In fact, I think we worked a lot longer building the dam than the dam actually lasted.

It was a period in our lives when we had plenty of time and plenty of energy. I doubt that any of us regretted the effort. We made a plan, worked at a common goal, enjoyed the fellowship and experienced the feeling of success at seeing that completed dam. It was worth all of the effort that went into it.

While I was growing up, Alford Druien and his family lived at Tanner where Mr. Druien worked for A.L. Hazel. The Druien's son, Dillon, was about my age and fit right into our neighborhood group.

One afternoon Dillon, Johnny Catlett, Doc Rock, Norman Rock and I were walking home from school when we passed Jim Blankenship's watermelon patch. You can imagine what thoughts came to five boys who had been cooped up in school all day when they discover one innocent and unattended watermelon patch.

Watermelon patch raiding was a tradition for young boys when I was growing up. Lots of people raised watermelons back then. If fact, all five of us may have had watermelon patches on our own farms, but that was not the issue. Most watermelon patches were so prolific in our neighborhood that no family could eat all of the watermelons they grew, but that was not the issue, either. The issue was the challenge of sneaking into a watermelon patch and getting away with an attack on an unsuspecting watermelon without getting caught by the farmer who probably would have given us six if he knew we wanted one.

The five of us had just gotten into the patch when we heard a noise in the bushes. We pretended to be scared and began to run.

Johnny, Doc, Norman and I cleared the fence and ran up the road. Dillon climbed straight up the fence and jumped from the top. His overalls caught on the top barbed wire and threw him against the ground.

He screamed and we ran back to him. He had broken his arm so severely that the bone was sticking through the flesh. For a moment we panicked for we could see he was seriously hurt and in pain.

There was usually no traffic on the road we had been walking, but God intervened. A car came along and took us to Dillon's house.

Dillon's dad asked him what happened and Dillon told him everything except about the watermelon patch. Dillon had to wear a cast for months, but when the cast came off the arm was fine.

When I was about six, Daddy traded for a new farm which joined my Uncle Ed and Aunt Cynthia Catlett's farm. Uncle Ed had twelve children. On the other side lived Roy Rock and his family of twelve children.

You can imagine the times we had. I spent all of my free time at Aunt Cynthia's playing with Lloyd, Johnny and David.

They had a nice pond where we swam in summer and skated in the winter. We had home-made sleds which we used to slide down Barren Run Hill or Aunt Nanny's hill. Both hills were straight down from top to bottom and made for some exciting fun.

Our favorite game was "hide and seek" which we played in Uncle Ed's big barn. Another game we liked was "corn cob fight". At school we played "town ball" and tag. As we grew older, of course, we liked to raid watermelon patches.

All of us had to help with the farm work, but when we were free we liked to spend our time together. We hunted wild grapes and hazelnuts or swam in the South Fork Creek at Logan's Bottom or Reeds Mill in addition to the games we played.

Retirement, "Changing of the Guard"; "Bunny" Ford and Donald on Donald's last day to sort the mail! December 29, 1989.

Two Cardinal Fans!
Donald and Jock Sutherland at a Virginia Tech/Louisville Basketball Game, 1988.

Two quilts made from Donald Mather's running tee-shirts
after his record runs across the state of Kentucky.

Emily Shelton,
Granddaughter

Sandra, our daughter, winning First Place,
Miss Nolin R.E.C.C., 1970.
Standing behind Sandra is Carolyn Baker, from Elizabethtown, Kentucky, the first runner-up.

Donald Mather after winning 4 medals in swimming at the 1989 *Kentucky Bluegrass Games*

Donald Mather after winning 4 medals at the 1988 *Bluegrass State Games* in Lexington

1987 Torch Runners for the Bluegrass Games in Lexington. Runners are standing in the stairway of the Old Capitol.

Bottom left to clockwise: Carol Proffitt, Theresa Gaines, Cindy Norton, Frank Ray, Susan Cox, Hopey Newkirk, Donald Mather, Glenn Easterling, Governor Martha Layne Collins, Evelyn Ashford, Larry Hayes, State Senator Ed O'Daniel, Curtis Ripey, Ken Hoskins, Martha Worful, Jim Green and Joe Washington.

1991 Lincoln Trail Regional Senior Games
held in Hodgenville, Kentucky. List includes the Director, Sport Chairs and some of the Senior competitors.

A Magnolia School trip to Mammoth Cave Park in the spring of 1947, my junior year.

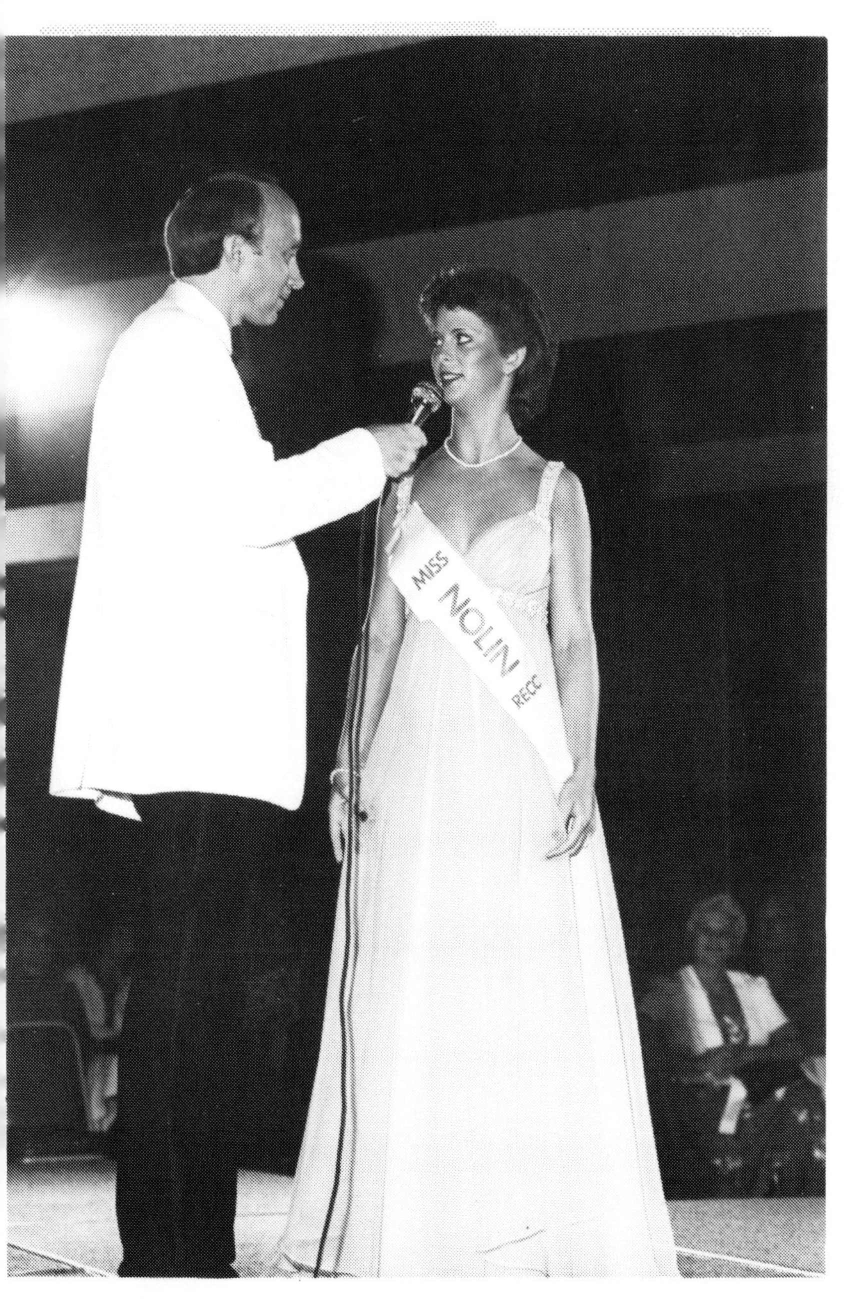

Mr. Ron Wolf, Master of Ceremony, at the 1983 Kentucky Miss Rural Electric Pageant at the Galt House in Louisville, Kentucky, interviewing Melissa Jo Mather, Miss Nolin R.E.C.C.

Various letters of Commendation and "Thanks"

United States
Postal Service
HODGENVILLE, KY 42748-9998

May 13, 1987

Mr. Donald Mather
U. S. Postal Service
Hodgenville, KY 42748-9998

Dear Mr. Mather:

The Postal Service has a proud tradition of serving the people of this nation and our community. Your professionalism has contributed to making the Bowling Green MSC the "best going." You can justifiably be proud to be one of the many employees who has made this a service-oriented organization through your dedication and commitment toward achievement of our goals of high standards in performance excellence.

Your 30 years of service are a milestone in your postal career. It is with great pride that you are presented this service award for 30 years.

Sincerely,

Ray McDowell
Postmaster

mw

cc:OPF

United States Postal Service

United States
Postal Service
BOWLING GREEN, KENTUCKY 42101-9992

May 18, 1988

Mr. Donald Mather
RR 01, Box 171
Hodgenville, KY 42748-9725

Dear Mr. Mather:

We have just been made aware of an incident in which you came to the rescue of an elderly customer while delivering your route on February 4, 1988. Mrs. Sam Walters had slipped and fell outside her home and was unable to move. She was exposed to subfreezing temperatures for one and a half hours when you found her. Your quick thinking and action in getting her inside, wrapping her in a blanket, and summoning an ambulance could very easily have saved her life.

You are to be commended for outstanding community service while in the performance of your official duties. Your actions have made all Postal Service employees proud and will serve as encouragement as we continue our daily efforts to improve the service we provide and the image we project.

I want to personally thank you for making our entire organization look even better.

Sincerely,

Kenneth Golden
MSC Director, Field Operations

OFFICE OF THE GOVERNOR
FRANKFORT, KENTUCKY 40601

MARTHA LAYNE COLLINS
GOVERNOR

September 22, 1987

Donald E. Mather
Route 1, Box 174
Hodgenville, Kentucky 40069

Dear Donald:

Just a note of thanks for participating in the 1987 Torch Run of the Bluegrass State Games. Your taking time to be a part of this event is greatly appreciated.

The Torch Lighting Ceremony heralded the opening of the Third Annual Bluegrass State Games which has become the premier amateur athletic event in our great Commonwealth. Our amateur athletes now have a place to excel and an event in which to take pride.

Please accept the enclosed photographs of this memorable event with my thanks and best wishes.

Sincerely,

Martha Layne Collins

Office of the Governor

The Lincoln Museum

The Lincoln Museum, Inc.
66 Lincoln Square
P.O. Box 176
Hodgenville, Kentucky 42748

Dear Donald,

The Board of Directors of the Lincoln Museum, Inc., would like to say "THANK YOU" and "CONGRATULATIONS" on a job well done.

The First Annual Walk-a-thon was a tremendous success due to all the work and worry that you put into it. We hope that this event can before long become an annual event that will find us raising not only money, but also public interest in the museum.

Again, our sincere thanks for your outstanding efforts.

Sincerely,

The Board of Directors
Lincoln Museum

IN ABSENTIA: Thelma Ford
Judge Tommy Turner
Rita Williams

Mr. Ronald Reagan
President
United States of America
Washington, DC 20500

Letters

Dear Mr. Reagan:

At a time when the Postal Service has been in conflict I thought you might enjoy a positive tone.

On February 4, 1988, my 71 year old mother walked out of the house to go to town. She slipped and fell, crushing her knee cap, blacking her eye, breaking her glasses and hurting the palm of her hand. Mother sat in 30 - 35 degree weather for about one and a half hours.

Her mailman was making his rounds and found her. He unlocked the house, got a chair near the inside of the door, got her in, wrapped her with a blanket, and got hold of family members. He stayed with her until the ambulance was ready to take her to the hospital.

My mother had surgery the next day and is doing fine, thanks to a person who took time to care.

When I called the mailman's superior the next day, the carrier had not told his superior of this heroic task.

The name of the mailman who helped my mother, Mrs. Sam Walters, is Donald Mather, Route 1, Hodgenville, KY.

I hope you see fit to write Mr. Mather and/or his superior for a job well done.

Judy Florence
1138 Flint Knob Road
Cave City, KY 42127

Upon receiving copies of the above letter and a response from the White House, Donald Mather was presented a Letter of Commendation and a Certificate of Appreciation from the Bowling Green MSC.

Former President Ronald Reagan

Certificate of Baptism

Certificate of Baptism

THIS CERTIFIES THAT ON THE 24th DAY OF October 1943

Donald Mather

WAS BAPTIZED INTO THE Baptist CHURCH OF Barren Run

Edgar M. Pottorff PASTOR

My son **Donnie Mather**, at 13, winning the
Kentucky State 4-H Speaking Contest in Lexington, Kentucky.
His Subject: "Modern Day Commercials".

Matt Shelton:
A 4 medal winner
at the
1987 *Bluegrass State Games*
in
Lexington, Kentucky

LaHoma on our wedding day,
June 28, 1959.

LaHoma and Donald toast on their 30th Wedding Anniversary

LaHoma and Donald at Donald's Retirement Dinner at
The Railsplitter Inn, December, 1989.

LaHoma, Ruth and Donald

Front Row: **Derek, Matt, Dolly, Nathan, Jessica** and **Abe.**
Back Row: **Mike, Donna, Bryan, Jo, Donald, Donnie, LaHoma, Ruth, Diana, Sandra** and **Kenny**

Seated: **Donna, Jo, Donnie, Diana and Sandra**
Standing: **Donald** and **LaHoma**

1945-46 Magnolia Basketball Team District Runnerups
Front Row: Coach "Pud" McClain
2nd Row: Stuart Pepper, Coleman Miller, Bill Lemons and Charles Waggoner
3rd Row: Donald Mather, Herbert Peace, Charles Akin and Kenneth Bell

***Magnolia Majors*: Quarter-Finalists in the 1947 State Sweet Sixteen**
Donald Mather, 7; Hobart Bowen, 66; Johnny Catlett, 47; Darnall McCubbin, 88; Kenneth Bell, 12; Charles Reed, 50; Bill Lemons, 00; J. D. Avery, 22; Stuart Pepper, 90; Coleman Miller, 80; Charles Ward, 11.

The "Deckers"
Grandchildren: Brett, 7; Michelle, 4; Courtney, 2.

Universal Studios, Hollywood, California
LaHoma, Donnie, Debbie Deering Clark, Rae Clark and Donald

Frank Ray with Donald Mather carrying the torch on Versailles Road on the way from Frankfort to UK Campus in Lexington for the *Bluegrass State Games*, 1987.

Aunt Cynthia picked a lot of blackberries and made jam. Uncle Ed was known to make blackberry wine from time to time. He also made sorghum molasses.

We kids had the sorghum eating process down to a science. We'd get a green cane stick and chew it a little. Uncle Ed would pour the fresh sorghum into a pan for us. We'd push the cane stick through the sorghum and eat it off the stick.

This is the second best way in the world to eat sorghum. The best way is with hot brown biscuits and melted butter on a cold winter morning.

Ah-h-h, Lord, You gave us so much when You gave us Kentucky.

What I remember most about Aunt Cynthia was that she laughed a lot and made the best brown biscuits I ever ate.

Lee Walters and Tom Druien owned farms close by. We didn't visit with them much, but they would hire us to put up hay when I got older.

Daddy was a good father. I worked hard helping him on the farm, but he never pushed me. By the time I was eleven, he had me cutting corn and putting it in shocks. When the corn was dry, the leaves would nearly cut your ears off.

In those days, we split our tobacco. I held the tobacco sticks while he put the tobacco on them.

Daddy also made tobacco sticks. I helped him saw the trees down then saw the logs into four feet, four inch lengths. Next, we pealed the bark off the red oak logs.

Finally, Daddy split each log into parts like a pie then using a special tool, he split and split until he had a tobacco stick. He was very fast at it. My job was to keep the splinters off the sticks. We made good money on our homemade sticks as they were much stronger than the sawed sticks which would break easily.

Jesse Tharp, grandfather of my writing partner, Sarah Bennett-Booker, lived in Magnolia. Every fall, he would drive his Model-T Ford all the way to our place to buy tobacco sticks. He said, "Ernest Mather's tobacco sticks were the best money could buy."

Mr. Jesse owned one of the first Model T Fords to come to Magnolia. As did most people back then, he knew a lot more about horses than he did automobiles.

One afternoon, Mr. Jesse and his wife, Ruby, were coming home from the store with their two daughters, June and Sarah Elizabeth, in the back seat. He turned the corner by the Magnolia School house too fast losing control of the car. It careened down the road and headed straight for a tree.

Mr. Jesse forgot all about the break pedal and began yelling, "Whoa! Whoa, blast you! I said, Whoa!"

The car did not "whoa". It hit the tree and climbed up the trunk before sliding back to earth and settling with a thud. Neither car nor passengers were hurt. Please, forgive me. I just have to say it - they don't build cars like they used to.

After our work was done, Daddy loved to fish and he took me with him. He liked to "set lines" so we cut short poles to stick into the river bank. Next, we took the short seine to the "Nathan Hawkins Branch" where we seined for crawfish and, occasionally, minnows which we put in our bucket.

One of us carried the poles and the other the bucket of crawfish and the fishing lines while we walked the short distance to our fishing place.

Two creeks, called the North Fork and the South Fork, come together to form the Nolin River. The North Fork is not very good for fishing, but the South Fork and the mouth of the Nolin make good fishing places.

We baited our hooks and set our poles, forty or fifty of them, along the banks of the South Fork. After setting our poles, we walked home and did our morning chores then back to the South Fork to run our lines.

Often we caught a big channel catfish which we would take home to eat. Daddy made this such fun.

When I was ten, Daddy gave me an interest in the tobacco. When we sold it, I got $30.00.

The first time we went to town, I talked Daddy into letting me use my money to buy a new bicycle. I paid $28.99 cents for it which left me a dollar and a penny as we did not have sales tax then.

We didn't have a car, but we found someone who brought the bike to our lane for us. Since I didn't know how to ride, I pushed it up the lane to our house. By the time I got to the house, my hands were numb because it was January and bitterly cold.

I learned to ride the next day. Some of the neighbor boys had bikes. We would go everywhere on those bikes. All the roads were gravel in those days so we had to be careful or the gravel would slide with us and give us a spill.

This bicycle was the only toy I ever had of any significance and I enjoyed it more than I can explain.

Our brother Madison had married by this time and had a child named, Wayne. We all thought he was something really special. Madison's wife was an excellent cook. She has always been known as the best cake maker in the country.

Madison grew fine tobacco and has directed the LaRue County Tobacco Show at the county fair for years. In his younger days, he was a good square dancer and square dance caller for the old traditional square dancing.

In February of 1941, my brother, Bob, was drafted into the army. He stayed in the army until July of 1945. He served in Africa, Sicily and Italian Campaigns.

When he left, only Leona and I remained at home.

My grandparents, Lloyd and Mollie Mather lived about a mile from us. Grandfather was small and had a mustache. He liked to play checkers, but was a slow mover. A game could sometimes take a lot of time.

Grandpa Mather was the son of Buck Mather who was the son of James Mather who was the son of Richard Mather who sold the Sinking Springs farm to Isaac Bush.

Daddy had a brother killed in World War I in France. He and Aunt Cynthia were the only children in the family to live to any age.

My mother's parents were David R. and Alma (Sissy) Hornback who also lived about a mile from us in the Barren Run section of LaRue County. Grandpa Hornback was jolly and had a crippled knee which made him walk with a cane. Mother had several sisters.

We started the Hornback reunion in 1976 at Freeman Lake. Between ninety and one hundred people attend each year. We cousins have a great time together.

Well, these were my beginnings, my roots. Not very exciting, perhaps, but solid, happy and full of fun, family and friends.

I learned to work hard, play hard, laugh, and share with others. I learned to appreciate others and learned who I was, who I am and who I would be.

It was a magical time to be a child, after the depression, but before the war. It was after the technical revolution began, but before technology became more important than people. It was after education and social contact became accessible, but before we crowded ourselves into cities isolating ourselves from our extended families until we lost our identities.

Yes, I have to admit, again, God blessed my roots.

CHAPTER FIFTEEN

A GOOD RUNNING YEAR - WITH A FEW UPS AND DOWNS

The running year started in 1984 with Fort Knox's *Bullion Bust Run* which began at the Grabowski Field House on the base. It was terribly cold and the winds were blowing. I won first in my age group and 33rd overall in the 5K. There were about 2,000 runners entered in the two events, the 5K and the lOK. The base commander gave the awards.

I had a score to settle at the *Run for Sight* in Meade County which was sponsored by the Lions Club.

During Roy McKamey's first year of coaching at LaRue County, LaRue County High School had a wonderful basketball team. The boys only lost three games at a total of six points.

Some of the players included Mitch Garrett, Lavelle Webster, Glen Decker, Kip Lee, Chris Rogers, Mike Otis, Dwight Rainwater and Rob Daley. Our daughter, Jo, was dating Glen Decker so I felt we had a special interest in the team. We followed their progress all year attending the games and participating in the *Big Blue Crew* which was made up of the fans and noisemakers for the team.

The week before the *Run for Sight*, Meade county beat our LaRue County team in the finals of the Regional Basketball Tournament in mid-March. I thought some of their fans were a little louder than was absolutely necessary given the circumstances. I informed some of the fans that I would be racing in the *Run for Sight* and if there were any 50 year old runners from Meade County in the race, they had better watch out. I was coming to get them. The Meade County fans got a hoarse laugh out of that.

The following weekend, I won my age group at Meade County beating my old friends Gene Priddy and Charlie Fetters, but there were no Meade County "oldies" to receive my revenge. Winning felt great, anyway.

I moved up a notch at the *Run with the Stars* at Bowling Green at the Greenwood Mall coming in 2nd to Don Sheumaker of Tennessee. I congratulated Don after the run. He's used to winning so it was nothing new to him. Tennessee has a lot of good older runners.

I had a winning streak of 22 wins and places going which ended with the *Ford Ranger* in Louisville. In fact, I lost three in a row afterwards.

I lost the *Old Kentucky Home Classic* to Bob Crow, a guy named Rowe and Owen Comer; although, I did receive a medallion with *My Old Kentucky Home* on it. I didn't do well in the *Kentucky Derby Mini-Marathon*, which I was running for the fourth time in 1984.

I ran at 1:49;50 which was a good time, but the race draws some world class runners in every age group. I never failed to run under 1:50:00 in the four times I had run in the race which made me feel proud.

In 1984, the race began on New Cut Road with 6,500 runners on the starting line. The news media and race officials have had photographs taken from low flying helicopters and three of the four times I have been able to identify myself in the picture. That must be some kind of record in and of itself. *THE COURIER-JOURNAL AND TIMES* have always given great coverage in the following Friday editions of the papers.

In the Leitchfield *Hospital Fitness Run* I began a long streak of running in which I won or placed. In Leitchfield I finished 2nd to Vern Hayes of Evansville. There were drawings for prizes at the awards ceremony. The Harley Howell family won about all the prizes.

Harley is a LaRue countian from Buffalo and is the son of "Talking Joe" Howell.

I won my age group at the *Burgin Beginning* in Burgin, Kentucky. The award was a medallion with a rising sun on it which was handmade.

I saw some old friends at the race, Jim Sharp, Barry Bertram and DeeDee Benthall among others.

This was a unique and interesting place to run. We ate in a little local restaurant in Burgin, which had it's group of local coffee drinkers. I started talking with them and said I thought there was a famous ballplayer from Burgin named Jack Coleman. They said I was right and he was still living in Burgin and owned a lumber company.

Jack was an All-American at the University of Louisville in the forties. He played on the team which won the N.A.I.A. national championship. He later played pro ball with Rochester.

At the race in Big Springs on a very hot day, I met Janet Omer. Her grandmother Highbaugh lived in LaRue County. Since Janet did a lot of competitive running, her grandmother had mentioned me to her. We struck up a conversation and I found her mother was Wilma Highbaugh who had lived at Hammondsville near Magnolia in our high school days. I had a great reunion with Janet's parents as they were there to watch her run.

Janet and I ran about two miles together before getting separated. In this race we competed only with the clock. A specific speed was set for gold, silver and bronze awards. If our running time was within the guidelines we won prizes regardless of how many runners came in at that time.

I won a silver and Janet won a gold. The prize was a running bag stamped with the prize we each received.

I ran into Janet at a lot of races after the *Big Springs Race*. She always did well in her age group.

Next, it was on to *Upton Days* where I finished third behind Kessinger and Barker. Eugene Barker's wife was from Glendale and he had attended Elizabethtown High School. The family ties caused him to want to come down to races in this area, though he had lived most of his life in Louisville.

I won my age group in the 5K race in the Elizabethtown *Dog Days Run* sponsored by the Junior Food Store. There were not enough trophies so I did not receive one.

Linda Switzer, the local Junior Food Store manager, kept insisting- until the company finally sent me a trophy. It was a large impressive trophy. Sometimes waiting pays off.

I finished 3rd to Paul Ennis and Owen Comer in the *Heartland Run* in Elizabethtown. LaHoma picked up our grandson, Nathan, who lived nearby to spend the day at the celebration. He loved the clowns and painted faces and other activities.

The Barren River Lake Park Run started near the Louie B. Nunn Lodge. It was a unique 3.1 mile race. I won a cute trophy with the year on it. I also beat Billy Hall Baxter that day.

After the race, Howard treated LaHoma, Ruth, Donnie and me to dinner at the lodge. They have the best food in the world at the lodge. Howard was always wanting to go back to eat there.

In my third *Steamboat Race*, I finished 5th behind James Carey, Bill Long, Phillip Hall and Owen Comer. In the Cow Days Race in Greensburg, I finished 3rd behind Vern Hayes and Owen Comer. The Greensburg newspaper always took the winners' pictures for the paper and we always ate at the Cozy Corner restaurant with Mrs. Edwards.

I ran 1st in the *Golden Armor* then ran the next day at Hardyville which was having its first festival with a one mile run. I won my age group and finished 19th overall. Charley Howell, the postmaster in Hardyville was the chairman of the festival. He had once inspected my city carrier route.

Gordon Poteet and Charlie Highbaugh were providing entertainment with some fine Bluegrass music. This little Hart County town was having a great time.

The *Casey County Apple Festival* in Liberty, Kentucky, had been hosting a race I wanted to take part in for a long time. Charlie Pearl, editor of the *CASEY COUNTY NEWS*, had invited me to run in their race several times. I made the run in 1984 and it was a good thing I did. It was the last year they had the road race.

The *Apple Festival* claims to have the largest apple pie in the world. It is baked in a huge copper pan and kept warm until time to eat it. There are literally thousands of people at the festival just waiting to eat some of the pie, including numerous politicians meeting people and giving out little gifts.

In 1984, Mac Trumbo was at the *Apple Festival* making tobacco sticks telling some outlandish stories which he said were true. He is a world class storyteller as are his brothers, Homer and George. As I said earlier, Mac has won the World Championship contest for railsplitting several times. If he and his brothers ever get tired of competing in physical contests, I suggest they try "Storytelling" competitions. I feel certain they would have to build a whole set of new trophy cases for their awards.

Mac was probably the best lineman to play football at LaRue County High School under Coach Clarence Caple. Mac even tried boxing at one time, but he said he wasn't too good at it as he had a glass jaw. I have a feeling kind-hearted Mac Trumbo just didn't like hitting and hurting people.

I finished 2nd in the race to Charlie Cheek of Louisville, but managed to receive two trophies somehow. After the race, I walked around awhile then went to get some apple pie. I almost got trampled getting it, but there was enough for everyone and I even got seconds!

Virginia Stewart was chairman of the *Railsplitter Run* for *Lincoln Days* in LaRue County in 1984. Virginia had always been involved in sports. The race route ran right by her house. I remember the first *Railsplitter Run* she was standing at her mailbox encouraging runners and passing out drinking water. As I passed by her, she shouted, "Go get'um! I'm proud of you."

I needed her encouragement about then and it helped me keep going.

Virginia says she got into running due to a massive depression she suffered three days before her fortieth birthday. It seems three days before the big day, Virginia woke up thinking, "This is it! This is the big 'Four, Oh'."

She started running the very same day. Virginia says she has never been a fast runner, but she entered the *Railsplitter Run* a couple of years. The second year she made up her mind to beat one of the local lady runners regardless of the cost. She was running steadily when she heard female voices moving up from behind. Thinking it was the lady she was planning to beat, Virginia doggedly pushed on. The voices drew nearer, regardless of how hard she was running. She refused to look back.

Soon the voices were at her shoulder and pulling ahead. When they passed, she discovered the voices belonged to two young women in their twenties who passed her as if she were standing still chatting as if they would never get another chance. They did not even glance in Virginia's direction.

Softball had been more Virginia's sport, but she noticed in her mid-thirties that someone had begun to move the bases farther and farther apart each season.

She finally began to suspect someone was coming in at night moving the bases between games. She gave up softball and took up tennis. Tennis was more strenuous, but you can't move the bases in tennis.

Soon after Virginia gave up running, Carol Haynes, Dooley Catlett and Angela Tucker talked her into "walking" the *Railsplitter Run* race route. Virginia told them she could not keep up, but they insisted, promised to walk slowly and assured her it would be fun. Over her misgivings, she agreed.

Just as she thought, in minutes Carol, Dooley and Angela were just little specks in the distance. A little more than half way around, she looked up and saw Carol, Dooley and Angela walking back toward her. They had crossed the finish line, waited for her, got worried and come looking for her. They walked with her to the finish line where she crossed the line dead last. The irony is that Virginia won her age group because she was the only one entered in her age group. She received a nice trophy.

Virginia plays golf now. She says that no matter where you hit a golf ball, in the rough, in the lake or on the green, it lays there and waits for you.

Virginia formed a nice committee for the *Railsplitter Run,* held an *Olympic* style awards ceremony with a two level box to stand on and played John Phillip Sousa music over the loud speaker. She introduced the "Lincoln Day Medallion" - the gold, silver and bronze.

Buddy Harpool and Tracy Gilliam who were running for the *Victory Athletic Club* in Louisville, were the overall winners of the *Railsplitter Run* in 1984.

Christie Jewell, 80, won the oldest runner with my grandson Derek Shelton, 3, the youngest runner in the fun run. Derek also was the first under six runner to finish so he received two awards. Derek had his face painted by an artist who had a booth set up for the celebration. He accepted his awards and was photographed with his painted face. He looked cute.

Lanna Jo Heath and Mike Otis were the first LaRue countians to finish in the 1OK.

When I stepped up to receive my gold medal, Virginia Stewart, Bob Brown and Charlie Fetters rushed forward to help me as if I were too feeble to climb upon the award box. Celia McDonald took a picture for the *LARUE COUNTY HERALD NEWS* which carried the caption "Local mail man, Donald Mather, helped to the winners box by jokesters".

Paducah, Kentucky, is nearly 200 hundred miles away from LaRue County down the Western Kentucky Turnpike. Lourdes Hospital in Paducah was sponsoring a race called the *Great Pumpkin Race*. Joe Shane, from the *Nautilus Sports Center*, was chairman of the race. I had received their literature in the mail and decided to enter.

Bill Rodgers, the greatest runner of all time, was going to be the guest runner. I had read about him for years and wanted a chance to meet him.

We left for Paducah from work and arrived just in time for the banquet for Bill Rodgers. He would also be speaking to us which was exciting. After the "Carbo-loading" (dinner), we were allowed to ask questions. I asked a couple, but there were lots of good questions asked.

Afterward, we were allowed to take pictures and talk with him. He autographed his picture for me: "Donald, Best Wishes for Smooth Running, Bill Rodgers".

Hey! I have dined with the best!

It rained cats and dogs all night. When we got to the Lourdes Hospital starting line, it was still raining; nevertheless, there were hundreds of racers ready to run. It stopped raining, but the race route was as slippery as oiled glass.

I placed 2nd to Bob Morton in my age group. Bill Rodgers, naturally, won the race overall. The awards were large hard plastic medallions with a large pumpkin, a shock of corn and other fall harvest symbols printed upon it. At the foot of the shock is the name of the race in orange. A stand to hold it upright was also provided. I think it is precious.

LaHoma and I came home by way of Kentucky Lake. While we were there looking around, we had a foot race. LaHoma beat me! I had to buy the dinner at the restaurant that evening. This trip was a lot of fun.

Why would anyone keep on entering a race in which they never win? I know don't either, but I kept entering the *River Banks Run* in Louisville.

The winners, Theron Kessinger, Wayne Collier and Ed Bridgewater, had won four times between them. I had beaten them in other races, but not the *River Banks Run.*

James Sallee went with me to the *Wendy's Classic* at Bowling Green. The start of the race was delayed a few minutes by David Mason the race chairman because of an electrical storm. There were four inches of water in the road and 4,000 terrified runners trying to stay out of the storm and avoid being struck by lightning.

I was terrified along with everyone else. I also felt sorry for David. A race as large as the *Wendy's Classic* takes months of planning, correspondence, and no small amount of money. All his hard work seemed to be running down the storm drains of Bowling Green, Kentucky that day.

At last the rain let up and we were on our way. After the race began, I realized I had forgotten to wear my racing number. I was so disappointed because even if I won, without the number I would be disqualified.

Neil, Anspagh, Dawkins and Sheumaker were just a few of the great runners in the 50-59 age group there. I got a trophy for just running, however. Long live the *Wendy's Classic*!

I finished 25th and won the oldest runner award and won my age group at the Munfordville *Bankers lOK*. It was awfully cold so the awards were given in the upstairs of the county courthouse.

The Candlelight Run in Louisville was a lot of fun. We held candles and ran across the river and back. I finished 3rd, but it was not competitive. I talked with some old friends Art Rousseau, Marilyn Scott and Charley Cheek.

The 1984 season ended with the *Life Begins at 40* in Louisville. This year, it began at the Douglas House and ran out into Cherokee Park. The course was sort of hilly, but fun. The Cherokee Club races are always accompanied by piles of food. Wally Bright brought his wonderful hummingbird cake.

I finished 2nd to Lou Sneider. Lou was a "track man" and has run in the *Nationals*, placing well several times. Lou was past sixty, but had a good running history and would compete well in the *Bluegrass Games* in the coming years. Lou had also written excellent informative stories for the *ROAD RUNNER'S MAGAZINE*.

The 1984 running year had been a good competitve running year. I was maintaining my conditioning and doing well in the competitions. Of course, I had a few down spells during the year, but the successes made up for the few disappointments.

CHAPTER SIXTEEN

A NOBLE SPORTSMAN AND MY YOUNG ADULT LIFE

I probably should have gone to college. I had an offer of a basketball scholarship to Campbellsville College, but none of my brothers or sisters had gone to college. They had done well, so I was a little hesitant to go.

I was sort of lost that first summer. After high school graduation, I had saved some money from my investments in cattle, hogs and tobacco so I began to think about buying a car.

During my teen years I hitchhiked to town on Saturday afternoon then found a neighbor going my way on the way back. In the forties, Hodgenville had a lot to offer us country people. There was a movie and a hang-out for young people called "The Luncheonette". On weekends and after school, it would be full of high school kids playing the jukebox.

Those young people who owned cars were very popular and were always hauling the rest of us around.

One of the reasons I was in a hurry to get my own car was a pretty girl from Louisville named Mardell Atherton. She visited her aunt, Mrs. Albert Hazle, in the summer. We dated a few times before I got a car which was difficult. We found someone to double date with which was really more fun, but I felt I needed a car.

My cousin, Lloyd Catlett, bought a brand new Oldsmobile toward the end of the summer during the State Fair. Lloyd asked me if I would like to go with him to the Fair in his new car. We planned to pick up his brother, Johnny, whom I had not seen since we graduated from high school in June. Johnny had gone to work at General Box Factory in Louisville and was living with another brother, Raymond.

We went up on Friday night. Since Mardell lived only five blocks away, I borrowed a bicycle from one of Raymond's sons and went over to see Mardell. She seemed pleased to see me so I asked her if she would like to go to the fair with Lloyd, Johnny and me the next day.

She said that she would love to go and she would find "blind dates" for Lloyd and Johnny from among her friends (This was during the time that no young lady would get in a car and go anywhere with three young men alone.). That evening we triple dated with Johnny and Priscilla Magruder, Lloyd and Doris Anderson.

Once we got to the Kentucky State Fair grounds, we decided to go to the Horse Show.

LaRue County native Jack Thompson had shown horses for years. Jack owned probably the most famous "fine harness" horse in the world, *Noble Kalorama.*

In 1941, he showed Noble Kalorama at Madison Square Garden in New York and won the *World Champion Fine Harness Horseshow.*

Jack lost both legs in service to his country in the Italian campaign during World War II. After a couple of years of rehabilitation, he readjusted his life to his disability and began to show horses once again.

On this evening, Jack was scheduled to show the famed Noble Kalorama in exhibition after the judging of all the other classes. At last the announcement was made that Jack Thompson and Noble were entering the ring. Everyone in horse circles and most of those who weren't knew Jack and the tragedy that had befallen him. As the big horse began strutting his "stuff", as only he could do, the crowd began to go wild. It disturbed the horse and the audience was quickly told to hold all applause until after the exhibition.

A hush fell over all of us as we watched the beautiful horse glide, pace and high step his way around the sawdust ring again and again. The courageous man handled the horse to perfection in spite of his disability. It seemed as if the audience stopped breathing during that triumphant display of beauty, grace and personal strength.

After Jack guided Noble Kalorama from the ring, the crowd stood to their feet with tears streaming down their faces and applauded and applauded. It was the greatest and most inspiring exhibition of any sport that I have been privileged to see.

We and our new friends had a wonderful evening. We triple dated again and again after that evening. In a few months Mardell and I stopped dating, but remained friends as did Lloyd and Doris, but Johnny and Priscilla continued to date.

After Johnny's tour of duty with Uncle Sam, they married and now have a successful marriage and three children.

By fall, I fell in love with a green 1947 Ford car. I bought it and found there were lots of pretty girls around home to date. There were always nice places to take girls back then, ball games, swimming, drive-ins and square dancing.

After my lessons at the elementary school, I loved square dancing. If I could find a square dance going on somewhere, that's where I would go .

I started dating a neighbor girl, BeeBee Tharpe. We dated and became very fond of one another, but she was very beautiful and popular so I had some serious competition. After a couple of years, we stopped dating. The Korean War was on, but I kept escaping the draft because I was farming. I wasn't really happy about my deferment, however.

In the meantime I had a couple of accidents with my car and traded it to Vance and Wilson Ford in Hodgenville for a 1951 Fairlane Ford.

I guess I was in one of those moods people talk about sometimes. I just seemed to feel restless. I wandered over to the recruiting office and inquired about the Air Force. Before I knew it, I had volunteered and would be leaving in two weeks for San Antonio, Texas.

I sold my car, cows, sows and pigs, put the money in a savings account and braced myself to learn to defend the good old red, white and blue.

On February 4, 1953, I was inducted into the Air Force. After one night in a hotel in Louisville, we were flown to San Antonio by way of Hong Kong, apparently.

It seemed as if we flew all over the country, making stops to add more Air Force recruits. This was my first time to fly and I loved every minute of it. When we landed at the airport in San Antonio, a bus was waiting to take us to *Lackland AFB*.

At Lackland they fed us, took us to our barracks and that was the last time anyone was nice to us for six weeks.

The first morning long before daybreak, we were given five minutes to be ready to fall out for breakfast. We had some of that S.O.S. stuff. You aren't supposed to like it, but I loved it.

For the next six weeks, we either guarded it, cleaned it or saluted it. We were always getting some kind of vaccination or having our teeth filled. Our non-commissioned officers, Corporal Hannah and Sergeant Hall, though lacking in anything which vaguely resembled maternal skills, managed to push, shout, lead and intimidate us through the program.

We took aptitude tests which qualified me for officer's training, but Sergeant Hall told me I would have to stay in the Air Force for five years so I declined the privilege requesting three schools, air weather, air traffic and stock records, instead. I got stock records school and was sent from the heat of San Antonio to the cold and snow of Cheyenne, Wyoming.

I made friends with Lee Leverett, Ray Kunze and Bob Linder who would be stationed in England with me. We parted for our twenty days leave before shipping out.

I took a train from Cheyenne to Louisville. I loved riding the train. Trains are so romantic, I wondered why they were not used by more people.

It was good to be home, but things had changed. I was no longer a kid. Mom said she wished I was back on the farm or was buying one of my own.

The family threw me a party at Lincoln Farm and everybody was there. It was a good time with family.

I was going to be away from home for three years!

I caught a train in Elizabethtown where Mom and Daddy and I said "good-bye". At *Camp Kilmer* in New Jersey I rejoined Leverett, Kunze and Linder among others we knew, then on to New York to board the *USS Henry Gilmer* for the voyage to England.

On the ferry out to the ship, we passed the Statue of Liberty. What a strange mix of feelings it caused to see it for the first time and to leave it behind all in a matter of minutes.

Once we were on the *USS Henry Gilmer*, we found we would have K.P. every other day. On the alternate day we were free to go up on deck. On one occasion when I was up on deck, I saw whales swimming in schools.

The first night I couldn't sleep and felt a little seasick, but it was nothing compared to what some of the men experienced. Adjusting to the motion of the sea took some time. We had to learn to walk and to hold our trays while we were eating to keep them from sliding across the table.

After ten days, we landed in Southhampton, England, where we got our first look at England and learned to be good guests of the English. We also went to the P.X. and saw our first English girls.
We got our orders. All of my group would be going to *Burtonwood AFB* near Warrington, Liverpool and Manchester, England. We boarded a bus for the trip, which would take nearly all day.

The war was in Korea, but we were trying to help keep world peace and watch the Russians from England.

It rained a lot and there was a lot of fog in Burtonwood, England, which is why Germany never bombed it during the war; they couldn't find it for the fog. I liked Burtonwood.

I was assigned to the *Material Control Squadron of Depot Supply.* We worked at Header House, the longest warehouse in the world. Linder, Kunze and I were assigned together, but Leverette was assigned elsewhere.

As I was introduced around the office, I discovered two other

Kentuckians, Roy Watson from Stamping Ground and Otho Cox from Kingdom Come. It made it seem more like home. I'd listen to English at work and Kentuckian at night.

On the weekend we went to Warrington to the dance hall above the *Pelican Pub.* The English girls came there from all over. I watched because I didn't know how to dance and they didn't know how to square dance. I also talked to girls. I especially liked one English girl, Marie Daw. She was from Liverpool which was only four miles from our base. Transportation was easy and cheap so we dated a lot.

Since I was a small child, I would faint any time I was sick which was not often. Sometimes this little condition could cause me no end of embarrassment to say nothing of scaring everyone around me.

One Sunday afternoon, I planned to meet Marie at the train station in Liverpool where we would take a bus to meet her parents.

I skipped breakfast, but ate chicken and ice cream for lunch. It is possible the chicken was tainted in some way because, just as we were about to reach our destination, I began to feel hot and sweaty. The next thing I knew, I was lying in a doctor's office wondering what hit me.

I had fainted on the bus and fallen out of my seat. The bus stopped at a doctor's office where some of the men carried me inside.

I had vomitted and was still terribly nauseated. The doctor said I would be all right, but that I must see the doctor on base first thing the next morning. He even refused to allow me to pay him for checking me over. He said, "Count it as English hospitality."

Marie took me back to the train and even rode the train back to Warrington with me, but I was so sick, I had to go back to the barracks.

Marie and I continued to date for a long time, but we eventually drifted apart.

About half way through my tour of duty in England, the Air Force went *Native Son.* This means that all of the functions which can be performed by local residents of the host country will be performed by civilians. Of the 320 G.I.'s stationed in our area all but twenty were declared "excess" and sent to other bases in Germany, Africa, Iran and those who spoke Spanish went to Spain. I was one of the twenty who remained in England.

I liked the English and they seemed to like me. They treated me like one of them. We were invited to their homes and enjoyed a fellowship and closeness I have always treasured.

About the time of the transfers, I was selected *Airman of the Month* for our division. It was quite an honor and I was very pleased.

In the fall of 1954, Otho Cox and I decided we wanted to go home. We requested Christmas leave and it was granted. We received a month's vacation which began December 1, 1954.

We took a flight that landed in Dublin, Ireland, Goose Bay, Labrador, and finally, in New York. In New York, we took a flight to Louisville. Cox's sister and her husband met us and took me to the bus station.

I rode the bus from Louisville to Elizabethtown then hitch-hiked to Hodgenville. I saw a lot of people I knew and got a ride home to my parents' home in Tanner.

I brought Mother a necklace from England. Through the years when she dressed up, she always wore the necklace. That necklace was precious to her and her loving it was precious to me.

I had a wonderful Christmas at home. I now had several nieces and nephews who had a tendency to spice up any family gathering. Too soon, it was over and I had to go back to New York to catch my plane to England.

We left *International Airport* to land again in Gander, New-foundland, where our plane got caught in snow drifts. We had to be plowed out of the drifts, but we eventually got free and took off for England where I would be another eighteen months.

All the fellows had to know how things were back in the States. The war was over in Korea and there was as much peace as the world ever knew.

When most people learn I have lived in England, they want to know if I saw the Queen. Indeed I did, and Prince Phillip, too. I stood within six feet of both of them and saw them quite nicely, thank you. They did not seem as intent upon seeing me as I was in seeing them, or they would have asked me to tea!

At the same time I was seeing the Queen and Prince, I saw the *Grand National Steeplechase*. I bet on three horses, Royal Tan to win, Irish Lizzard to place and Tudors' Line to show.

In the *Grand National Steeplechase* the horses go around the track twice. I climbed on top of a ten foot fence to keep track of my investment.

At the three-quarter mark, five of the 37 starters were left. All three of my horses were still in the race with Royal Tan leading. My horses finished 1-2-3 with Royal Tan winning. My lucky day!

I went back the next two years, but never won again. It is an exciting race, but horses fall and lose their riders. Seems cruel, now that I think of it.

Six months before I was to come home, I met another English girl, Chris Johnson, from St. Helens near Liverpool.

She was Catholic and I a Baptist, which may have been our only problem. Her father was a coal miner and we "got on together". Chris and I had some very good times.

It seemed that Chris and I were always going to someone's wedding and reception. I was best man three times while I was in England.

Sometimes Chris and I went to Southport-on-the-Sea and to Blackpool, a city on the sea, and sometimes to New Brighton above Liverpool. We grew very fond of each other. I gave her a Pekingese puppy. I had hoped to see her again after I left the Air Force; we wrote letters but a reunion was not to be. Sometimes marrying outside your own country works - sometimes it doesn't. I'll never know.

I vividly remember the pretty flowers and nice girls in England, the older English people who were so nice to me, the Bobbies, the two-tiered buses, and the trains with seats facing each other in compartments. I fondly remember the pubs where we would go to talk and sing. I remember *Header House*, the *U.S.O. Club* and *N.C.O. Club* that could get the best bands to come and play on Saturday night.

I played on the squadron basketball team and was picked to play on the All-Star team. We played some English teams and were never beaten. I saw two LaRue County boys over there, David Hutchinson and J.E. Cox who is now Hodgenville's police chief.

I remember the teamwork of Americans and Englishmen working together. I was delighted with the English and their tea breaks; 10:00 o'clock, 12:00 and 2:00. The English loved their hot tea.

When I had to leave to come home, it was a bitter-sweet blessing. I had to tearfully tell my friends good-bye. I had worked with these people for three years and they had become an important part of my life. It was tough.

My co-workers and friends gave me a party before I left. Charley Price, the old Scotsman with whom I had worked, had written a poem about *Header House* that he gave me. The others gave me a large, silver mug with an inscription: "To Don, from your many friends, Burtonwood, England". Everyone was there - the clerks, section heads, Air Force personnel, our captain and, of course, Chris. They were sad, and I was too.

Leverett, Linder and I flew back to New York together. We had three weeks leave and were not assigned to bases, so we parted at *International Airport.* After that, I heard from Linder occasionally at Christmas time.

It was good to see Mom and Dad. I squeezed them both. Mom fixed a big supper. We ate then sat and talked. They had gotten older, I thought. Dad and I went to the State Fair at the new fairgrounds near the newly completed Interstate Highway 65 South.

When the three weeks ended, I went to *Homestead AFB* about 18 miles south of Miami, Florida. I loved Florida. Because of the heat we were allowed to wear shorts and short sleeved uniforms to work. There was a swimming pool behind the barracks which helped me catch up with my swimming every afternoon after work.

I had saved a good bit of money during my stay in the Air Force, but I did not want to buy a car until I came home; therefore, I did a lot of hitchhiking and riding with other servicemen. I had made up my mind to retire at the end of my first tour which was only five months away.

I contacted Carol Thurman, whom I met before I went into the Air Force while she was visiting relatives in LaRue County. She was in college in Birmingham, Alabama. She, her parents and I went to Key

West one Sunday. Mr. Thurman offered to help me find a job with the Border Patrol after I left the service if I wanted to stay in Florida.

While in Florida, I got a good suntan, went deep-sea fishing and went to the dog races a lot. Carol and I saw the North-South football game at the Orange Bowl in 1956.

While my time in the service had brought a world of new and fascinating experiences, I felt it was time to go home. I was ready to pick up the threads of my life, put down some roots and get on with the future, whatever that would hold.

I left the Air Force in February. After stopping by to see Carol on the way back, I caught a bus to LaRue County and home.

CHAPTER SEVENTEEN

A TRIATHALON STRUGGLE AND A SHOWY QUILT

As the racing season of 1985 began, I did not realize I was entering a pivotal year in my life as an athletic competitor. I also did not realize how busy, expensive or productive this year of change would be.

1985 would be a year of trying new things, of nearly frantic activity and a year of involvement in new ventures. During the year, I would investigate Kentucky from border to border and competition to competition.

The regular racing schedule began as it always did with the *Tumbleweed Classic* in Louisville. I finished 25th overall and 2nd in my age group to Tom Wolf of Indiana. We enjoyed the Mexican food and the opportunity to socialize with fellow *Cherokee Road Runners*.

The *WAVE 970 Run* was an exciting race, but I didn't do as well as I wanted. We finished Wally Dawkins, Jim Carey, Frank Meade and Donald Mather in my age group. Everyone was given a beach towel with a big running shoe on it.

My next race took me to Gallatin, Tennessee, for the Rotary Club's 6th Annual *Great Sumner County Run*. I finished 84th overall and 2nd in my age group. After the race we stopped in Goodlettsville to load up on firecrackers and eat at the *Cracker Barrel*.

Then it was back to Louisville for the Cherokee Running Club's *Leprechaun Run.* I won my age group and received a green trophy.

In the *Lions Club Run* in Radcliff, I finished 2nd to Joe Uhlig and won the oldest runner award. The race was held at the Colvin Community Center. The overall was won by Jim Raprock and Susan Bonnett in the women's division.

At the WHAS *Crusade for Children Run* on an extremely windy day I ran into lots of the people I knew from running circles; otherwise, I came away a loser. The Sutherlands, Sneidners, Careys, Gene and Lil Priddy, Carl Dohn, Janet Omer, Bill Ulrick, Don Coffman and Dave Murphy were all there for the run.

I will discuss the runs for the record in the next chapter and go on to the next regular season run at Mammoth Cave, *The Earth Run,* where I won my age group. The race is held in the picnic area of Mammoth Cave Park where there is lots of shade, which may have contributed to my successful race.

I received a medallion which was square and especially made for *The Earth Run.*

We got to visit with Kenny Morris, his wife and daughter, Kennetha. Kenny coached basketball at East Hardin High School at one time.

At the next race in Glasgow, I had developed an allergy and really should have stayed home. I couldn't breathe and choked up along the way.

Ray Parella, Ken Combs and Lane from Tennessee got the awards. It was a matter of getting all the "big boys" in one sack.

We went on to Bowling Green for the *Big Red Run,* which was named for the Western Kentucky University mascot. There were a lot of pretty college girls helping with the race. I won my age group, beating Strickler, who had beaten me the year before.

It was also in 1985 that I took the tee-shirts I had been given for the races I had run to Mrs. Icy Davis who lived in Green County. I ask her to make a quilt out of the tee shirts which had the name of each race on the front.

She cut a thirteen inch square out of the front of each shirt and sewed them together. It took 49 tee-shirts to make the quilt, but the quilt was very large and very colorful. A few years later, I put the quilt on exhibit at the *Lincoln Day Quilt Show* where it received a lot of attention from quilt lovers.

We had an old bicycle we bought at one of Fred Lobb's sales. It was a three-speed girls' bike and nothing to try a triathalon with, but I got it out and rode it down the road a mile or so.

Since the wheels went around, I guess I thought that qualified me to participate in the up-coming triathalon in Green County. I dumped the bike in the back of the old truck and told myself I would go down to Green County and watch the race, at least.

The old Ford truck could have used some radiator work because it got hot on the trip to Green County - real hot. I stopped at a grocery store and got some water to try to cool down the truck.

I wasn't far from Greensburg, but I had to drive through Greensburg to the American Legion Park on the other side. By the time I got there, the truck was hot again. I parked it, deciding I would worry about it later.

Paul Ennis and his crowd gleefully said they knew that sooner or later, I would try their triathalon. Once I got there with my bicycle, there was no turning back. Of course, I had taken the precaution of putting my swim suit on under my clothes just in case I was overcome by the desire to participate.

I must have been overcome because I was signing up for the race before I thought about it. Green County has the most challenging triathalon in the Commonwealth of Kentucky and I guess it was as good a place to start as any.

The committee had designated a 55-59 age group and there was only one other competitor entered in my age group, a Hager fellow from Richmond. If I didn't win, all I had to do was finish and I would get a big trophy.

The race officials announced the race would start in ten minutes and that the swimmers should follow them. There were fifty-five of us trooping along the river bank. We walked about a half mile then got in the water with our "life-savers" on and waited for the signal to start swimming.

The signal came and I started swimming. I soon found out the river was not deep and, like the others, I could lean forward and walk fast so that it was like running in water.

The water run lasted about eleven minutes and I was in the middle of the pack. I had probably done more actual swimming than any of them. I was a good swimmer having done a lot of it as a kid.

I went to the truck and put on my running shoes and suit. The temperature was in the nineties, so I wore a cap to keep my head cooler.

I got on the bike and started down the road to Greensburg out Highway 88. Then I discovered the bike would not change gears. I was getting passed right and left.

I finally got to Highway 88, turned left and felt sick after a couple more miles. I stopped near a trailer and asked a man for some water. He gave me a big fruit jar of water. I drank most of it, but it smelled slightly of antifreeze and I didn't want to add poisoning to my list of woes.

I thought I might feel better if I rode slowly for a while. I did. I rode on, but had a terrible time getting any speed out of the old bike.

Before long I reached the eight mile marker where I was to turn left. The course was roughly square which would eventually lead back to Greensburg. I rode through a narrow road where there were people along the road offering water to the riders.

At the second square turn, I promised myself that when I finished the biking, I would just quit. It was a 32 mile ride and I had made it 25 miles.

I saw a store and stopped for a candy bar. The lady fixed me a couple of glasses of water. The last six or seven miles were pretty tough, but I made it back to Greensburg

It had been thirty-eight or thirty-nine years since I had ridden a bike. At the courthouse, I pushed the bike, drank some water and hit the road for the ten mile run.

My legs were shaky so I walked a while to try to get them back. There wasn't a breeze stirring and the heat was oppressive. As I reached the bridge, I met tired runners coming back.

I crossed the Green River Bridge and immediately turned right. The crops were beautiful along the road, but the corn was ten feet high which knocked out any hope of a breeze.

At this point, I saw no runners. I was hopelessly alone. I walked a lot, but finally came back to within a few miles of the bridge. I kept telling myself there would be water somewhere around the bridge, but when I got there the last water stop had closed.

I went another mile and stopped at a house. There was a well in the yard, but the pump wouldn't work. I knocked on the door. A beautiful dark-skinned angel opened the door, took one look at me and said, "What have you been doing? Playing ball out in the hot sun, I guess?"

I explained quickly and asked for some water. She brought a pitcher and a glass. I drank two glasses. I thanked her and told her she had saved my life.

Back on the road, I ran and walked a couple more miles. The organizers of the race from Druthers Restaurant discovered that I was still out, so they brought some Sprite and checked on me. I had less than two miles to go.

When I got within a half mile of the finish, Paul Ennis and Billy Squires came out and ran back with me to the finish line. They made me feel great, applauded me, gave me water and brought me a big trophy.

I had my picture made with Paul Ennis and the Macy twins, Karen and Sharon, whom I have known a long time. I was pleased to see LaHoma had driven down to see me cross the finish line. She told me later the whole family was worried about me trying something like this without practicing or borrowing a decent bike.

Dan Lindsey from Morehead had won the previous year and was holding the lead in 1985, but developed a charley horse a couple of miles from the finish line.

If I were into biking, I would love to do triathalons.

I finished first in my age group at the Cherokee Road Runners *Run with the Hogs* in Louisville. The race was held in Butchertown with the aroma of meat and lard filling the air. I had been away from Louisville running for a while so seeing old friends was great.

I finished 2nd in the *Fort Knox Trail Run* in the fall. Our grandson, Matt, went with us. He had not been around the military much, so he was fascinated by them.

On the way home our car overheated. We stopped at a store to cool it down. Joe Uhlig came along and helped us. He was working at Fort Knox as a tank mechanic. He was still running, but didn't race any more.

I chaired the *Railsplitter Run and Walk* in 1985 which kept me from entering the competition.

My last regular race of the year was the *Turkey Trot* in Glasgow. I finished 2nd and won a nice plaque. By now the den wall was covered with plaques and I loved every one of them!

CHAPTER EIGHTEEN

A NEW CHALLENGE AND A RECORD RUN

By the Spring of 1985, I had been running competitively for five years. I had seen many different and beautiful places in Kentucky. I had gained experience and met many people in my age group who, though we had competed with each other, had become life long friends. While I had never become disenchanted with competing, I was beginning to feel as if I had accomplished about all I could on the regular running circuit.

The familiar restless stirrings of looking for a new challenge initiated a period of self-evaluation. I got out the scrapbooks and my running records and began to study them closely. Soon I realized I was drawing close to a "Record".

I had run in many festival races, most major runs and had competed yearly in several of the most well-known races in the state. I believed I was about ready to set a record for running in the most counties in Kentucky. I decided I would set a goal to run in every county in Kentucky.

I soon found my goal was unrealistic as many counties do not offer organized races. For example, I discovered one county where I had not run was planning a festival. I called the festival chairperson and asked if they would be having a race along with their festival.

She said, "No, but on the Fourth of July, we all run across the street. The first one across gets a silver dollar."

I passed on that one.

I took a map of Kentucky that only listed the county names and using a crayon, colored in the ones in which I had run an organized race. After studying the map for a while, I thought I might be able to set a record by running in each county or the county which bordered it.

I asked Iris LaRue from the *LaRue County Chamber of Commerce* for help. She found out where festivals were being held in the counties I needed to complete my record. In addition, I used Kentucky tourism magazines and the Kentucky Parks schedules to set up a week to week schedule so I could finish in one year.

People in Kentucky are so kind and supportive of each others' interests. I called one chairperson who said they were not scheduling a race, but to give her a week to see if she could get one started. She was unable to get a race going on such short notice, but she tried.

In addition to my regular running schedule, I would need to run in eleven counties more in order to set my record. After lining up these remaining races, I realized this was going to be an expensive undertaking without a sponsor.

The cost factors were staggering enough, but I would have to be blessed enough to find the vacation time from work, stay well and avoid injury. Our cars would also have to stay in running condition in spite of their age and the rapidly increasing number of miles my running was adding to their speedometers.

I took a deep breath and plunged in, having decided to try to finish in one year.

Our first run off the regular circuit was the *Hillbilly Festival* in Pikeville, Kentucky, sponsored by Citizens Bank of Pikeville. The founders of *Hillbilly Days* were Howard Stratton and Grandy Kinney. Proceeds from the race, handmade quilts and other things, went to the Crippled Children's Hospital in Lexington.

At noon on Friday, I took a half day vacation. Donnie, LaHoma and I boarded the old '77 Chevy wagon and headed up the Bluegrass Parkway to Lexington where we would pick up I-64 and eventually the Mountain Parkway.

All along the Mountain Parkway we had seen beautiful

mountainous terrain, coal mines and coal trucks hauling the coal away. Houses were built on ledges of rock along the highway which must have given the owners wonderful views of the valleys and hills around them.

As I have said before, to Kentuckians, no matter how high the mountain, its called a "hill". Whether hills or mountains, Eastern Kentucky provides some beautiful scenery and very kind people.

We stopped to eat dinner so when we reached Pikeville it was getting dark. The festival was in full swing. It did not take long for us to become lost in the crowd along the blocked streets.

A man must have thought we looked lost because he stopped and asked if he could help us. I told him we needed a motel or hotel. He led us to one of the local motels which had no vacancies, but the motel owner called another motel and found a room for us.

We were told there was good music in the park downtown. After unpacking we drove as close to the park as possible then walked across the Big Sandy Basin. The course of the Big Sandy River has been changed for some reason and all we saw was the dry basin.

There was a huge crowd. One of the local men told us some of the people enjoying the festival "hadn't been out of the hills all year".

The music was a mixture of Bluegrass and Mountain music. It was great and we enjoyed ourselves very much.

We watched the people and they watched us. Soon, some of them came over to talk to us and welcome us to the festival. They turned out to be nice, friendly people, just like Kentuckians are supposed to be.

The next morning I picked up my tee-shirt and looked at the trophies to be given away. I hoped I would win one of those trophies in the lOK. There was a nice crowd for the race and I actually saw someone I knew.

I started the race running pretty well, but the mountain air made a difference to me. I came in 4th to Bradford from Virginia, Warren McFadden from Paintsville and Staggs from near Pikeville. I won no trophy this day. A nice lady from Citizens Bank gave me a cap with their name on it, though.

We stayed another night. We took part in the dancing in the park, then went to a movie. We had dinner in the rooftop dining room at the Landmark Inn. The view from the window was breathtaking, and the food delicious.

On the way back we stopped at Natural Bridge Park and climbed the hill to reach the top of the bridge. It was beautiful. We added a lot of pictures to our collection.

The following weekend, the Scottsville Women's Club was sponsoring the *Jacksonian Run* called the "hilliest little 5K in Kentucky". The Scottsville Women's Club offered superior management for the race. Awards were 5 deep in all divisions with silver cups for the winners of each age group. Everything about the race seemed to run exceptionally well.

I won my age group and one of the silver cups. I was so glad. The overall winner was Darrin Kinder in the men's division while Kathy Van Meter from Bowling Green won the women's division.

Sharon Garland from Laurel County was in the race. We also renewed acquaintances with Mark Lowry II, a professor at Western Kentucky University.

LaHoma went with me on this trip, happily anticipating dinner at the Louie B. Nunn Lodge at Barren River State Resort Park. As I have said before, the food is delicious.

The following weekend found LaHoma, Diana, Nathan and me tooling down the Western Kentucky Turnpike to Rosine and the *Bluegrass Run*. We were going north, south, east, west and back again. We were crisscrossing the state time and time again keeping up with the "record schedule" and my regular list of yearly runs.

Rosine is a small town with a country store and a nice park. I finished 3rd to Ivan Reynolds of Evansville and Tom Foster from Owensboro in their 5K run. After the race we visited with Ray Rayl, the excellent over 60 runner from Evansville, Don Ferguson from Rosine and Kathy Van Meter from Bowling Green.

Later we stopped at Caneyville to visit Gay Hazle's drug store. Gay and I had played together as boys. It was good to see him.

From there we went on to Rough River State Park where we

ate and went swimming. The water felt so refreshing after the run that morning. It seemed to help wash the muscle soreness away.

Our schedule took us to Morehead for the *Citizens' Bank 5 Miler*. Dan Lindsey was chairman of the race and Dave Wottle of Olympic fame would be giving out the awards. It was a very big race.

I finished 2nd to Harold Love of Lexington in my age group. The overall winner in the men's division was George Nicholas of Dayton, Ohio. In the women's division the overall winner was Maria Pazarrentas. My old friend Hopey Newkirk finished 2nd.

There were a lot of good mountain runners in the race. Tommy Smith of Corbin, Frank Cornett of London, Jeff Collier of Partridge and Phil Lucas of Beattyville to name only a few. We really enjoyed the Morehead run.

The *Poke Sallet Festival* in Harlan, Kentucky, would be a momentous occasion. I enjoy nearly all sports. Over the years, I have kept up with most of our state's athletes of note. Perhaps, because we Kentuckians are so enamored of basketball, we seem to produce at least our fair share of noteworthy athletes in all sports.

Harlan, Kentucky, was the home of Wah-Wah Jones, who led the home town team to the high school championship, then went on to be an All-American at the University of Kentucky and competed in the 1948 Olympic competition.

The Poke Sallet Run was sponsored by the Mountain Trails Health Plan, Inc. of Harlan, Kentucky, and was held on June 29, 1985.

It was a long drive to Harlan. LaHoma and my grandson Abe Devore went with me which helped make the trip more fun.

We decided to spend the night at the Pine Mountain State Park. It is one of the most beautiful places I have been. I wished we could have stayed a week. All of Kentucky's State Resort Parks are beautiful and it seems that everyone has a favorite.

Some people think Jenny Wiley State Resort Park is the most beautiful. Others think the Cumberland Falls Park is the only place to vacation. Many people say there is no better food cooked anywhere than at the Barren River Resort Park. For me, the jury is still out on my favorite park. I guess it is only fair to say, I never visited a Kentucky State Park I didn't like.

In the morning we drove over to Harlan for the race. The starting line was near the courthouse, so we didn't have trouble finding the location.

When the race began, we ran for about a half mile along a fairly level course. Suddenly, out of nowhere we began to run straight up. We came to our first "hill". Those "hills" can be deceptive, as we've said before. This had to be the "mother of all hills", but what can you expect in Harlan County?

I lost my wind and barely made it to the top. To keep going, I told myself that somewhere, somehow this thing had to go down again. Sure enough, once we made it to the top, it was downhill the rest of the way to the finish line.

I won my age group and LaHoma took a lot of pictures for the scrapbook. We also met Emily Bailey, organizer of the race. I told her why we had driven so far to race. She thought my idea for setting a record was great. She was so excited for me and so supportive; I hope she reads my book.

We also met Charlie Harris who ran the race with his dog on a leash. He and his dog must have had a better running system than the man and his dog who passed me in my first *Golden Armor Race* a few years earlier.

After the race we heard two bands play the "Poke Sallet Ballad" then we ate "poke" in the street at an outdoor cafe. We used a lot of vinegar and it was pretty good. The next day there was an article in the Louisville papers. A reporter had interviewed a Harlan County native who said it "took a lot of poke" for him. He said he had to have it at least twice a year.

I'm certain everyone in Kentucky knows what "poke sallet" is. In LaRue County, we refer to any of the family of green vegetables such as mustard, kale, spinach, collards or poke as "greens". Our mountain neighbors to the east refer to the same vegetables as "sallet".

A housewife might say, "I'm cooking a big pot of sallet for supper tonight." This could mean you were having anything from spinach to poke.

Herein hangs another tale. To all Kentuckians, except those who have been corrupted by too much television or too many years in cities, the evening meal is "supper". If we go out to eat in a restaurant, we "go out to dinner". If we eat at home, we eat "supper". If you're planning to have sallet for supper, you'd be right at home in Kentucky.

The word "sallet" may be an early American corruption of the word "salad". This is about all I know on the subject. If you want to know more, you will just have to go to the *Poke Sallet Festival* in Harlan, Kentucky, and find out for yourself.

The following Saturday we took the Western Kentucky Turnpike to Sebree, Kentucky, which is in Webster County between Madisonville and Henderson.

I was getting closer to my record, but it was getting really expensive to complete this goal without a sponsor. However, LaHoma and I were having a lot of fun and meeting some wonderful, interesting people.

The race at Sebree was held on the Fourth of July and was appropriately called the *Firecracker Run.* We drove some of the last miles of the trip in the dark which enabled us to see gas wells burning at night. It was quite a sight.

THE SEBREE BANNER NEWSPAPER sponsored the *Firecracker Run* which was chaired by Betty Catlett. It was a coincidence that I have a cousin named Betty Catlett Rose.

I chose the 5K run of the three options. I finished 3rd in my age group. In the western part of the state there is stiff running competition from some good runners from Evansville. They are really tough and make an exciting race.

I visited with Glen Menser and Ray Rayl who were competing in the race as well. Betty Catlett, thoughtfully, sent me the results of the race which appeared in the *SEBREE BANNER.*

The following week, I was on my way back to Eastern Kentucky for the race in Maysville. I went alone which turned out to be a good thing because the old station wagon gave me trouble. We had been blessed in that the old wagon kept on rolling for us, but about five miles from Maysville, I realized my car lights were very dim and I could not see very well.

I sort of limped into Maysville, or just outside to a fast food restaurant. I ate, then found I could not start my car. I tried to sleep, but couldn't. I got out and ran a couple of miles. When I came back to the car, a couple of teenaged boys were driving around. I asked them to help. They jumped the car and it started.

I drove into town to find the starting point for the race, then found a closed service station where I parked and spent the night. When the morning came, I saw the Ohio River and the view of the bridge sometimes used on KET-TV. It was beautiful.

The station manager arrived and promised to check my car. I cleaned up, dressed and ate at a nearby restaurant, then went on to the race headquarters where I met Bill Hornback from Ohio.

John Knebenow was race chairman. The race was an "out and back" along the Ohio River. I had hoped I would run into some of the Maysville basketball team who had beaten us in the second round of the State Basketball Tournament when I was in high school. None of them seemed to have gone into running, unfotunately. I would have loved to beat them in a race!

I finished 2nd in my age group, then went to check on my car. The station manager said I had a loose alternator belt. He tightened it and charged the battery. My bill was six dollars. God is good, isn't He?

The following weekend we were scheduled to take the long drive back to Eastern Kentucky, but we stopped off for the *Daniel Boone Run* in Winchester, first.

As we drove into town, the balloon race was in progress. I ran the lOK finishing 3rd to Roland Anspagh, who has held a national record in the 3,000 meters, and Harold Love. Since only two awards were given in each age group and I had not won one; I was eligible to enter the 2 mile race.

Our Grandson Matt Shelton went with us on this trip. He and I ran in the two mile race. I won 1st place and was awarded a trophy and a running print.

After eating, we drove on to Hazard down the Mountain Parkway. I would be running in Jackson at the *Honey Festival* the next day.

We had reservations at the La Citadel Motel. The La Citadel is located in Hazard straight up the "hillside" about a mile. You can imagine the view from the windows of the motel.

When we went through the front door of the motel, I noticed a lot of people milling around who appeared to be about my age. One of the ladies smiled when she saw me and started in my direction.

We had walked into the middle of the 1945 to 1949 Hazard High School Class Reunion. I, apparently, looked like one of their classmates. The lady welcomed me home to Hazard. I explained that I was not who they thought I was and that I was there to race the next day in Jackson. They seemed to be as interested in my running as I was in their reunion. We began talking.

I told them I had played on a team that went to the State Basketball Tournament in 1947 and thought Hazard had played in the same tournament. They agreed that they had, indeed, played in the tournament and that I could meet some of the players the next day.

We ate dinner (we were not eating at home so we didn't have supper) at the La Citadel restaurant. Later we sat by the swimming pool.

The next morning, I was forced to go to Jackson by myself because LaHoma and Matt were so carried away with the La Citadel Motel. I found the race headquarters and who do you suppose was the first person I recognized? It was none other than Roland Anspagh who had heaten me the day before.

We raced around the Pan-Bowl. I came in 3rd to Anspagh and a local person, Wireman. I talked to Phil Lucas from Beattyville who said there was going to be a race in Beattyville the next day. Roland Anspagh said he was going over for the race and invited me to go along. I said, "No thanks. You've beaten me enough for one weekend!"

I got some honey for winning in Jackson, so I took my honey and went back to the motel to go swimming with Matt. Later we went to a movie at the Fugate Amusements between Hazard and Jackson. After the movie we went bowling. When we returned to the motel, we watched the Hazard group have their reunion around the swimming pool.

At check out time the next morning, we were greeted by the chairperson of the reunion who gave me a key to the city of Hazard. What nice people the Hazard High School class of 1945 to 1949 turned out to be.

With the honey from Jackson, running print and trophy from Winchester, and the key to the city of Hazard, we took the Daniel Boone Parkway to Manchester, London, Somerset, Columbia, Greensburg and home.

The *Tobacco Festival* in Carrollton was my next stop. I met the race chairman, Dan Carrico, who turned out to be a relative to Nancy Marcum, a high school classmate of LaHoma's. When he discovered who I was and why I was racing, he welcomed me to the *Tobacco Festival Run*, which was in competition with another race in Madison, Indiana, on the same day.

I finished 2nd in my age group to Mel Harper. I had never beaten Mel in a race. The following year I would beat him in the *Triple Crown Race* called the *Run for the Arts.*

The *Mud Run* was a half-marathon in Shepherdsville. It was the easiest half- marathon I ever ran. Owen Comer and I ran together swapping leads several times. He finally beat me in the last quarter mile. I finished 3rd.

At this point I had three more races to run to enable me to set the record. I was tired and we had spent a lot of money; but I was too close to quit.

I'd been looking forward to the *Apple Festival* in Paintsville, so we headed down the Mountain Parkway again.

Not everyone is enthusiastic about running. As we reached Paintsville, I asked two firemen where the race would be held. One of them thought a while, then said he didn't know. The other said he didn't know either. I asked where I could find the newspaper office. They said there were two papers, which one did I want. I decided I'd better try to find the race headquarters for myself.

After driving about two blocks, we saw the *Apple Festival Run* banner hanging across the street.

Paintsville is Warren McFadden's hometown. We talked with him and made some new friends as the race time neared.

The race was an "out and back". Some of the first runners turned around too quickly. The race officials had a hard time deciding how to handle the mistake. Finally, they added three minutes to the time of the first seven runners. I won my age group and my name was called for an extra prize, a running bag.

The chairperson for the race was Rick Roberts. He was a colorful character who wore Reebok shoes and shorts which looked like the British flag, the Union Jack.

While we were eating lunch, I got into a discussion with some of the local men. Someone mentioned that the singer, Crystal Gayle, was going to be Grand Marshall of the parade as she was born in Butcher Hollow not far from Paintsville.

I told one of the locals that if he saw her to let me know because I wanted to go out and give her a kiss. Two or three minutes passed and several shouted to me, "Okay, Big Boy, here she comes!"

I was on the spot, so I dashed out into the street. I soon thought better of trying to give her a kiss. She had almost as much security as the President of the United States. I walked up to the convertible she was riding in and asked if I could shake hands with her. She said, "Sure."

We shook hands. She said, "My, your hands are sure cold."

It wasn't exactly what I had in mind, but it was pleasant and reaffirmed my opinion that she is a nice lady.

We bought a half bushel of apples and went home.

Greenup County is Jesse Stuart country. It is also the home of Don Gullett, a former baseball pitcher for the Reds and the Yankees. Don is retired and farms in Greenup County. My next to last race in my record setting schedule was to be held in Greenup County.

We spent the night in Morehead then arrived in Greenup County in time to get a haircut before the race. Their festival was called *Old Fashioned Day* and the race was sponsored by the Lady of Bellefonte Hospital. No cost was involved in entering the race.

I liked the race very much. My time was 44:10 for the 10K, and I placed 2nd in my age group.

The National High School Cheerleader Champions in 1985 were from Greenup County and in the parade that day. I got their autographs. They were: Missy Wells; Laurean Hall; Nicki Bates; Joanie Price; Annette Steele; Tonya Cockran; and Michelle Aldon. They were such pretty girls.

In the summer of 1985, I participated in the *Bluegrass Games* in Lexington. I met a man from Fort Thomas, Merle Nickell. As we talked, he told me about teaching at Buffalo. He was also the basketball coach there in the early fifties. He remembered our mayor, R. K. Keith, Mr. Edwin Harvey, "Sawdust" Childress and Spider Reed. He asked how they were doing.

I told Merle about my plans to set a running record in Kentucky and that I needed to run in Covington. Later, I got a letter from him telling me about four or five races before the end of the year. The most appealing race would be held in Covington on Thanksgiving Day. It was called the *Elks Run* and it would be the 76th running of the race. This is the third oldest race in America.

I had one more race to go for my record, but I would be able to get a little rest as this was the 11th of October and my last race was scheduled for Thanksgiving Day.

LaHoma could not go with me for the race on Thanksgiving Day as she would be cooking Thanksgiving dinner for the family. I invited James Sallee to accompany me.

This would be a fantastic race to finish the record. Jerry Traylor would run the race on crutches. Jerry had run across the United States some 3,200 miles on crutches. I saw him run and talked to him after the race. Jerry is the most amazing person.

When I got Jerry's autograph, he wrote a note which said "Live Life with Joy". Those were poignant words. I was thrilled to finish this dream of mine, especially on Thanksgiving Day.

The next morning when James and I ate breakfast, we saw a LaRue Countian, Vicky Jewell, working in the restaurant. After eating, we hurried to the Latonia Shopping Center where the race would start.

There were 2,500 runners warming up in the extreme cold. I had purchased some new running shoes for this race, a pair of Tiger X Caliber G.T.'s, but they were not my problem. My problem was that

I had been so busy working and stripping tobacco, I had not had enough practice.

When I crossed the finish line, I threw my arms in the air. This was a special and proud moment for me. I had set my record. I had done what I set out to do. I looked down onto the street where I found a penny with Abraham Lincoln looking back at me. I took it as a sign that God had been with me and helped me finish my race. I was ready to go home to where I belonged - to Hodgenville, Kentucky.

Some of my friends had been keeping up with what they probably thought was a crazy escapade. However, Celia McDonald from *THE HERALD NEWS* sent her sports editor to do a special on me.

There was a nice photograph with a headline which read "Ambitious Mather Finishes His Trek Around the Bluegrass Over Thanksgiving Day". The writer and photographer was Robin Milby, who has great potential as both a writer and photographer. I really think a lot of this young man. I wish him all the best.

In addition to the sense of accomplishment, I found myself thinking about what I had learned from the effort of running all across Kentucky. I know I came away from the experience with a heightened awareness of the beauty of Kentucky and its people.

I saw the mountains, the lakes, the rivers, the bluegrass, the pretty ladies, many of the great local festivals, most of the tourist attractions, the magnificent national and state parks and the plain old everyday fields, streams, trees and flowers. Kentucky must be the most beautiful place on earth.

I was privileged to meet people from every corner of Kentucky. Kentucky's people are involved. They are great basketball fans, lovers of music, appreciate the Kentucky Derby, are involved in just about every sport and, for the most part, are dedicated to keeping Kentucky the best Kentucky can be.

We found wonderful restaurants, motels and hotels. We met so many nice runners who are nearly all good sports. I had also participated in some great races.

In addition to what I had learned through sight and sound, smell and touch, I had also learned something about my inner self; something spiritual.

I believe that for every feat or accomplishment, we pay a mental and physical price. Without God's approval and provision, we cannot be successful at anything, yet, with God, we can do anything.

If someone were to ask me what God's purpose was in helping me run so many races and how he helped me find the money to pay for the activities, I could not answer, even today. I know that God was with me all the way and I feel his full purpose will unfold in His time. It is enough for me to know that God is with me today, yesterday, tomorrow and forever.

At this point, with some experience behind me, I would like to present some awards of my own. I believe the best runner I have ever met is Bill Rodgers. Stan Cottrill gets the award for the most determined runner. The most popular runner would go to either Wally Bright or Swag Hartel. The best race award goes to the *Wendy's Classic* in Bowling Green, Kentucky. The best race director award goes to Gil Clark. The best state games goes to the *Bluegrass Games* in Lexington. The best local festival goes to *The Lincoln Days* in Hodgenville. The best running course goes to the *Military Challenge* in Louisville. My favorite competitor would have to be the "Jolly Jogger", Paul Ennis from Greensburg. The best female runner is Priscilla Welch from Great Britain. She was the winner of the 1987 *New York Marathon.* I met her in Bowling Green, at the *Wendy's Classic* the year she won there.

CHAPTER NINETEEN

THE BLUEGRASS GAMES AND A NEW CHALLENGE

Governor Martha Layne Collins was responsible for initiating the *Bluegrass Games*. In a progressive and far reaching plan, Governor Collins made a move to lend her influence to an activity which held the potential of uniting Kentuckians in a common effort. In addition, the games provided an arena for Kentuckians to demonstrate their skills, win recognition and enjoy each other.

The *Bluegrass Games* also provides another tourist attraction in a state which is burgeoning with spectacular scenery, historically significant areas and landmarks, good food and sporting events equalled by none. I cannot help feeling that Governor Collins' foresight and enthusiasm for the people of Kentucky as demonstrated in the development of the *Bluegrass Games* is still helping Kentucky and her people move into the twenty-first century.

The story is told that Governor Collins was attending a celebration in honor of two Kentucky athletes who had competed spectacularly in the 1984 Olympics. As she observed the activities, the idea came to her that Kentucky provided the nation with an unusual number of fine athletes in all sports. Apparently, it also occurred to her that Kentuckians needed an arena to demonstrate their talents.

Governor Collins surrounded herself with experts in a variety of sports asking them to develop the *Bluegrass Games* for the people of Kentucky to enjoy. The *Senior Games*, which are competitions for older athletes, are an off-shoot of her original idea.

The 1985 *Bluegrass Games* were held in Lexington and were responsible for providing me with a new love - race walking. One of the first events in the *Bluegrass Games* of 1985 was a race walking event. There were only five walkers entered in the race and it was the only race of its nature in the games, but I was intrigued by it.

When the race results were posted in the *LEXINGTON HERALD LEADER* the next day, I made careful note of the winning times for the 1,500 meters. The following week, I went to the track and marked off 1,500 meters and began practicing. Eventually, I timed myself and found I could compete with anyone my own age, at least.

With visions of trophies and gold medals dancing in my head, I sat down and wrote the director of the *Bluegrass Games*, telling him age groups for the walking events would increase fairness to older runners. It could also increase the number of people participating in the races, if walkers felt they had an equal chance of winning. No one wants to enter an event just so the winners will have someone to beat.

When I received my booklet the next year, I found my letter had been given consideration. There would be age groups in the Bluegrass Games race walking events. My age group would be 50 and older. It was an improvement, but could still use some fine tuning.

All people over fifty are not created equal. There is a noticeable decline in strength and endurance, even for the physically fit, which seems to occur in about five year intervals. Unless the sixty year old is unusual, he/she will not be able to compete with a fifty year old.

If event directors would set the age groups after thirty-five in five year increments, we might see many more older people exercising and working toward competitions which give 70, 75, 80, 85 year olds a fair shake. In order to do this, we will have to change how we view aging. EVERYONE OVER FIFTY IS NOT CREATED EQUAL!

Another reason I decided to take up race walking was my poor showing in the running competitions. Early in my running career as an older runner, I found my best shot at the shiny trophies was in developing stamina, strength and endurance.

I had been in the winners circle over the past six years, not because I was fast, but because I could set a pace and hold it for as long as it took. I was not, and never had been, a sprinter. Remember the number of times I had been edged out by runners who could sprint in the final half or quarter mile?

I had entered the 800 meter and 200 meter races in the 1985 Bluegrass Games only to be embarrassed by some track specialists who were better sprinters. Nevertheless, I had a wonderful time and got to participate in the parade of athletes.

I marched into the stadium with other LaRue Countains. Coach Jack Mitchell had brought along Brandon Claycomb, Casey Sparrow and Tommy Mitchell. Tommy Mitchell won a bronze medal in the high jump. It was a proud moment for all of us as we marched into the stadium.

Regardless, seeing the games planted a seed. I was gearing up and getting ready for the next year of the Bluegrass Games.

My grandson, Matt Shelton, had been playing just about every sport and for a 9- year-old, he had a very good arm. I asked his mother, Donna, to check to see how far he could throw a softball.

When Donna told me how far Matt could throw the softball, I knew he could be competitive in the Games. She mailed his entry form entering him in the 50, 100, 200 and 400 meter, softball throw and the long jump. I entered the race walk, discus, shot-put and triple jump just in case I decided to try them.

The Radisson Hotel in Lexington was renting rooms for half price so we planned to stay two days. We went up on Friday, checked into our room, then went to Shively Field for the pre-opening ceremony.

Hank Aaron, Wilma Rudolph, Peter Vidmar and Governor Collins were all making ceremony opening speeches. Matt enjoyed this very much as he is a fan of all sports. Later Matt and I marched in the opening ceremonies with the track and field competitors wearing our track and field tee-shirts. Our sponsors were Coca- Cola and Valvoline. Wilma Rudolph and Peter Vidmar carried the torch and lighted the flame to signal the start of the second annual games.

There had been a mistake made on my entry form which forced me to file a protest on Friday evening. The following morning the race officials had me straightened out, but it caused me to have to compete on the outside lane.

There were about ten walkers in the race representing several age groups. Bob Hicks broke first. I got behind him and shadowed him for the first three laps. On the fourth, I tried to pass. I got even with him, but I couldn't get around him. Bob finished 1st, but I was a close 2nd. It was a thrill just to be in the Bluegrass Games.

I received my silver metal then went to watch my grandson compete. Matt finished second in the 50 meter run, 1st in the softball throw and second in the 100 meter. In the long jump, he jumped farther than anyone, but fell. His next two jumps weren't as good.

Matt finished the day with three medals to my one. We had reason to celebrate. We called Matt's parents to tell them how well he was doing. They promised to drive up on Sunday to watch the final competitions.

Sunday afternoon I competed in the triple jump and the shot-put. Matt continued with the 200 and 400 meter runs. When the *Bluegrass Games* ended, Matt had won one gold, two silver and one bronze medal, while I had won one silver.

The headlines in *THE LARUE COUNTY HERALD NEWS* the following week read: "Shelton Wins 4 Medals in Bluegrass State Games". Now you know that had to make a little fellow feel proud.

When the 1987 *Bluegrass Games* rolled around I was ready for the race walk competition. I was a torch runner in the 1987 games, but more about that later.

My grandson Matt was also competing. I was scheduled to take part in the walk while Matt was scheduled to compete in the running events and softball throw.

Early Saturday morning we went to Shively Field, where the Games were held, to register and pick up our tee-shirts. Matt's parents, Donna and Mike Shelton, and his two brothers were there to watch and take pictures. Donna took a picture of Matt and me in our running gear.

We met so many of the people we knew from past race competitions. We visited with Phil Lucas, Don Coffman and Mrs. Jean

Wright, who was the chairperson for the track and field events.

Before long we started warming up for the competitions ahead. I met some of the other race walkers. When the race began I broke 5th in a field of 40 walkers. The age groups were badly arranged which meant I would be in the 40-59 age group which meant I could not be competitive. I did finish 8th overall, but I was disappointed for I would have been 3rd in the 50-59 age group.

Matt was having a marvelous day, however. His age group was 8-9-10 year olds and Matt was 10, which gave him an advantage. He won the gold in the softball throw and the gold in 100 meters. He set *Bluegrass Games* records in both of these events. He also won the 200 meter run.

On Sunday, he tied for 1st in the long jump with Brian Wingfield, who had been the big winner from the year before. Brian was awarded the gold because T.A.C. rules specify that in case of a tie, the second best jump is the deciding factor. Three gold and one silver medal in one season is excellent competing. In two years of competing in the Bluegrass Games, Matt had won 4 gold, 3 silver and 1 bronze medal.

In the 1987 *Bluegrass Games* the family participation had increased. Diana and Nathan went with us as did Donna and Mike and their three boys, Matt included. The kids were having a wonderful time at the motel the night before the competitions.

The next morning our little group went to Shively Field where the track and field events are held. Nathan and I were entered in the 1500 meter race walk; we were early so we were able to watch a few other events before ours began. We watched Buddy Harpool win the 1500 meter run.

Eventually it was time for our event. There were 43 entered in the race walk of all ages and sexes. Troy Givens and Judge Embry were entered and broke first. I fell in behind them, but got a bit winded because I started too fast. I finished 3rd behind Judge Eugene Siler of Williamsburg and Barnett from Lexington. I received a bronze medal.

Nathan, who was eight years old, finished eleven seconds out of third place which meant no medal today.

My next event was the 200 meter run. I thought about not competing, but at the last minute, I decided to go ahead as planned. I'm glad I did. I finished second for a silver medal. Matt and Nathan competed in the 100 meter, but won no medals.

We went back to our motel, ate and swam. The next morning we swam until almost noon then ate and returned to Shively Field for the competitions.

My first event of the day was the 100 meter. There were only three of us entered. I finished 2nd for another silver medal. I won a silver in the high jump as well. At this point a reporter from *THE NEWS ENTERPRISE* came to our area to interview me.

He took a picture of me holding my three medals. When the large color photograph came out in the paper I stood holding my three medals, but I won four before the day was over.

Nathan barely missed winning a medal and Matt finally won a gold medal for the long jump. In three Bluegrass Games, Matt had won 9 medals.

Another LaRue Countian, Brooke Sullivan, won a bronze medal in the 100 meter run. During the Lincoln Days Celebration Parade, Mrs. John Sullivan drove John Keith's Mercedes convertible with Brooke, Matt, John Michael Sullivan and me riding in the back. A sign on the side of the car said: "Bluegrass Game Winners". There were six stars on the sign, one for each medal we won that year.

In 1988, Matt won state champion in the *Bluegrass Games* long jump competition. I carried the torch again and won silver medals in the *Bluegrass Games* 100 and 200 meter runs and the high jump.

It was also in 1988 that LaHoma won first place in the Kentucky Health Department talent show for a skit she did in which she mimicked Tammy Faye Baker. With tons of make-up and a few other changes, she looked just like Tammy Faye. The whole family was so proud of her.

In the summer of 1989, I wanted to try something new in the *Bluegrass Games*. I had trouble deciding between track and field and swimming. In the *Bluegrass Games*, one can only participate in one sport, but as many events within that sport as one wishes. If I competed in swimming, I would have to miss the track and field events. At last, I chose swimming.

I went up early on opening day to watch some of my friends carry the torch from Frankfort to Lexington. Afterward, we ate together at the University of Kentucky football field parking lot. Some of my old track and field buddies wanted to know why I wasn't entered in the events this year. I assured them I was still around, but swimming this year.

On Saturday, I competed in the 100 meter free-style in which I placed 3rd in my age group. An hour later, I competed in the 50 meter breast stroke, again, placing 2nd.

I planned to get a good night's sleep, but was too keyed up from competing.

On Sunday, I placed 3rd in the 50 meter free-style. In my last Bluegrass Games competition of the 1989 season, I finally won a gold medal for finishing 1st in the 50 meter butterfly. I took my four medals home with a great feeling of accomplishment.

CHAPTER TWENTY

RACE WALKING, A NEW LOVE

After my introduction to race walking at the *Bluegrass Games*, I began looking around for opportunities to walk and learn.

It was spring before I found a walk in which to compete. Glasgow was holding three races and one of them was a race walk. I have to admit, I was scared. I don't like losing and I wasn't sure what I would find when I got to the race headquarters, but I went anyway.

There were about 40 racers taking part in the walk. When the race began I was in front. This was thrilling after spending so many years lucky to hold on in the middle.

We were walking in a square from the start to the finish line. When I made the first turn, I looked back. There was a girl in 2nd place, but not close. I quickened my pace to prevent her from gaining if she made a move.

Soon, I saw the finish line ahead of me; three blocks, then two, then one. I poured it on. The crowd loved it. I won the race!

It was the first time I had ever won the whole race.

Someone suggested I run in the 10K as well, but I was savoring the moment. I was like a kid at Christmas; I didn't want the feeling to end. I had found a new love.

Ohio County Judge, C.B. Embry, watched me win the walk that day. It must have looked like fun, for he soon took up the sport himself. Judge Embry and I met again and again, soon becoming great friends.

My second walk was at Bud's Lake in LaRue County.

Shirley and Bud Eastridge developed and own Bud's Lake, which offers recreation, sports, fishing and swimming with a chance to enjoy the outdoors. They were having a *Bud's Lake Day* with competitions and contests. Shirley asked me to help her chair a race which would take place during the frontier games.

I told her I would love to help if she would allow me to hold a race walk. She agreed and we began developing an entry form with a map to Bud's Lake on the back. I took the form to several races.

We eventually had five entered in the walk, twenty in the fun run and fifteen in the longer run. I wish we had had better luck with the turnout. We tried, but probably could have used more publicity and more time to get ready.

Races tend to be growing concerns. Each successive year seems to see a larger and larger turn out. It takes some patience and faith, but most well-managed races do tend to pay off in the long run.

I won my second walk and am indebted to the Eastridges for more practice and a fine race.

I could find no more walks to enter until the 1986 *Bluegrass Games*.

I found another walk at Fairdale about a month later. The walk and the run they were having were scheduled to begin at the same time, which is not good race planning. Some competitors have a tendency to cheat in walking in that they run and walk rather than walking the whole distance.

The *Fairdale Walk* was an "out and back", but there was little indication of where the turn was to be made. I must have done it right, for I held the lead except for two people ahead of me who were running almost as much as they were walking. Eventually, they were disqualified. I won the race receiving a beautiful plaque, a free meal at Shoney's and a tee-shirt.

I saw Swag Hartel and his wife at Fairdale and was able to sign up several runners for the *Railsplitter Run* in October.

The *Mothers Against Drunk Driving* sponsored a walk in conjunction with the *Golden Armor Festival*, which I entered. There were about 15 walkers in all.

The race officials had organized this race the way a race should be organized. Their attention to detail included a police car to lead the race which helped to prevent those who attempt to run instead of walk from succeeding in their efforts to win unfairly.

I walked right on the bumper of the lead car, but held a comfortable pace without speeding. I won the race and got the biggest trophy I ever saw.

In 1986 the *Railsplitter Walk* was held on the 12th of October. There were about 23 walkers. There were some experienced walkers in the race which made the competition much stiffer than usual. I started in 2nd place, but was in 3rd by the half-mile marker. I finished 3rd overall to Troy Givens and C. B. Embry. We were very pleased with the way the first *Railsplitter Walk* had gone.

The following week Scottsville held a *Walk With Christ*. There were 150 people entered in the walk, but I felt I was prepared to compete. I finished 2nd overall to C.B. Embry, Jr. I also won my age group so I went home with two nice trophies.

I finished 3rd overall to C.B. Embry and David Buckman from Lebanon in the *Turkey Trot Walk* in Glasgow.

I did not compete again until the spring of 1987 when I started my year with the *Old Kentucky Home Classic Walk*. There were only 11 people entered, but I won overall which is always a good feeling.

During the Kentucky Derby Festival, a walk called the *Ramble for the Roses* was held at Holy Rosary Academy in Louisville. There were 2,500 people entered in the walk, but I finished 5th overall. Not bad for a man my age, if I do say so myself.

My old friend, Troy Givens, from Charlestown, Indiana, sent me an entry form for a walk to be held in Charlestown. I entered and finished 3rd to Troy and a man who beat me in the *Ramble for the Roses*.

I competed next at Starlight, Indiana, in the *Strawberry Festival*. It was a confused four mile affair in which runners and walkers began together which fostered some cheating. One of those disposed to cheat was eventually disqualified. I finished fourth overall.

In the fall of 1987, I competed in the *Champions on the Move* at Bellarmine College in Louisville in another race walk. The campus was as beautiful as the weather.

In a field of 600 walkers, I finished 3rd overall, but would have won if I had not taken a wrong turn and gone two blocks out of the way. I enjoyed the pizza and music they provided.

The following week I entered the *Turkey Trot Run/Walk* at Glasgow. I chose to compete in the walk finishing 3rd overall to David Buckman of Lebanon and C.B. Embry of Beaver Dam. Out of the three races held that day, I was judged "Best Grand Master Participant". I won a $25.00 award and a medal.

Three races were scheduled for Columbia. When I arrived for the races, I saw David Buckman, but to my relief, I found he was competing in the one mile run so I would not have to compete against him. I won my walking event, receiving a $25.00 gift certificate and a plaque.

Two weeks before Christmas, I entered a two mile walk in Louisville called the *Jingle Bell Classic*. I was the overall winner in this one. It was very colorful as we ran or walked with little bells so we jingled when we moved.

The following week, I entered the walk at the *U.K./U.L. Scholarship Run/Walk*. There were 200 participants. Dr.'s Roselle and McSwain started the walk by firing a gun. I finished first and won the overall award.

One of the events in which I had the most fun occurred in the spring of 1988 in the *Walk America* at Elizabethtown High School. It was a ten mile walk to generate money for the March of Dimes.

One of the things which made it so much fun was that groups of people from factories and businesses walked in groups. G.I.'s from Fort Knox's "Charlie Company" also walked.

Each group wore tee-shirts with their company name on them. I decided to just run the ten miles. I started out in 1st place. Soon everyone ran. I finished 5th overall from a field of 850. The walk made nearly $40,000.00 in entry fees and sponsorships.

From Elizabethtown, I went to Corydon, Indiana. I saw a few old friends among the 54 walkers. I finished 5th overall and won a stoneware mug.

In 1986 I had done more running than walking; however, by 1987 I did more walking than running. Because I was becoming involved in other competitions and events, the number of running competitions I entered in 1986 was greatly reduced over previous years and would drop drastically again in 1987.

I chaired the *Railsplitter Run* which kept me from competing that year and I was adding more and more walks to my schedule of activities.

I did manage some satisfying competitions, however. I finished 1st and 18th overall in the 45 and over in the *Lions Run* in Radcliff. I won my age group at *Super Run II*. In the *Run for the Arts*, I beat Mel Harper for the first time. I won my age group at the Earth Run at Mammoth Cave Park.

I was late registering for the 13.1 mile *Kentucky Derby Mini-Marathon*, but the race director, Gil Clark, helped me get everything together. I appreciated his help a great deal.

I picked up my race packet and got to the starting line. A helicopter hovered over us taking pictures of the start. I was lined up with Marilyn Scott. We talked a while before the gun went off.

In big races where there are lots of runners, the start of the race can make one kind of drunk. The runners aren't in step and it gives one the sensation of rocking in a boat. I must not have been feeling too well, for this bothered me more than usual.

I ran okay for about three miles, but when I reached Iroquois Park, I knew something was wrong. For one thing it was entirely too hot to be running thirteen miles. I ran another mile, but something was telling me to stop.

I stopped and walked a while, then started running again. I just wasn't up to running for some reason, so I quit for good. I had run in 184 races and finished every one of them, but today I just quit.

I was disappointed, but when I found out how many of the runners became ill, hot, fainted and so forth, I was glad I hadn't pushed it any farther.

Swag Hartel and his wife were standing near the trees. They encouraged me to get back in the run, but I was finished. Mrs. Hartel gave me some coffee which I drank as I cooled down and watched as runners passed me by.

I finally jumped in and ran out of the park to New Cut Road where a man named Crossfield gave me a ride downtown. He was watching his wife race. He and his wife came to run in the *Railsplitter* later on.

LaHoma and my mother-in-law were glad to see me at the finish line as they had been worried. We joined the race party with Gene and Lil Priddy on the Belvedere.

I finally got back in the swing of things with a 2nd place to Owen Comer at White Mills. I won my age group in the *Pioneer Days Run*.

Gil Clark managed the race at Fort Knox where I won my age group and 7th overall in the 5K. I won a big trophy which came from Jim Hutcherson's Sports Shop in Radcliff.

I only ran once in 1987 and in 1988 not at all. I had turned my attention to race walking, the *Bluegrass Games* and the *Senior Games*. These activities were new, interesting and allowing me to face some new challenges.

CHAPTER TWENTY-ONE

TORCH RUNNING

As I was thinking about and preparing for the 1987 *Bluegrass Games*, the idea occurred to me that it would be fun to help carry the torch used to light the "Olympic fire" in the stadium at Lexington. The torch was carried from the capitol steps in Frankfort through the stadium gates in Lexington, where the fire was lighted and the games began.

My grandson, Matt Shelton, and I had competed in the *Bluegrass Games* the first year in 1985 and again in 1986. We were preparing to compete again. I had learned to love the Bluegrass Games.

The first year had been great, but I was afraid the Games would not continue. In 1986 the *Games* turned out to be even bigger. More sports had been added and even people with disabilities were given an opportunity to participate.

The 1985 *Games* drew 20,000 participants. In 1986 there were 25,000 athletes participating. Though I did not know it at the time, there would be 30,000 participants in the 1987 *Games*. The *Bluegrass Games* rank second only to the *Empire State Games* of New York state in terms of the amount of participation. We Kentuckians may be second in size, but I doubt we rank second to anyone in enthusiasm.

I really wanted to carry the torch. I had watched some of my friends and acquaintances, such as Joe Hasse and Tommy Smith from Corbin, David Mason, chairman of the *Wendy's Classic* in Bowling

Green, Gordon Coe from Louisville, Don Coffman from Frankfort and many others carry the torch.

I eventually called Ann Coffee, who was on the *Bluegrass Games* Board of Directors. I told her about my running and race walking. I also told her about my grandson participating in the games and how well he had done. She said they might like to do a feature story on my grandson and me.

I left my phone number and waited. Time passed and nothing happened. I sent my entry form and entry fee in so I could participate in the race walk and possibly another event. I soon received a letter acknowledging my entry in the games with information on hotel rates and the map giving the location of the events. There was also a note from Ann Coffee telling me that if I were interested in carrying the torch to call a number she sent along.

My wife received the mail that day. She called the number and was asked if I still wanted to be a torch runner. She told them I would be thrilled. They said they would love to have me and asked for my shorts and singlet size because they would be providing a running suit for the runners.

When I came home from work, LaHoma said, "I have a surprise for you." I knew right away what it was.

In a few days, I received a letter from Governor Martha Layne Collins congratulating me on being chosen as one of the torch runners for the 1987 Games. She also sent a schedule of events and directions to call Charley Jones at her office if I had any questions. She promised a very exciting day for me. She kept her word. It was a very exciting day.

I had not been running much in the past year, so I got out and practiced in the 90 degree heat to be sure I could go at least two miles or whatever I would be required to do in carrying the torch. I also checked my running shoes.

After some deliberation, I knew I would either wash the shoes or go buy some more. I decided that the occasion called for a new pair of shoes.

I drove over to the mall in Elizabethtown a few days before the *Games* to visit the Athletic Attic. I had no more than gotten in the store than I noticed a pair of red, white and blue Reebok shoes.

I tried on several pairs of shoes, but my heart longed for Reeboks. I finally gave in and told the sales lady, I wanted the Reeboks if she would throw in a pair of socks. She said she couldn't give me the socks, but she gave me a ten percent discount. I guess she thought I was a senior citizen.

It just bubbled out that I would be wearing the shoes to carry the torch for the 1987 *Bluegrass Games.*

She said that was a coincidence as she had sold shoes to another gentleman who said he would be carrying the torch for the Games. I asked if it was Joe Washington. She said it was and asked how I knew.

I had read *THE NEWS ENTERPRISE* that day and had seen an article about Joe's being chosen as a torch runner. I did not know him, but knew he was a gymnastics coach and assistant football coach at Fort Knox High School. I looked forward to being on the team with Joe. After suggesting my sales lady watch the opening ceremonies on KET and Channel 41 out of Louisville, I tucked my purchase under my arm and left the mall looking forward to my latest adventure with great anticipation.

The torch runners had been directed to meet on the University of Kentucky campus at the K-Men's Lounge. There we would receive our new running suits and would be transported to the Old State Capitol in Frankfort by van. In Frankfort, the torch would be lit for the journey to Lexington and the ceremonies to be held in the stadium.

LaHoma and I appeared to be the first to arrive at the K-Men's Lounge, but soon another car pulled into the parking space next to us. I recognized Joe Washington instantly. We introduced our selves and looked at our feet. Lo and behold, we had on identical red, white and blue Reebok shoes.

Joe has a warm bubbly personality. He laughed and said, "These shoes are going to make us soul brothers!" And they did.

Other runners began to arrive from all directions. Hopey Newkirk from Owingsville was there with her husband and mother. I had met Hopey at runs in Winchester and Morehead. She is a very fine runner who has won the *Metro-Marathon* in Louisville. She had also run the *Boston Marathon* in 1981 and 1987.

Frank Ray, who was an excellent runner in the 50-54 age group, lived in Richmond, Kentucky, where he was girls' basketball coach in the high school there. Ray came over to talk and catch up on the news.

LaHoma took my picture with Hopey, Frank and Joe in our new Bluegrass running outfits which were red and white. Our shoes even matched.

Susan B. Cox from Lexington came over to our group and we introduced ourselves. We found out later she had run the *Iron Man Triathalon* in Hawaii the year before placing 2nd in her age group. I passed the torch to Susan near the airport on Versailles Road later that day.

There were two van loads of runners to be driven to the Old Capitol by state police officers. A place was available for LaHoma so she rode with us in the van. We were all so excited about the day and this new experience.

We were escorted inside the Old Capitol building. The first person I saw was an old friend, Carol Profitt's mother. She told me Carol was one of the runners. I met Carol's fiance, then I saw Carol. I was so surprised to see her, I had to give her a hug.

Carol had been a great athlete before an automobile accident left her paralyzed from the waist down. Carol, with the courage of the truly great athletic competitor, was now competing in wheel chair racing events. She would be one of the torch runners on this occasion.

A photographer lined us up on the stairway, eight on each side of the stairway with Carol at the bottom. We had our pictures made from every conceivable angle; then Governor Martha L. Collins climbed the stairway and stood near me.

Joe B. Hall, Dr. Bob Davies, Evelyn Ashford, Skeeter Johnson, Mayor Jim Burch, Jessie Laine and others posed with us on the stairway. LaHoma took dozens of pictures. After the picture taking, we relaxed our face muscles and waited for the next event.

We met Sue Feamster and Ann Coffee, directors of the Bluegrass Games who were lovely people. Next, we filed outside and stood in a line across the top steps of the Capitol building. Dr. Bob Davies called our names as each of us waved to the huge crowd that had turned out for the opening ceremonies. Among the crowd were 1,700 "pacesetters" (Pacesetters were senior citizens 55 and over.).

After introducing the torch runners, Dr. Davies introduced Evelyn Ashford who spoke about her Olympic experiences. Jessie Laine then sang the National Anthem and Governor Collins lighted the torch held by Jim Green. Jim is a graduate of U.K. who was once considered the fastest human being in the world. Jim started the run and we would all have a part in it.

Jim is a sprinter, so he soon passed the torch to Serena Wingfield, a senior high school student who had won three titles in the previous year's State Track Meet.

I kept a diary of everything that happened that day. Now, I am so glad I did for I would not take anything for it. I asked each of the runners to write a comment or two in my diary of whatever they were thinking at the time.

Serena passed off to Curtis Ripy, Jr., a Senior at Kentucky State College. He ran the toughest two miles of the race - all uphill. I did not envy him.

Curtis passed off to Larry Hayes, secretary to Governor Collins. Larry wrote in my diary: "I hope to be in as good shape as you are when I am your age".

Larry passed off to Martha Worful from Lexington, a very pretty lady who works as a librarian and is married to Doug Worful who is the nephew of a former deputy sheriff of LaRue County, John T. Worful. I had met Doug at a run in Harrodsburg.

Martha passed off to Joe Washington, who would run one mile as a "warm up". A runner had failed to appear; therefore, Joe would run twice.

Joe passed off to Senator Ed O'Daniel from Springfield, Kentucky. I had known Ed several years from past running meets. Ed passed off to Cindy Norton.

Cindy sat on the same seat with me, so we had time to get acquainted. She is the daughter of former University of Kentucky quarterback, Rick Norton. She wrote in my diary that she was a senior at Henry Clay High School, played soccer and worked at Kentucky Horse Park. Cindy passed off to Ken Hoskins. The "p.r." times he wrote in my diary were really impressive.

Theresa Gaines took the torch from Ken. Theresa is a roller skater and a lot of fun. She wrote in my diary that she was "the scared skater" and asked me to pray for her. She survived and passed off to Hopey Newkirk.

Hopey wrote in my diary that she was "thrilled to be a part of the torch run". Hopey passed off to Carol Proffitt.

It was difficult for Carol to handle the wheel chair and the torch, but she made it two miles. She wrote in my diary that it was an "honor to be a torch runner for the Bluegrass Games". She later said that she had the "greatest feeling inside" because of her love for Kentucky and racing.

Frank Ray of Richmond took the torch from Carol. Frank and I have a lot of mutual friends. He is easy to spot at races for he often wears orange and black and is a member of Hager's Hagglers Running Club. LaHoma, Frank and I ate lunch together after the torch run.

It was my moment in the sun. I would take the torch from Frank. I got out of the van early to stretch and loosen up. The excitement and nervousness began to build inside of me. Of all the miles I have run, all the awards I have won and the good times I had doing it, I never experienced a prouder moment than when Frank handed me the torch.

Frank smiled and clapped his hands as I adjusted the torch in my right hand. What a place to exchange the torch. The hand-off had taken place in front of the Castle near the Airport Motel and Restaurant on Versailles Road just outside of Lexington.

There were policemen on motorcycles in back of me. A police car was in front and in back with the two vans behind. People drove past in cars shouting encouragement. It was extremely hot and the sweat soon started flowing, especially into my eyes. I normally wear a cap when running, but I hadn't wanted to mess up our uniforms.

The torch was heavier than I thought it would be. I had to switch hands occasionally.

I passed off to Susan Cox. She took the torch and we exchanged compliments then away she went.

I caught my breath, boarded the van, drank a Coke and ate the blueberry pie Curtis Ripey gave me.

We followed behind Susan Cox. I marveled at how graceful she appeared as she ran. She wrote in my diary that her friends had been such an encouragement in her life and said "I love to meet friends like you who enjoy life and fun and fitness. Keep smiling and moving."

Later on the van, Susan told us about the rigorous training she had undertaken to prepare for the *Iron Man* and the qualification process she had gone through to become eligible. She said her friends had raised money to help her take her family with her to Hawaii. There are fascinating people in running.

Joe Washington took the torch from Susan for his second run of the day. Joe passed off to Glenn Easterling of Ashland.

Glenn works for Armco Steel and is a T.A.C. official. His ambition is to be an official in the Olympics.

After Glenn's run we all got out of the vans and ran the last two miles together. At Shively Field, we posed again for pictures with our hands clenched together showing the thrill of victory.

After the posing and the picture taking, we showered and relinquished our new uniforms to be washed and dried while we ate the picnic provided for us in a tent near the K-Men's Lounge.

I ate, picked up my packet for the games the next day and practiced my race walking in the parking lot with an audience.

LaHoma left to find the rest of the family, who were coming up to watch the ceremonies, while I socialized with the other runners.

Evelyn Ashford, the fastest woman in the world, would carry the torch into the stadium with sixteen torch bearers following her. We were seated in the end zone so we could watch the preliminaries, but would not be obvious to the crowd. I sat with Evelyn Ashford.

Evelyn said her ambition was to run again in the 1988 Olympics then turn to something else, but that sports was her life. Her husband was out on the field taking pictures of everything. He waved to her.

With all of her accomplishments, she seemed thrilled to be the torch carrier for the *Bluegrass Games*. She said it was a first for her.

Soon the Bluegrass banner was brought through the gate carried by some famous Kentucky athletes: Kyle Macy, Mel Turpin and Jim Masters who were former U. of K. basketball players; Phil Hart, a track official; Melinda Cumberledge, Miss Kentucky, was also in the procession.

Next came the *Athletes Against Drugs* which included Wah-Wah Jones of the 1948 Olympics.

Next, the different sports followed. Each sport represented had its own color. Tee-shirts were provided for each participant in the color of the sporting events in which he/she was entered. It was colorful as one sport changed to the next; soccer to track and field, shooting, swimming and so on. Finally the *Kentucky Long Rifles* came into the stadium surprising everyone by shooting blanks into the crowd. It woke up the 12,000 spectators.

Eventually, six thousand people marched onto the field and sat on the grass in front of the podium.

Governor Collins was introduced. She told how the games were conceived after the 1984 *Olympics* in Los Angeles, California. She went on to say that as the celebration for the home-coming Kentuckians who had participated in the 1984 Olympics took place in Louisville that day, she began to think about an *Olympic*-like event for the people of Kentucky. After months of hard work, she made the *Bluegrass Games* a reality.

Governor Collins is to be congratulated for initiating the games. The *Bluegrass Games* are something all Kentuckians can be proud of. I remember how proud I was at the first Games to hear former Governor Happy Chandler sing "My Old Kentucky Home" and to see Bob Beaman, world record holder in the long jump.

At the end of Governor Collins' speech, she announced that the torch would soon arrive in the stadium carried by Evelyn Ashford and sixteen runners from across the state.

Joe Washington and Cindy Norton lighted the torch for Evelyn who began to lead us into the stadium. Joe and Cindy were behind Evelyn and Susan Cox. I was behind them and so on. The spotlight was on Evelyn and all the lights were out in the stadium.

Cawood Ledford and Ann Coffee were doing a play-by-play account for Channel 41 T.V. Relatives at home were taping the activities for us.

The crowd stood and applauded. What a proud moment that was!

We turned left and moved toward the podium and went to stand by the placards for each runner. Evelyn ran slowly to the furthest end zone and back again. As she ran, each of us saluted her, then turned to face the podium.

Evelyn was met by Tamara McKinney, a Kentuckian who had been in the Olympics as a downhill skier. Evelyn lighted Tamara's torch, then they lighted the huge flame which signaled the opening of the Games. The finale included a laser light show.

We were invited to the President's Room for a reception where we met and talked with so many fascinating Kentucky people.

Later, as we were talking with Mr. and Mrs Joe B. Hall, I mentioned the fact that I had two daughters who had been winners of the *Miss Kentucky R.E.C.C. Pageant* and that I believed Mrs. Hall was the first winner of that pageant. Mrs. Hall said she did not remember being the first; however, it had been awhile. Mr. and Mrs. Hall seemed as if they were having such a good time together.

I received pictures of our experience from the governor's office. I had to make a new scrapbook with just the *Bluegrass Games* and the torch running.

In 1988, I was again a torch runner. On August 30, 1988 I reported to Wildcat Lounge where Don Coffman gave me a tee-shirt to wear. Some of the other runners were Ernest Southworth, Chuck Gullo, Roy Hines, Peggy Dearborn, Scott McBrayer, Bill Austis, Judy Ziegler and Becky Deloreto.

The Casey County High School Band played "My Old Kentucky Home" and the National Anthem. Governor Wallace Wilkinson made a speech and lighted the torch which started us on the way to Lexington.

The program that evening was held in Commonwealth Stadium. Michael Jordan of the N.B.A.'s Chicago Bulls was the guest runner. Don Coffman, captain of the torch runners, led us into the stadium. Don lit Michael Jordan's torch and together they lighted the flame which symbolizes the beginning of the *Bluegrass Games.*

Again, I collected pictures, experiences and wonderful memories.

CHAPTER TWENTY-TWO

GAMES, BOARDS AND A BUSY SENIOR

Before I could turn around a time or two, a new challenge presented itself - the *Kentucky Senior Games.*

The *Kentucky Senior Games* is a spin-off of the *Bluegrass Games.* While some of us "Seniors" competed fairly adequately in some sports because of the age grouping, organizers saw a need for a sporting event which was designed especially for older people.

The *Kentucky Senior Games* was established as a non-profit organization with volunteer leadership. There are some weaknesses in this approach which will be discussed later.

The *Senior Games* are held four times a year offering different sports for each season. In the winter there are basketball and ice skating events.

In the fall there is swimming, golf and related sports. In the summer, lawn bowling, horse shoes and billiards are offered. In the spring the track and field events, race walking, tennis, softball and football throws are provided. The logic of seasonal competitions is obvious in that seniors tend to be more weather sensitive.

In order to qualify, a competitor must be 55 or older. Competitive categories are further defined in five year increments.

I sent in my entry fee which allowed me to compete in three events. I chose the half-mile race walk, the one-and-one-half mile race walk and the softball throw. I also entered my quilt made of racing tee-shirts in the arts and crafts quilt show.

On opening day, a ceremony was held to recognize people from each district. I was the only participant from the Lincoln Trail District.

After the ceremony, there was a *Fun Walk*, which I won.

The competitions began. The first event was the softball throw. Paul Baynes and I warmed our arms up by playing pitch and catch. It didn't take long to realize I would have to settle for a silver medal as Paul's first throw went 210 feet. My best throw was 160 feet, but I won a silver medal right at the start.

The quilts were judged next. Everyone was really impressed by my quilt made of running shirts and I won first place.

There was a banquet that evening for the Senior athletes. Paul Baynes from Louisville sat with LaHoma and Me.

Paul was recognized as a champion. He had competed in the *National Senior Games* in St. Louis where he won the softball throw.

My antenna went up, instantly. If there is anything to win, I want a chance to win it.

Charley Daniels, chairman of the *Senior Games*, said that any of us who finished 1-2-3 on the state level would qualify for the *Nationals* the following year in St. Louis. I had already qualified in the softball throw, so I relaxed and enjoyed my dessert.

After the banquet, there was a dance. LaHoma and I danced until about midnight. The Romance novels are always talking about the heroine and hero "dancing until dawn". Dancing until midnight at the *Senior Games* is pretty romantic, if like everything else, you make a few adjustments for age.

The weather had been hanging around 100 degrees for much longer than necessary the summer of 1988. Because of the heat, we were told to report to the track at about daylight; otherwise, we might have danced until dawn.

We set our alarm clock and, being a little anxious, we set it an hour earlier than we had planned. We got to the football field way too early. I took the opportunity to practice a little.

The first event was the 800 meter run. I was not entered in this event, but I was feeling great and asked if I could run it as a warm up. I was given permission to do so and won.

I won the one-and-one-half mile walk, but not by much. I won the half-race walk easily.

After my last event, the officials took my picture with my medals and another one of LaHoma and me holding up my quilt to go in the *SENIOR NEWSLETTER*. I finished the competition with one silver and three gold medals and had qualified for the Nationals in 1989.

In February of 1989, my wife and I traveled to Owensboro to compete in more *Kentucky Senior Games*. This time I would be competing in basketball in the floor shooting and the free-throw shooting.I had gone to the Hodgenville Elementary School and practiced on their outside basketball court with some of the kids who are usually up there playing after school. I thought I had a good shot at the gold.

The headquarters for the *Senior Games* in Owensboro was the Executive Inn. LaHoma and I love an occasional weekend at the Executive Inn relaxing, eating the good food and seeing the excellent entertainment provided. We especially like to spend the weekend when George Jones or Tammy Wynette are performing in concert.

This trip was strictly for the competition in the games.

I was able to spend some time talking with Charley Daniels and Cyndi Sturgeon from the *Kentucky Games*.

I finished 2nd in the floor shooting event; in the free-throw event, I won the gold. We received our winning medals at a lovely dinner held in our honor. The Owensboro Senior Citizen Club was in charge of the program which included music and humorous skits that were very entertaining.

In just a few weeks after this competition, I received my invitation to participate in the *National Senior Olympics*. I had qualified in the 800 meter run, the 1500 meter race walk and the 5000 meter race walk.

Unfortunately, family circumstances prevented me from practicing as I would have liked to do. Regardless of feeling unprepared, I intended to attend the Nationals in St. Louis.

I had two opportunities to compete just before going to St. Louis, the *Frogtown Hop* in which I finished 1st and the *Mile Race-Walk* in which I finished 3rd to David Buckman and C.B. Embry, Jr. I walked the mile in 8:41 which was an excellent time, but Buckman and Embry are much younger than I.

LaHoma and I would be leaving for St. Louis on Father's Day. We first attended church, then had dinner with our family at Holiday Inn North in Elizabethtown. We had a wonderful meal and fellowship with our children, grandchildren and in-laws. I received many cards and my children gave me a new warm-up suit to wear in St. Louis. What a pleasant send off!

After the meal, LaHoma and I went home to load the car for the trip to St. Louis. We were not traveling light. It looked as if we were planning to stay a month though we would only be staying a week.

The opening ceremony was to be held on Monday at 6:00 p.m.; therefore, we had plenty of time. We took our time and arrived at Washington University about two hours before the ceremony was to begin.

Participants would be spending the week on the Washington University campus in a dorm next to Wohl Center where everything having to do with the Senior Games took place.

After getting our things up to the dorm room, LaHoma and I went to Mudd Field where a picnic was provided for the athletes and guests. There were more than 3,500 athletes competing. It was an impressive sight to see all those older athletes excited, involved and enjoying the festivities.

No sooner than we arrived we met a contingent from Kentucky. Among those we met first were Eugene Nolans and Neville Dodd from Bowling Green.

Gail Wigginton was passing out tee-shirts and golf shirts for us to wear in the opening ceremonies to show that we were from Kentucky. We joined the Nolans on the grass for our picnic.

We athletes would march into Francis Field, the site of the 1904 *Olympics* for the second annual *National Senior Games*. I joined my fellow Kentuckians to march in with the other 47 states, Taiwan, England and Canada.

Our state had 46 senior athletes competing in various events. The Nolans marched in the front carrying the banner of Kentucky while Neville Dodd, Merle Nickell, Gail Wigginton and I marched in the rear.

As we marched by the crowd in the stands, we all said in unison, "Hi, ya-all!" The crowd clapped and seemed to appreciate it.

The speaker who spoke at the program which followed the march of athletes was Marty Glickman, radio sports announcer, former track star, football player and basketball player.

He teased us about our marching. He said Americans marched worse than anyone else.

Marty had been in the 1936 Olympics which were held in Berlin. When he marched into the stadium, the athletes looked up into the dignitaries box and saw a little guy with hair on his forehead and a little mustache which reminded them of Charley Chaplin. Little did they know on that date how different from Charley Chaplin Hitler would prove to be.

He reminisced about running in the *4 x 100 Meet Relay*. On one side of him, at the start, was a Frenchman and on the other, a young Japanese man. The Japanese man shook hands with him, smiled and wished him good luck. After the relay, which the American team won, the young Japanese man shook his hand again and congratulated him.

Six years later, during the war, Marty read where this same Japanese man, a former Olympian had been shot down over the Pacific and killed. Marty was then wearing the uniform of the United States Armed Services. Marty said he broke down and cried as though he had lost a close friend. Athletes develop a deep and warm rapport with fellow competitors during competitions such as the Olympic Games.

I could understand his feelings as I have made such good friends over my years in running and other competitions. They become like family.

I spoke to Marty, briefly, after the ceremony. Of course, there were many others waiting to do the same.

The *National Senior Games* attracted a lot of famous atheletes, some still competing and others there to lend support and see what was going on. For example, we met Ed Benham who had been a jockey in his younger days. He had ridden horses at Keeneland, Churchill Downs and Latonia Race Tracks in Kentucky. Ed began running when he was 70 years old. After twelve years of running, he had amassed 120 national titles in running. In 1989, he was nearing his 82nd birthday, still active and competing in the running events in the Senior Olympics.

On our last day in St. Louis, LaHoma and I had breakfast with Ed and his wife. Ed was witty, quick minded and kept his weight at his horse riding weight of 110 pounds. Both he and his wife were delightful Christian people.

We also met Tony Quici, a senior from New Mexico, who rode a three-wheel bike from New Mexico to St. Louis, a distance of 1500 miles. His amazing ride was intended to generate interest in Senior Games and demonstrate that older people can still do unusual things, stay physically fit and compete in sports and games.

Another delightful new friend was Jean Benear from Tulsa, Oklahoma. Jean was a 62 year old race-walker who wore running shorts made of material which resembled the American flag. All of us began calling her "Miss America".

Other interesting race-walkers were John Bointano, who was a cousin to Brian Bointano, the Olympic Ice-Skating champion and Patricia Farrar, wife of a former Governor of South Dakota and two-time gold medal winner.

One of the high points of this experience was Gail Wigginton, who was the Kentucky Director of Games official. She helped keep all the Kentucky athletes comfortable and inspired. We really learned to appreciate her. Those of us in track and field really loved her.

My first competition in St. Louis was the 1500 meter race walk. There were twenty-three of us on the track at the same time. There were three race-walkers from Kentucky, Emil Motten from Hopkinsville, Henry Shillinglass from Hawesville and me.

I broke out about 7th, but to get an award I would have to keep up that pace to finish 6th. I couldn't keep it up long enough so I finished 11th out of the twenty-three with a time of 09:45.

I had walked much faster at other races, but I was so aware of the judges who were stationed at various points around the track to check that we were race-walking correctly that I don't think I was really walking as well as I could.

If we received three warnings or three points we would be disqualified. I certainly did not want to get disqualified.

My anxiety about disqualification caused me to be so conscious of each step that I'm certain it affected my performance. I would have gotten used to it after a while, however.

I guess eleventh wasn't too bad when you consider that each of those athletes had placed first, second or third in their home states.

Bointano won the gold.

I was scheduled to run in the 800 meter run, but I decided to drop out and rest for the 5,000 meter race-walk the next morning.

I felt more at ease the next day after competing once. I joined the others at the starting line thinking I might make a better showing.

The 5000 meter would start on the track. We were to circle the track twice, go out onto the street for two-and-one-half miles, then come back on the track for one final lap to the finish line.

When we lined up for the start, Sister Mary M. Weaver from Denver, Colorado, was in the very front row. We had talked with her several times and found her to be a lovely person, inside and out.

The track judges required her to pin up her habit so they could see her knees as they were determined every competitor walk correctly. In order to determine the correctness of the race walk, the judges must have a full view of racers' knees, legs and feet. As could be expected, she handled it all with grace and good humor.

The race started. I felt I would do better this time. After one trip around the track, I felt more confident.

My pace was about the same as Jean Benear, the lady with the stars and stripes shorts - our "Miss America". I decided it would be wise to use her to pace myself, so I stayed behind her for the two laps around the track. Once out on the street, I tried to pull ahead of her. She must have been holding back a little for I soon found I was not going to be able to pass her.

Almost from the start, I began having trouble relaxing my legs. I assumed the problem stemmed from the extreme heat and nervousness from having the judges watch us so intently.

I finished about thirty-eight seconds behind Miss Benear, but I was the first Kentuckian out of 341 race-walkers. I was 9th in my age group and 52nd overall. My time was not good enough to win a ribbon or a medal, but I thought my first effort was pretty good.

The St. Louis Post Dispatch covered the games very thoroughly during the week. They gave the 5,000 meter race-walk top billing. A big color picture appeared on the front page of the paper. I found my cap in the picture. I was in the fourth row from the front.

Since my competitions were over, LaHoma and I took in some of the tourist attractions in St. Louis. We went to the zoo one evening where we enjoyed a box supper, then danced to music by a band playing mostly music from the 40's and 50's in honor of us "Seniors".

There we met Barbara McQuitty, USNSO National Games Director and Ken Marshall, who handled the publicity for the games. Ken was known as the "Silver Fox" as his hair was solid silver.

We went to the Muny Outdoor Theatre to see Tyne Daly in *Gypsy*. The following day, we took a boat ride down the Mississippi River and walked to the base of the St. Louis Arch - Gateway to the West.

We left St. Louis and the Senior Olympics with many pleasant memories and high hopes of qualifying for the 1991 Games, which were scheduled to be held in Syracuse, New York.

Shortly after returning from St. Louis, I received a telephone call from Charley Jones from the Kentucky Senior Games asking me to serve on the Board of Directors for the Kentucky Games. I told him I would be delighted to serve on the board.

I hoped that on this committee I could help to make the games better. I felt we needed to promote them better in our own state. I was hoping to see Kentucky represented by a much larger contingent in the 1991 *National Games.*

I love competition. I love to win and I love to work to better my own performance. Of all the events open to senior citizens, I love track and field events most. As a *Senior Games* board member, I hoped I could do my part to advance opportunities in the State of Kentucky.

CHAPTER TWENTY-THREE

RETIREMENT - THE END OR THE BEGINNING

In 1989, I was entering my sixtieth year of life and beginning to think about retirement. I had enough years of service to retire, but compulsory retirement was still several years away.

The issue began to weigh upon my mind. If I retired, what would I do with my life. If I did not retire, I would miss some of the things I had been wanting to do for a long time.

I have been blessed with good health and was very active. I am concerned for the welfare of others and am deeply concerned for the welfare of the Commonwealth of Kentucky. I began to think in terms of running for public office.

It seemed to me to be a new and wonderful challenge. The challenge of the run for office could be very exciting, but once in office, I could help to make things better for the people of Kentucky. Of course, I had a decided interest in senior citizens and programs which would benefit them.

LaHoma and I talked about my idea to run for office. She did not give me a lot of encouragement. Perhaps her faith in the outcome was less positive than mine or maybe she was just tired of all the hard work I had put her through supporting me in my efforts.

Regardless, I knew deep in my heart she would stand with me whatever my decision. I still had a year to think about my goals, platform and method of campaigning.

One would think that a man contemplating retirement would see some signs of life slowing down a bit. Wrong! If anything, it seemed I was involved in more and more.

On April 1, 1989 the *Lincoln Museum* was scheduled to open its doors for the first time. All of our family had been very active in supporting this venture.

LaHoma's aunt, Thelma Ford, had been one of the town's most dependable volunteers in the Chamber of Commerce and in the museum effort. Her name will forever be linked with her loyal support of the town and its efforts of revitalization.

Once the museum opened, she applied her considerable knowledge of history and the Lincoln era to providing informative and interesting tours of the museum.

My mother-in-law had been actively supporting the museum effort by buying memberships for herself, our children, our grandchildren, her grand sons-in-law and many memorial memberships.

In 1988, I had an idea of putting on a *Walkathon* to raise money to be used in helping to purchase the building and to buy some wax figures of Lincoln from another museum.

I quickly gained support from the Chamber of Commerce and received some vital encouragement from Iris LaRue, who had been most active in promoting the county, *Lincoln Days* and the museum. Iris went to the newly formed Lincoln Museum Board to get approval for the Walkathon.

I preferred to hold the *Walkathon* after the weather cooled down in the fall, but did not want to interfere with the Lincoln Days Festival. The deciding factor came when the band director of the LaRue County High School Band of Hawks said the band would be free to participate on the 29th of October.

Once the Museum Board agreed to back my *Walkathon*, I set about to give them the best, most unusual and most heavily awarded event I could manage.

I decided to give awards for best sponsorship, oldest, youngest, most unusual costume and to each school in the county in the order of their participation. I encouraged people with disabilities to participate. I began mailing out entry forms to friends I knew in running, the handicapped, clowns, a person to walk backwards, beauty queens, champions of all sorts, military people, politicians and Lincoln look-a-likes.

Celia McDonald, owner/publisher/editor of *THE LARUE COUNTY HERALD NEWS*, was most helpful with advertising in *THE HERALD NEWS* as well as arranging advertisements in neighboring papers. J.C. Ragland agreed to videotape the walk.

I secured donations of about 50 nice prizes including a quilt, "Seven Sisters", donated by Oda Mae Vaughn of Vaughn's Nursery. I sold chances on the quilt to raise the income for the event.

The weather had turned cold and rainy, so I prepared a "back-up" walk by receiving permission from school officials to hold it inside the high school if it rained. It did not rain, thank God.

Our race began at Lincoln National Park where Lincoln was born and ended three miles away on the Public Square in Hodgenville in front of Lincoln's monument. It was cold. It was especially cold at 7:30 a.m. when we began registering the walkers.

We had an excellent turn out; 263 walkers with various and asundry champions, politicians, handicapped, old, young, the dedicated and the casual. The Band of Hawks played music and the National Anthem.

I had arranged for ten torch walkers to lead the Walkathon. They were high school students who had excelled in some field.

Representative Bill Ark borrowed the torch from the *Special Olympics* in Frankfort. Murrell Smith and I welded two barrels together and painted them white. Next, we inserted an outdoor grill in the top of the barrel and added some fuel in the grill. We set the barrels in front of the Lincoln Monument. We would light the fuel in the barrel with the torch carried from Lincoln Park.

I bought caps for the torch carriers with *Lincoln Museum Walkathon* written on the front. Shonie Thomas, two time long jump and high hurdle champion of Kentucky, was the lead torch carrier.

My grandson, Brett Decker, won the youngest walker. Christie Jewell won the oldest, while Mary Lois McFelia won the quilt drawing.

LaHoma and I even won a dinner for two at the Green Bamboo restaurant.

Everyone seemed to have a wonderful time and we raised $3,000.00 for the museum effort.

When the museum opened in April of 1989, my family and I felt a great sense of accomplishment.

Courtland "Corky" Cox had retired from the LaRue County school system and became the first museum director. Because he was retired, he felt he had time to get the museum off to a good start.

Again I was faced with new reasons for retirement. Time and skills learned over a lifetime contribute to the common good. I was to think back over this issue many times in the year ahead.

As I have mentioned in earlier chapters, 1989 proved to be an eventful year. The *National Games* and being asked to serve on the *Senior Games* Board to name a couple. Sometime during the year, I received a letter from the Louisville Post Office telling me there would be a seminar for all employees eligible to retire.

In September, our 10th grandchild was born to Melissa Jo and Glenn Decker. To our surprise, she was a beautiful red-haired child whom her parents named Courtney Gail. My mother, Glenn's mother and LaHoma's aunt Lillian had been red-haired so we should not have been surprised. She was a gorgeous baby and smiled all the time.

I must have stopped and taken stock. With ten grandchildren, the idea occurred to me that I might be getting old.

One day I figured up how many miles I had walked or run since 1964 when I first began working for the post office. It came to enough miles to go around the world twice. Maybe, I had earned my retirement, at least, for awhile.

Subsequently, I attended the retirement seminar in October. My questions were answered and I felt more secure about the idea. I had a retirement conference with Marty Van Fleet in Louisville, signed the papers, then came back to Hodgenville to give my letter of resignation to Postmaster Ray McDowell.

Instead of a Christmas dinner, we waited until the last day I would work, the 29th of December, 1989 and had a retirement dinner.

Appropriately, the dinner was held at Sharon and Ken Taylor's Railsplitter Inn. I had eaten lunch at Sharon and Ken's other restaurant, The Duck Inn, for many years.

On the last day of work, of course, I had mixed feelings about retiring. My patrons had showered me with good wishes, pleasantries and even some letters, notes and gifts. There was a very special gift from Gene and Angie Tucker, which now hangs in my den.

Barry Minton from *THE HERALD NEWS* followed me on my last day of work interviewing me and some of my patrons. He attended my retirement dinner and wrote a nice article for *THE HERALD NEWS* with a picture he had taken in front of "Red" Hazle's store. I had grown up with Red near Tanner Store.

My retirement dinner was such a pleasant experience. Ray McDowell presented me with an achievement award and a Cross pen set and spoke approvingly of my work at the Post Office. LaHoma gave me a Cardinal (University of Louisville) sweat shirt and two tickets to the Kentucky/Louisville game the next day. Three of my children attended, Donna, Diana and Jo, along with fellow workers and former workers.

After the presentations, I was asked to say a few words. To my surprise I had to fight back a tear or two.

I told how, as a little boy living on a farm a third of a mile off the highway, I had looked forward to going to get the mail. I told of how Howard Gardner had impressed me and in his quiet way, had influenced my life. I shared some of my times with Howard and ended my speech by saying I hoped someone had watched me and that I had had a positive influence on someone else. At least, I pray that I have.

It was over. I was retired after thirty-three years and nine months with the Federal government.

I felt strange not having to get up to go to work so I began looking for something worthwhile to do. I was determined now to run for office. I sent for the appropriate papers from the Secretary of State in Frankfort, but every time I started to get the papers notarized, something would come up to stop me.

A lot of people were finding out about my desire to run for office and were encouraging me to run. However, LaHoma did not want me to run and with all of the interruptions, I was not sure God did either.

I missed the paper filing deadline for 1990; so I tucked the desire to run for office away for a future date.

I turned my energies toward working for the *Senior Games* and the *Bluegrass Games*.

In June 1990, Les Reynolds and I were unanimously voted onto the Board of Directors of the State Senior Games at the meeting in Lexington. Other members of the board included: Betsy Whitt; Charley Daniels; Gail Wigginton; Carole Kramer; Cyndi Sturgeon; Kitty Parker; Carol Marek; Sherrill Brakmeier; Jeff Hockberg; Rugh Parks; Linda Vernon; Patsy Tooley; Terri Graham; Mary Jane Sharp; Mabel Ballinger; Lori Nicholas; Tom Doty; Charlie Jones; and now Les Reynolds and I joined them.

Les had competed in St. Louis and won a gold medal for his age group.

I found it very easy to become friends with all the board members, though we came from all over Kentucky. We have had several meetings and the rapport has endured.

After our first meeting, I was determined to develop *Regional Senior Games* in my own district. I called the Director of Aging at the Lincoln Trail District Area Development office, Nancy Addington. Nancy went to work immediately on developing the competition. Gail Wigginton came in from Owensboro to explain the ground rules for regional meets.

We formed a committee and picked our sports chairmen and began looking for a place which could accommodate the games, sponsors and media attention. We knew we would have to have good sports chairmen, an opening ceremony and a beauty queen or two to give out the awards.

Finally, we decided to have all the games in LaRue County except for the swimming events. Nancy arranged to use the E-Town Swim Club pool for our swimming competitions.

We raffled off another of Oda Mae Vaughn's quilts to make money and nearly all of the county banks helped sponsor our events.

In September 1989, we held our very first *Regional Senior Games* with the opening ceremonies held at the Senior Center in downtown Hodgenville.

After several discussions with her father, Kristie Hicks, the reigning Miss Kentucky Teenage Beauty Queen, would hand out the awards.

It was an unlikely day for the *Games* as it rained extremely hard in the early morning. We had a short opening ceremony where we introduced Kristie to the crowd and gave her a gift. Nancy Addington and Judy Cederholm made short remarks. I told the people gathered about my experiences in St. Louis.

We had the drawing for the quilt. Lo and behold, the winner was, again, Mary Lois McFelia who had won the quilt at the *Lincoln Museum Walkathon.*

Our sports chairmen were: Carol Haynes, Danny Owens, Carl Riggs, Lanny Crain, Danny Atherton, Junior Puryear, Pat Noe, Harry Quesenberry, and Joe Warren. I won the one mile race walk overall while Roberta Rock won the overall women's class. I also won the javelin throw and the softball throw.

The following week, Fred Shelton and I went to the E-town Swim Club for time trials. We both qualified in five different swimming events.

Stewart's Restaurant in Hodgenville gave all of us who had participated or chaired one of the events in the *Regional Senior Games* a free meal. We ate and talked about future games.

A lot of people qualified for the *Senior Games,* but only five of us participated on October 8th and 9th. Mycia Bell, Fred Shelton, Wendell Groves, W.T. Hazle and I went to Lexington to the opening ceremonies at the Bell House. Mayor Scotty Baesler was the guest speaker. I think he may be governor some day - remember the name.

At the end of the day, I had seven gold medals, Fred Shelton had six gold medals, Wendell Groves had two medals and Mycia Bell had one. Our district had won 16 medals. In the evening we celebrated at the Fayette County Senior Center with a meal and dance. The music was from the 40's and 50's which, of course, is the best music ever written.

The *Kentucky Senior Games* was a struggling organization with limited funding from the state and small sponsorship. In November of 1989, when the State Board met at Cumberland State Park for two days, we drew up a budget and the qualifications for a full-time executive director before we adjourned.

I was offered the job as a volunteer executive director on a part time basis, expenses paid. I was thrilled and would have loved to be able to accept, but with no salary, I felt I could not afford to do so.

It is my feeling that, as a culture, we do not value our older people as we should. I am also afraid that most of us older people do not value ourselves the way we should. When we begin to think of ourselves as worthwhile we will begin to participate in activities designed for older people and will demand equal treatment under the law. We will also begin to demand our share of the available resources.

I competed in as many race-walks as I could find in 1989. I was the overall winner in the *Bowling Green Corvette 2 Mile Walk*, 2nd overall at Franklin in the *Garden Spot Trot*, and the overall winner in the one mile *Walk For Christ* at Scottsville, where I beat David Buckman from Lebanon for the first time, and I met Joe Zwick from Middlesboro.

At the *Railsplitter Walk* in Hodgenville, I finished 3rd overall, while my grandson Nathan finished 4th overall. Gene Harrison was 1st and C. B. Embry was 2nd. I decided it was too hot to compete in the one mile Fun Run and the saw-pull later in the day.

I race better in cooler weather, so as the weather cooled, I prepared for a huge, historic competition at Cincinnati, Ohio, on Thanksgiving Day. There were 3,000 runners and race walkers entered in the event.

This had to be the coldest day I have ever raced. I wanted to win very badly. I was extremely nervous. I had hopes of beating Joe Vitucci who had done a 1OK walk in 60 minutes.

All the runners and the walkers took off at the same time. I raced on the side walk to avoid being run over. After a couple of miles, I realized I was doing very well. I only saw one other race walker and he was no more than three or four steps in front of me. I knew he was not Joe Vitucci because Joe is about my age and the man ahead of me was much younger.

I kept very close to this man who had very good form for a race walker. When we approached the end of the Bailey Bridge over the Ohio River, I saw him slow a bit. I began to believe I could pass him.

As we left the bridge with about one-and-one-half miles to go, I passed him and "turned it on" for a while. I lost contact with him after that. By the time I reached Pete Rose Way, I was still feeling very good. I kept pushing and finished in 59:17. I thought I was the first race walker.

LaHoma was there to meet me. I told her I thought I won. When the awards were announced, the winner was Dick Fenci and I was 2nd overall. Joe Vitucci came in well in the back this time. I was well pleased with my award of a brandy snifter with a gold inscription which read "2nd overall, *Thanksgiving Day Walk* lOK".

My last race of 1989 was in Chattanooga, Tennessee, the *Karen Lawrence Race*. The proceeds were to go to the Danny Thomas Leukemia Hospital. Karen Lawrence began the race, but died a year later of leukemia.

While we were there, LaHoma and I met and had a picture made with the Karen Lawrence family - her mother, father and twin sister. On the walls were hundreds of pictures of each year's race dating back to 1979. Karen's sister now chairs the race.

It is a two mile walk and a four mile run. I finished in 19:00 and was the overall winner. It was good to finish the year with a solid win and to feel that we were helping a good cause. We left Chattanooga with fond memories and eating at the Cracker Barrel, one of our favorite restaurants, didn't hurt anything either!

In the Spring of 1990, I went to Hopkinsville to be keynote speaker at the *Pennyrile Area Development District's Senior Regional Games* banquet. There were 450 people in attendance and over half of them had competed in the Senior Games. I received some very nice gifts, including a country ham and an opportunity to visit with Sonja Caldwell and Patsy Tooley.

I also went to work, part-time, for Gross Diamond Center. I was interviewed by Mike Gullo, who is a cousin of Chuck Gullo, with whom I had carried the torch in the Bluegrass Games in 1988. At the age of sixty, I became a rookie in the diamond business. Since I would only work part-time, I would still have time for the Senior Games.

Nancy Addington, Judy Cederholm, Lorena Russell and I began meeting for our 1990 games. As this was our second year, we were having more people getting behind us.

We gained sponsorship from Lincoln National, Magnolia, Buffalo, Peoples' and Farmers' banks. We also had Dow Corning, Houchen's Market, Bell's Grocery, the Railsplitter Restaurant, Po Folks Restaurant and Geneva's Florist. We also got a very generous gift from Hardin Memorial Hospital, due to the efforts of Fran Arnold, public relations specialist.

With these fine sponsors, we were able to provide excellent *Regional Games*. We doubled our entries over the previous year and our older people were beginning to get excited about our games. We encouraged everyone to go to the *State Games* and compete at that level.

The *State Games* were to be held a month later on the Northern Kentucky University campus, June 14-16, 1990. There would be a banquet and a chance to see Rosemary Clooney and the Cincinnati Pops Orchestra in concert.

Ten people registered from LaRue County alone. This had been a dream of mine since 1988, when I had gone to the Games as the only participant from my area. I knew that if I could get people interested, we could win the *Games* as a team.

LaRue County had had some individual state champions, but never a sports team champion. The ten of us who represented LaRue County in the *Senior Games* were a bunch of battle scarred athletes from years past.

For a brief two days, we rolled back the clock to compete in numerous events. Some of those heroes were: Pete Marcum, former LaRue County jailer who was recovering from surgery for a melanoma; Alvis Shelton who, the year before had open-heart surgery; Adrian Russell who was 70 years old; Mycia and Edgar Bell, the husband-wife team who won their age group in walking;

Donald Thurman, who won his age group in bowling; George Dorsey, silver medal winner in bowling; R.B. Smith, won a 4th in his age group; Lorena Russell won two medals before her knees started bothering her; and me, who fought my way to seven medals.

The ten LaRue County people totaled 36 medals before they finished and were declared the "Winningest County Participating at the Games".

I have proof that dreams do come true, even if it means waiting until the "twilight years" or "zone" as the case may be.

CHAPTER TWENTY-FOUR

I DIDN'T WIN THEM ALL

Since we have come this far together, it is only fair to share my moment of crushing defeat as well as the times when I made a good showing. It isn't easy for me to talk about it even now. In fact, I'm not sure I have given up on the idea yet.

It is very difficult for a positive thinking person like me to waste time thinking about negative things even for a short time; but to devote precious chapter space to a failure is difficult indeed.

Psychologists tell us that it takes both failure and success to make us emotionally healthy people. They also say we probably learn more from our failures than we do successes. It makes sense, I suppose.

Throughout my lifetime, I have loved to compete and have tried everything I was big enough to try. I have failed occasionally, but have succeeded more than I have failed, thank God.

I have failed and I have succeeded and I can tell you with no hesitation that success is a lot more fun. For that reason, this is going to be a short chapter.

Since I first began running, I had wanted to try to run across Kentucky. I knew this would not be an easy feat. My favorite runner, Stan Cottrill from Hart County who has run across everything which can be run across, had to make several tries before he made it.

I knew that if I made it, I would be the oldest runner ever to have run across Kentucky. Though I was dazzled by the possibility of another "record", I wanted to be certain that if I were the oldest runner to run across Kentucky, I would live to tell about it. I decided I should try part of the run first, then decide if I wanted to try the whole thing.

I talked with Freda Shelton, who was connected with the M.D.A. I told her that if I could run from Louisville to Hodgenville and felt pretty good about it, I would try to run across Kentucky and raise money for the M.D.A. Freda called the Director in Louisville who said if I made it from Louisville to Hodgenville we would get together on the project.

In the late spring of 1986, I planned to do the practice run. For obvious reasons, I chose the last weekend which would be cool enough to try such a long run.

Joe Warren and Lewis Perkins had agreed to help by driving along and watching out for me. I took Friday off from work and rested all day. I ate two pizzas in the afternoon, then went to meet Joe and Lewis at Druthers Restaurant in Hodgenville.

I took three pairs of running shoes, a sack of bananas, some oranges, cookies and a cooler with my own water. I also took an extra warm-up suit. We were as well equipped as we knew how to be.

We planned to arrive in Louisville, eat dinner, meet with the M.D.A. official on the *Belvedere* then start my run back to Hodgenville at 8:00 p.m.. My goal was to arrive in Hodgenville the next morning at 8:00 a.m. If successful, this would be a 62 mile run.

It looked like rain all day, but it would not stop me from making the attempt. If it just drizzled and sprinkled, it could help keep me cool and keep me from becoming dehydrated.

Joe, Lewis and I got on the *Belvedere* early and waited for the M.D.A. official who soon arrived. We agreed that if I made a successful run we would cooperate in obtaining sponsors, but if I failed we would drop it. He told me that he "admired" my courage. We said good-by.

I was already dressed for the run with Ben Gay and Vaseline rubbed on all of the places which might get sore. I left the *Belvedere* running.

I had only run two blocks when I stumbled stepping up on a two inch curb and nearly fell. How embarrassing! I was planning to run 62 miles and here I was nearly falling flat two blocks from the starting point. The idea crossed my mind that it might be an omen, but I rejected it and turned my attention to the task at hand.

Every two miles, Joe and Lewis were supposed to be waiting to give me water and find out what I would need at the next stop. They were always right where they said they would be. Lewis would run out to give me a cup of water. I drank it on the run.

After about eight miles, it began to rain as if it would never get another chance, so to speak. The rain felt good on my body, but it showed no signs of letting up. There was a lot of lightning which caused near blindness with every flash. Fortunately, I had a sidewalk or path to run on most of the way, so I did not end up backside down in a ditch.

When I reached Kosmosdale, there was water standing in the road ankle-deep. I just knew I was going to develop blisters, but I never did.

The plan had been for a couple of runners to meet me on the last part of the run to help me by running with me. I knew by the last leg I would need all the encouragement I could get. Some of my grandkids would run with me in the final stretch. We had also planned for a police escort to meet me and bring me into town. My nephew, Gary Mather, was planning to videotape some of the last part of the run.

I had a singlet made which read: "Belvedere to Hodgenville, 1986. 1929 Vintage - Age 57." I was going to put it on just before I ran into Hodgenville.

When I reached the Last Chance Liquor Store, I had run 20 to 21 miles. I wore reflectors on my cap and shirt, but the rain had played havoc with all of that.

Joe and Lewis were waiting for me with water and a banana. Just as I took them and ran off, I heard Joe say the truck wouldn't start.

I knew Joe would manage some way. I wondered how he would get help at that time of night, but I just put my faith in God and Joe and ran on.

It had grown very dark with the cloudy sky and there were few cars on the road. Each time I met a car, the lights left me blinded for a while.

When I reached the tank on display to mark the boundaries of the Fort Knox Military post, I knew that two mile stretch to the top of Muldraugh Hill would be very taxing. I made a quick decision to walk to the top of the hill and save my energy for the rest of the trip.

At midnight, LaHoma was coming over to see about me and bring James Sallee, who was going to run with me to keep me company. I finally got to Muldraugh and there were Joe and Lewis waiting for me.

Joe had gotten the truck jumped to start it and was afraid to turn it off for fear it would not start again.

I ate some cookies and started to change my shoes when LaHoma drove up with James. James and I took off together. I felt fine and had a lot of strength left, but my knees were sore. I thought it might have been caused by the ten miles of rain I had run through and the dropping temperatures.

I began to run and walk. I made it to Fort Knox and told James that I didn't know if I should punish my knees like this. A mail carrier makes his living with his knees and an injury could leave me sidelined in my career as well as in competitions.

Oh, how I dreaded to quit. I just hate it when my heart and my common sense get into a conflict. My heart is every bit as strong as my head, maybe more so in some situations; but I was too smart to end my career and all of the things I love to do out of pride.

James and I began to "fast-walk" and talk. The traffic had slowed a lot, so we could run in the road some of the time. I told James I was going to give it a "good shot", anyway.

My knees did not improve. I was beginning to feel little shocks go up my legs from my knees with every step. When we reached Radcliff, I told James I had better quit.

Joe had promised to meet us at the Waffle House on the other side of Radcliff so we kept going to meet him there. When we arrived, Joe was there with the motor of the truck still running.

I told my crew that I knew I could make it to Elizabethtown and probably all the way, but I couldn't chance running on my sore knees. I finally said, "I'm going to quit".

The disappointment was terrible. I went to the car and LaHoma got me some coffee. For about two minutes, I thought I was going to lose consciousness, but the coffee brought me around.

I thanked Joe and Lewis and apologized for failing. They had helped me run 38.4 miles and I had made good time. It was only 3:00 a.m., which would have left me five more hours to finish the run.

James rode back with LaHoma and me. When we reached Hodgenville, we stopped and told C.M. Davenport not to expect us as we had been forced to quit.

I got home and collapsed on my bed. The next day, I took some long soaking baths to work out the soreness. In a couple of days, I was fine.

I think, under better circumstances, I could have made it. Anyway, I'm grateful to the people who helped me try. They have offered to help me again if I want to try again.

Who knows. Where there is life, there is time. We just might try again before it is all over.

Now, as far as I'm concerned, enough has been said on this subject.

CHAPTER TWENTY-FIVE

BAND, BEAUTY CONTESTS AND GRANDKIDS

When children come along, young parents work so hard to feed them, clothe them and provide a house for them to live in it is hard to keep up with all the changes. It seems they leap from the cradle to first grade to beauty contests and band concerts to adulthood. It all happens so quickly, many of us parents feel as if they grew up in the split second it took to turn around.

In our family, the signal our children were growing into teenagers and quickly becoming adults was when they joined the band. LaHoma and I joke about spending twenty-one years in the high school band.

Donna was our only child not interested in band, but band membership is not a requirement for family membership. We loved her just as she was and her interests were every bit as important as band. It is just that with four children in band, we seem to think of band as a signal of growing up, independence and the development of personal interests.

When Sandra played clarinet in the LaRue County band, it was directed by Gene Hoggard who was considered one of the best, if not the best, high school band director in the state. Sandra became a majorette, practicing on the car port and in the yard for hours on end. When time for the LaRue County Fair came, Sandra's baton routine won 1st place.

During Sandra's junior year, the band won the *State Band Tournament* at the Kentucky State Fairgrounds. Her majorette squad also won the State Contest.

As with our other girls, Sandra went through a period of time when there was the "boy friend of the week", but her first real boy friend merits some discussion because he crossed our lives again years later.

Sandra and Gary Guthrie, from Sonora, dated for a time. When he went to college they drifted apart, but they have remained friends over the years.

Gary took a job with a radio station in Louisville after leaving college, where he made a tape blending the voices of two singers, Barbara Streisand and Neil Diamond, who had separate recordings of the same song, "You Don't Bring Me Flowers". He played it on the radio and it was a "hit". Word got to California where Streisand and Diamond, who had never met, cut a record of the song, which has become one of the all time best sellers. Streisand and Diamond sang the song on the Music Awards the following year.

It was a thrilling moment for our family as we watched T.V. that night. We would not see Gary again for a long time, but it would be a memorable moment when we did.

It was a happy time. Sandra, Donna and Diana were in high school. Mom and Daddy still lived on a farm not far away. My brothers and sister and their families were well and happy and close enough to keep tabs on us and we on them. Our kids loved to go to Pa and Granny's to eat.

Mom was such a good cook and could whip up a great meal with chicken dressing, chocolate pies and sweet muffins. On such occasions, the grandkids would play games while the grown-ups played horse shoes, went fishing or just sat in the shade and talked.

On Mom and Daddy's fiftieth wedding anniversary, we invited the children, grandchildren, in-laws and Dad's sister and Mom's sisters to our house. It was a grand occasion which yielded stacks and stacks of pictures for the scrap books.

Daddy's driving wasn't the best, but he came by often to check on all of us kids. He just wanted to see how we were doing from time to time.

In 1970 Sandra was a senior in high school. You'll just have to forgive a dad's pride, but I thought she was just beautiful, as I think all four of my girls are beautiful. I encouraged Sandra to enter the Nolin R.E.C.C. beauty contest as I felt she had a good chance of winning. Sandra checked the date and told me she would be in band camp and did not feel Mr. Hoggard would let her leave for the contest.

Mr. Hoggard took band camp seriously, as he did anything associated with the band. (This is probably why his bands won everything coming and going.) I don't think any man alive has a chance against a determined mother, so LaHoma talked to him about it. He agreed that it would be a great opportunity for Sandra and said we could come for Sandra just before the contest, but we had to bring her back immediately after the contest. We were delighted to do so.

On the evening of the contest we packed her bathing suits, evening gowns and the other necessities in the car, drove to Camp Crescendo and picked up our little Beauty Queen.

As we sat waiting for the decisions of the judges, LaHoma and I thought she had a good chance of winning. Soon our daughter, Sandra, was announced the winner. So, I'm not the only one who thought she was beautiful, smart and talented.

She received a kiss on the cheek from Mr. Clem Tharp, the Director of the Nolin R.E.C.C., a silver vase and one year scholarship to Elizabethtown Community College.

After band camp, Sandra was taken to Louisville by Mrs. Wilma Jenkins where she was completely outfitted for the state competition in August. The co-op reporter came out and took what seemed like hundreds of pictures for the local papers and the Nolin Coop newsletter.

Sandra did not win the state competition, but you will never convince me that she was not the prettiest, smartest and most talented of the competitors.

Sandra had been dating Kenny Devore for some time. When she graduated from high school, she and Kenny became engaged. She took advantage of her scholarship and enrolled in the E.C.C. School of Nursing.

After she received her degree, she and Kenny were married at the First Baptist Church in Hodgenville by the Reverend Kenneth Hayes. Kenny enlisted in the Navy and Sandra left for the Great Lakes with her new husband.

We still had four children at home with Donnie just a busy little fellow.

It was about this time that I placed 2nd in the LaRue County Tobacco Show to my neighbor Bob Devary.

Jo was playing on a very good girls softball team, Charley's Angels, coached by Mrs. Trumbo and Mo Druien. Over a period of three years they were to lose no games and win twenty-seven. They also won several tournaments.

One of the last Charley's Angels teams went to the State Tournament at Madisonville, Kentucky. We washed cars to make money for the cost of the trip. At this time the team was coached by Jerry Helm. As many parents as could went along with the team. We stayed at Morton's Gap where the kids and the parents had a great time. The team did not win, but we had a great time.

Donna Gail married her childhood sweetheart, Mike Shelton, her senior year in high school. Donna finished high school, then entered nursing school at Elizabethtown Community College as Sandra had done.

Sandra's son, Abe Devore, was our first grandchild followed by Donna and Mike's son, Matt. Matt looks somewhat like his mother, but he has his daddy's coal black hair. Donna and Mike lived near us, so we got to see a lot of Matt. Matt was a good baby and grew into a fine athlete. Donna graduated from nurse's training and got a job at Hardin Memorial. Our first two adult children became nurses.

Donnie was in school by then and very active in 4-H. He won the speech category four or five times in the County 4-H over the years. When he was twelve he won the county contest, the regional at Bardstown and the state in Lexington at the University of Kentucky by speaking on modern day commercials. He was able to win the 4-H talent show five times and was once regional runner-up.

For one of the talent competitions, Donnie had been secreting himself away in his bedroom for weeks. We knew he was getting ready for the talent competition, but we had no idea what he was planning. Donnie does not like to have anyone watch him rehearse which means opening night is usually the first time we see his program.

On the night of the competition, Donnie was introduced. He did a "lip-sync" and dance to one of Michael Jackson's songs. LaHoma and his grandmother, Ruth Nichols, were sitting in the audience seeing the act for the first time. When he finished there was a moment of silence, wild applause, then every head in the house turned to look at LaHoma and Ruth who were sitting open-mouthed themselves. We did not know he could dance, nor did we know he could put on such a professional looking show. Again, his parents stood amazed!

Diana played softball on the church softball team, played the piano for the Wesley Meadows Methodist Church and in 1980, married Mark Phillips. We were concerned about her education, but she worked at Golden Corral Restaurant for several years and worked her way through E.C.C. in Computer Programming. Her son Nathan has grown into quite an athlete in his own right. He plays soccer and shows a great deal of potential as a gymnast. Nathan likes to stay overnight with us and play checkers and cards with me. He also likes for me to tell him scary stories.

Jo played J.V. basketball her freshman and sophomore years, but went on to other things after that. Jo played saxophone in the band and was elected band president her senior year. Jo was also an honor student and was selected, along with Terri Druien and Theresa Crawford, to compete in the Girls' State Academic Competitions.

When Jo was a junior in high school, LaHoma, her sisters, brother and I talked her into entering the Nolin R.E.C.C. beauty contest. All of the family went to show our support. After the contest activities, in which Jo looked like a winner to her daddy, the girls went off stage to change clothes for the announcement of the winner; a drawing was held. Jessica Pearl, Sandra's youngest child (Abe, the oldest, had been joined by his sisters, Dolly and Jessica.) won the girl's bicycle. We were thrilled.

Jo led the girls back on stage where eventually Paula Garrison was announced as the "runner-up". We held our breath until Jo Mather was announced as the winner. LaHoma and I must have clung to each other for five minutes. Eventually, we found we could still actually walk and went to congratulate Jo. While we were backstage hugging and taking pictures, another drawing was held and I won the microwave oven being raffled. Jo was awarded a crown, a silver vase and $150 toward the purchase of clothes for the State R.E.C.C contest. This must have been one of the Mathers' lucky nights.

The following week Wilma Jenkins and Mickey Miller came to interview Jo and take pictures of her at home. Judi Perry from *THE LARUE COUNTY HERALD NEWS* wrote a nice article which included a picture of Jo and Paula together.

At the state pageant at the Galt House, Jo was not the winner. Again, I thought the judges were terribly misguided in their decision, but no one asked for my opinion.

After graduation in 1984, Jo married her childhood sweetheart, Glenn Decker. Glenn was quite an athlete in high school. He pitched and played shortstop on the baseball team and quarterbacked the first LaRue County football team to beat Elizabethtown in twenty years.

Jo won a scholarship to Georgetown College, but Glenn was more important. They married at MeMommie's (the name the kids gave their grandmother Nichols) house with all the family there.

One summer, Donnie went through all of our pictures and memorabilia to make scrapbooks for each of the girls for Christmas.

Many changes have occurred over the years. We have faced and weathered some troublesome times, had many successes and many joys which have made the bad times seem not so bad after all.

Sandra and Kenny have three children Abe, Dolly and Jessica Pearl. Donna and Mike have Matt, Derek, Bryan and Emily. Donna is a registered nurse and Mike is a machinist at Crucible Steel in Elizabethtown. Diana Lynn is a computer programmer at Dow Corning in Elizabethtown where she lives with her son Nathan.

Melissa Jo and Glenn have a son, Brett and two daughters, Michelle and Courtney. Jo works in the Circuit Clerk's office in Hodgenville and attends college at night. Glenn works for Coca-Cola in E-Town.

Donnie is married to Kim Blair and lives in Bowling Green where Kim teaches and Donnie attends Western Kentucky University. Donnie is majoring in theater arts and has acted in several of Western's plays and projects.

We are proud of our children and our grandchildren. They have been a joy to us and a gift from God. This is not to say that there were not times we did not walk the floor and spend a lot of quality time in prayer on their behalf, but they are ours and we love them.

CHAPTER TWENTY-SIX

HOLLYWOOD AND "PUTTIN' ON THE HITS"

By now each of our children could probably write his/her own book. In selecting material for RUN KENTUCKY RUN, I have found so many dear, precious and funny stories which I have been forced to leave out. It has not been easy to decide which stories would be included and which would be left for another time.

I eventually decided to include some of those events in which LaHoma and I participated in some significant way or were, at least, present when it happened.

Our trip to Hollywood is just such an experience. It all began when Donnie decided to enter the *Puttin' on the Hits* contest in Louisville in September of 1986 while he was still in high school.

There were 55 contestants on the first night of competition. When the contest judges began the eliminations the group was cut to sixteen. Donnie was one of the sixteen chosen to continue.

The 1st, 2nd and 3rd place winners of the contest would be invited to go to California to appear on the *Puttin' on the Hits* television show which is recorded in Hollywood.

On the second night of the competition, the judges selected the top three contestants. Donnie's "lip-sync" of Prince and the Revolutions and their song, "Kiss" had put him in 2nd place. LaHoma and I were so stunned, we sat perfectly still in our seats for a few minutes.

We eventually got to our feet and went to congratulate our son. After hugging him and joining in the excitement, I noticed a young man who looked a great deal like the television personality, Dick Clark. I asked him if he were related to Dick Clark. He said that Dick Clark was his father.

His wife joined the conversation and complimented our son on his fine performance. We found out that Debbie Clark had a couple of Country Western records on the market and she had an aunt who lived in Columbia, Kentucky. We suggested she attend the Lincoln Jamboree in Hodgenville when she came to visit her aunt.

Donnie was given a trophy, records, a tee-shirt with *Puttin' on the Hits* written on it and some other prizes. We went home excited and happy. The local newspapers gave him a great write-up and he was invited to perform twice more.

Weeks passed without hearing from anyone from the *Puttin' on the Hits* television show, but Donnie was confident that he would, sooner or later, hear from the show.

One night, the call came. Donnie was asked about his school schedule and if someone could come with him to California as he was a minor and required a chaperone. A contract arrived.

Because this was a once-in-a-lifetime opportunity (knowing my son as I do, I'm not certain this was a "once-in-a-lifetime" thing at all.), I was allowed to take time from work to make the trip. We would be gone ten days and return on Christmas Eve. It was an all expense paid trip for two, so I paid my own plane fare, but that turned out to be all I had to pay.

THE NEWS ENTERPRISE did a feature story on Donnie. Sharon Johnson from THE ENTERPRISE and the photographer, Mike Douglas, went to the Mall in Elizabethtown where Donnie was performing one Friday night to take pictures.

When Donnie's act was announced that evening, the audience was told about his trip to California. He did a "Prince" and a "Michael Jackson" routine. There was an impressive response to his act. Later, the girls asked for his autograph.

Donnie loved to perform, but he was not quite ready for the "Teen Idol" role. He was gracious to his new fans, but the surprised look on his face made me think he might call on his running skills from earlier years and bolt for the nearest exit at any moment.

When the paper came out, there was a half-page picture of his performance with a caption referring to him as the "Great Pretender".

LaHoma helped Donnie up-grade his costume to better match some of the outfits worn by Prince in his videos. He wore a black leather jacket, vest and bell-bottom pants with big white buttons. Donnie looked good in the outfit.

On the fifteenth of December Aunt Thelma, Donna and MeMommie took Donnie, LaHoma and me to the airport in Louisville. We were not traveling light.

We had enough clothes to last a month. If fact, if we left anything at home at all, it was sheer oversight.

It was Donnie's first plane ride and it had been a long time since I had flown. On the plane we met Paul Hornung, the football Hall of Famer. We asked for his autograph.

At International Airport in Los Angeles, all the contestants were taken to a nearby hotel where it seemed as if the room was full of "lip syncers" and their luggage. There were contestants from all over the United States, Canada and one from Mexico. As we got acquainted, we found the age range ran from 15 to 40 for the contestants.

Soon we were loaded in two buses and driven to Universal City to our hotel, the Sheraton-Universal. It was a beautiful hotel.

We had no more than set our suitcases in our rooms than Donnie wanted to go sight-seeing. We went to Universal Studios where we saw films being made and the sets of some famous movies such as JAWS, BATTLESTAR GALACTICA, THE THREE AMIGOS, the house from PSYCHO, a King Kong exhibit and the parting of the waters featured in EXODUS. We spent the evening visiting with other contestants.

The following day, Donnie went to rehearsals. There were only eighty other contestants as there had already been some eliminations from the original 180.

There were three levels of competition. Round one was a prize of $1,000, round two was a prize of $5,000 and the final round was an additional $25,000 dollars. Six contestants would perform on each show. The winner went to the semi-finals to compete with five more winners. In the grand finals, there would be only five contestants.

After rehearsals, Donnie wanted to go to the Hard Rock Cafe. We ate and looked over the rock memorabilia of Elvis Presley and others. Donnie carved his initials with hundreds of others on the table where we ate.

We called a cab and went shopping. The cabbie gave us his card so we could call for him by name when we wanted to go back to the hotel. In a city of 12,000,000, I thought that was a nice gesture.

The second day Donnie met other contestants and attended more rehearsals. Everything had to be timed down to the second. On this day, he also met Allen Fawsett, the emcee of *Puttin' on the Hits*.

On the third day we took the "Oscar Tour". We saw Hollywood, Beverly Hills, the star's homes, Farmers' Market and Century City.

There were very few on the bus because of the time of year; therefore, the guides spent more time with us personally.

Donnie was impressed with the Dorothy Chandler Pavilion where the Oscars are given. I think LaHoma was more impressed with the Farmers' Market. I was impressed with the Coliseum where the 1984 *Olympics* were held.

At Mann's Chinese Theater and the Hollywood Walk of Fame, Donnie took pictures of the stars of his favorites; Walt Disney and Michael, for example. We all enjoyed the stars' homes. Donnie took as many pictures of us as he could.

On Wednesday night of our first week, Donnie and the other contestants were invited to perform at Womp's Restaurant. The winners would receive prizes and we would all receive a free dinner.

The contestants wore the costumes they would wear on the TV show so it looked a little like Mardi Gras in the restaurant that night.

Rac Clark, whom we had met in Louisville, was there and Allen Fawsett introduced the acts. When Donnie finished his act, Allen Fawsett said, "Not bad for a white kid".

The Everley Brothers act won out of the 40 acts performing. The Everley Brothers act would be on the same TV show as Donnie. There was a drawing and I won a $25.00 gift certificate to eat at Womp's again and a long playing record.

After seeing his competition, we felt good about Donnie's chances in the televised competition. I was impressed with the "Mr. Magic Act", "Lionel Ritchie", "Skeebo" and "Janet Jackson", who was played by Sherry Kelly.

When we first arrived in California, LaHoma had called Mark Greer, who was living in Los Angeles, and Gary Guthrie, who was living in Scottsdale, Arizona. We had written to each of them earlier about our plans and had been invited to spend some time with them.

Mark had played on my church softball and basketball teams. Later, he went to Western Kentucky University where he had been W.K.U.'s mascot "Big Red". Mark made plans for us whenever we had time from Donnie's rehearsals and performances.

While LaHoma, Donnie and a pretty contestant named Debbie Brennan went to see the Johnny Carson show, Mark and I went to a Lakers' game.

The Lakers were playing the Portland Trail Blazers. It was a good game and we had good seats near the front. It was great seeing Magic and Jabar and their coach, Pat Riley, who had been one of "Rupp's Runts" at the University of Kentucky.

Mark planned to come to the taping of Donnie's show on Friday afternoon and invited us on a boat ride on Huntington Bay to see all the homes on the bay decorated for Christmas.

The next morning, Donnie had a final rehearsal at the studio. We went early and watched on a monitor in a special contestants' room.

Donnie would be competing with the Everley Brothers, who had won first prize at Womp's, his friend Janet Jackson, the Jail Birds, the New Edition and the Boston Girls' (Midnight Illusion).

Donnie was the last contestant on the show and had drawn center stage out of the three triangular shaped stages. We were seated in front of his stage. All of the performances were so good. I kept the other contestants' scores and knew Donnie would have to be perfect or one point less to win. When his scores were announced, he had scored 89 out of a possible 90 points.

Allen Fawsett came on stage and announced there had been a tie for second, but the Winner was "Prince and the Revolution. It's the Kid." "The Kid" was the nickname the other contestants had given Donnie.

Donnie was given an envelope with $1,000.00. Allen said, "You can take this back to Hodgenville, Kentucky, with you and come back and compete for $5,000.00 on the next show."

After we returned to the monitor room where the contestants had gathered, I was so thrilled, I had to hug the Boston Girls and Sherry Kelly. All the contestants were so supportive and kind to Donnie.

Mark was waiting for us. We went back to the hotel to change clothes for our trip with Mark and his cute, bubbly wife, Jenni.

The homes around the bay were beautiful. There were many boats riding around. The other boaters would call out "Merry Christmas and a Happy New Year!" It was the coldest night while we were there. Fortunately, we were dressed properly and wore big gloves Mark provided. We rode about thirty miles, then docked at a restaurant for dinner.

After seeing a movie at Mann's Chinese Theater, we walked along the *Pathway to the Stars* then went to the Hollywood Wax Museum. I had to stand and look at Clark Gable and Vivian Leigh for a long time. I had loved GONE WITH THE WIND.

On Sunday we went to a nearby Methodist Church, the Toluca Lake United Methodist Church in North Hollywood. The pastor had gone to school in Lexington. Afterwards, we used my gift certificate to eat dinner at Womp's Restaurant.

On Monday, Donnie would be competing in the semi-finals in the afternoon. Gary Guthrie had called and said he was trying to schedule a flight to L.A. so he and his daughter, Tyler, could come to see Donnie's show.

Donnie's competition in the semi-finals were a PeeWee Herman duo, a Madonna act, a tramp and a Cupid. Donnie performed second in this show. Just as LaHoma and I took our seats, we saw Gary and Tyler three rows back from us. We waved and the show started.

Cupid did his act in a polka dotted diaper with hearts pasted to his chest. He danced around and pretended he was going to shoot a little arrow into the air.

His score beat Donnie's. Donnie was disappointed, but took it fairly well. He had come a long way from his "grumpy bell" days.

After the show, Gary and Tyler took us to eat at Hamburger Hamlet. We caught up on the events of the years since we last saw each other. Gary pointed out Weird Al Yankovic who was kind enough to sign an autograph and pose for a picture with Donnie.

The following day, we went to Disneyland. We saw Captain E-O, the Matterhorn and the Haunted House. There was so much to see. I finally gave out and let them have it. I watched people while LaHoma and Donnie continued to enjoy the exhibits.

Afterwards, we met Mark after work and went to their home and on to Tony Roma Restaurant where we had a wonderful meal. The Greers had made our visit to California a pleasant one.

The final day in California, Donnie and I went to NBC Studios with "the Everley Brothers" and their mom. It was a fun day complete with souvenirs.

While we had seen Rac Clark every day at rehearsals, we had not been able to see his wife, Debbie. We had missed several calls from her at our hotel. Finally I called her back. She had watched both of Donnie's shows over the monitor and was thrilled for him. She had sent us her records and said she would love to sing at the Lincoln Jamboree. We also discussed the possibility of their coming to Kentucky as Grand Marshals of the Lincoln Days Parade.

We saw Dick Clark at the finals that evening, but he left quickly. We found out he had the flu and had to leave because he was so sick.

The final show was very good. The winner was an act called "Houston" who played a double roll, half Lionel Ritchie and half Diana Ross. He was good. I have seen him on TV several times since that night. His career must be doing well.

As we were leaving, Rac Clark came to us and said, "There's someone wanting to see you." He took us to see Debbie. She had been unable to see us because Rac, as producer of the show, did not want contestants to think there was anything dishonest about the show. If the contestants had known Debbie was from Kentucky, they might have felt the results were rigged. Believe me, the show is fair.

We were so glad to see her. We spoke again of her coming to Hodgenville, took more pictures and hoped to see them again soon. We did.

As a member of the *Lincoln Days Committee*, I was fortunate enough to be allowed to invite Rac and Debbie Clark to come to Hodgenville and serve as Grand Marshals of the *Lincoln Days Parade*. We had a good visit with the Clarks and Debbie sang at the Lincoln Jamboree.

After ten days, the contestants had become very close. The young people usually went to the hotel pool and talked and talked. The older people did the same thing elsewhere. We barely went to bed until it was time to board the buses for the trip to the airport. At 1:30 a.m., we were on our way to the airport and home.

There was a lot of hugging and handshakes before we left.

Donna and her family met us in Louisville. Matt, Derek and Bryan each had to carry one of the bags to the car.

When we got home, we found that Diana and Nathan had decorated our house with Prince Memorabilia, black and white ribbons and a sign saying, "Congratulations Donnie and Welcome Home". It was a perfect home coming.

We went to Christmas Eve services at church. Everyone was so happy and even Brett Decker was singing.

When Donnie's shows were aired on channel 41 in Louisville and channel 34 in Campbellsville, we had a family party.

Donnie has talked to several of the contestants on the phone since the trip to Hollywood. He has also received letters from fans who saw the show. He has an impressive scrapbook of the trip.

We enjoyed our first trip to Hollywood; however, if Donnie continues to pursue his current career plans, it may not be our last.

CHAPTER TWENTY-SEVEN

FAITH AND THE SOURCE OF OUR STRENGTH

I have always said that it took three churches to get me saved. I made my profession of faith at a revival at the Cumberland Presbyterian Church in Magnolia when I was a seventh grader. I later joined the Barren Run Baptist Church.

Baptists must be Baptized, but it was the dead of winter which made a baptismal service in the creek below the church an unpleasant consideration for all concerned; hence, we went to the Baptist Church in Hodgenville and used the baptismal pool in the church.

It may have taken three churches, but it only took one Christ and one honest heart.

When LaHoma and I married and moved to Hodgenville, I joined LaHoma at the First Baptist Church in Hodgenville. We knew we wanted a Christian marriage and we wanted to help our children grow to adulthood with Christian roots.

When I joined Brother Ginn was pastor, followed by Dr. H.E. Coker and then Brother Kenneth Hayes. Brother Hayes encouraged me to take a more active part in the church. I joined the bus ministry.

As the Bible says, we went out into the highways and byways with our two new church buses and brought people to church. People began sending their children, some of whom had never been in church before.

Each bus had a driver and two church workers. I drove. Judy Sidebottom taught songs to sing on the way to church and Dale and Mary Gaines Morris rode with us to help with the children.

I felt this ministry was needed and the work was what today's church should be doing. When the church fails to reach out to the young, the church fails.

Some of our church members didn't like the children coming to church without their parents, the slight disturbance they caused from time to time, or something about it. They would do such things as park their cars where the bus was supposed to park and lock the car doors.

I know I am not called to "judge another man's servant", but it was extremely difficult to look at those cars with their locked doors and not think about "offended little ones", "necks" and "mill stones".

I was also on the finance committee, the nursing home ministry, the youth ministry and the jail ministry. I often went with Kenneth Devore to minister in the county jail. Eventually, LaHoma and I became Sunday School teachers to the seventh and eighth grade girls and boys.

I had the boys and she taught the girls. I really had to start studying my Bible seriously then.

In 1972, I was ordained as a deacon with Larry Pursiful, David Stearman, Jack Mitchell, Mike O'Bryant and Sam Stewart. The next year, I was elected chairman of the deacons.

My deacon board chairmanship was probably the most rewarding job I ever had. Serving the Lord's supper, being in charge of meetings, holding prayer meetings, giving my testimony in front of the church, visiting my church families, visiting new people who moved into our neighborhood and serving on all the church committees was so rewarding. Serving the Lord is always rewarding and makes me feel so good.

We began a prayer breakfast on Sunday morning. We also brought in Jimmy Rogers' Gospel Singing Group to sing gospel songs. They were great!

I also coached the men's softball team. We had some good players and some good teams. Later, I coached the boys church league and we won the church league and the League Tournament as well.

In a few years Dr. Isaac McDonald became pastor and we continued to work in the church.

I believe in serving God in every way God leads me to serve. I believe that each of us has a work to accomplish on this earth and that work may be as simple as driving the church bus, but it is a necessary and vital part of God's plan for us and our lives.

We are not all called to be Billy Grahams, but we are all called to do whatever God has planned for us. I would not even want to speculate on what happens if we refuse to do the job God chooses for us to do.

I'm glad to do my part and am infinitely grateful that I know God walks with me throughout everything I do in this life.

God has been good to us. I learned to pray in good times, when in doubt about the future, when we were competing and I prayed for other people. I often wonder how much better the world would be if everyone prayed every day. I feel certain we would see some changes in the world.

My family and I were in church the Sunday Morning someone came to tell me my mother had suffered a stroke and was very ill. I hurried out of church and to my parents' home.

She never recovered fully from the stroke, but lived another five and one half years. She refused to go to the hospital so she did not receive much therapy except what she did herself.

I took for granted Mom loved me and knew I loved her, but I had never told her in words. When I realized I might be losing her I quietly and tearfully told her I loved her.

Dad had been a powerful man. With a little help from us with the wash, grocery shopping and other things, he managed quite well for four years. One day in town, Dad fainted. He was rushed to the hospital.

Daddy had developed hardening of the arteries so that his mind would come and go. When he was better, we brought him home.

With both parents in bed at the same time, we hired someone to stay with them in the daytime and the four of us alternated weeks staying at night.

This was probably the most difficult time of my life. It was a trying time for all of our family. It took about all of the faith, prayer and courage any of us had to get through it.

A year later, Daddy died a week short of his 85th birthday. I had arrived about noon and was helping my sister, Leona, give him a bath. We turned him on his side and noticed a change come over him. He gurgled and died.

Brownfield Funeral Home was in charge of the funeral and they made him look as he had fifteen years earlier. He was buried at Barren Run Cemetery in the community where he was born, lived and raised his family.

Four months later, Mother followed him. She was very sick and I knew the night before that the end was near. I rushed to her house when I got off work to find her much worse. She recognized me and I was glad. Two hours later she died.

Bennett-Bertram Funeral Home handled her funeral and they made her look young, too. I was glad. Mom was buried at Barren Run also.

Another sad day, was the day their farm was sold and their things divided or sold. It had been our home for forty years, then in a few short hours it was gone.

CHAPTER TWENTY-EIGHT

ANOTHER CHALLENGE-ANOTHER RACE

The years have been so full since I began running on that warm Sunday evening in 1979 that I don't think I could have squeezed one more activity into those years if I had turned it sideways and shoved. Nearly thirteen years of wonderful people, challenges and excitement.

I collected enough tee-shirts to make a second quilt of running shirts and the shirts from the *Bluegrass Games* and *Senior Games*. Mrs. Veechie Davis of Green County quilted it for me.

I entered it in the "juried exhibit" in March of 1991 at Hillbilly Heaven in Bardstown called the *Festival of Quilts*. My quilt was selected to be on the WHAS television news coverage of the event.

I have had McCoy's Studio in Hodgenville make a print of my two quilts, side by side. There are 104 shirts in the quilts and they are quite colorful. The name of the print is *Run Kentucky, Run*.

In 1985 and 1986, I chaired the *Railsplitter Run* for Lincoln Days. The committee and I made changes which made me very proud. In fact, I wouldn't mind serving on this committee again. I still have some ideas to make it better.

While I was on the Lincoln Day committee, I was able to get Rac and Debbie Clark to come to Hodgenville as Grand Marshals. Debbie also performed at the Lincoln Jamboree and did so well and looked so beautiful.

In September of 1991 we had our third *Regional Senior Games*. The participation was small.

Henderson, Kentucky, had placed a bid with the Board of the Senior Games to host the *Senior Games*. Becky Russell, Lisa Crooke, Marcia Spreckels and two young men named Darin and Allen made Henderson's bid most attractive by telling us what Henderson had to offer. Henderson was chosen as host city.

The opening ceremony of the 1991 *Games* was held at South Junior High School. Marvin Posey was the emcee and Jimmy Feix was the speaker. Bailey Gore from Murray carried the torch into the stadium and lit the flame.

LaHoma and I videotaped interviews with many of the participants and enjoyed playing them over and over.

When the games began, our LaRue County people began to win immediately. Some of us had to cut short our track and field competitions to get to the swim meets because they were held at the same time.

Fred Shelton and I competed in several swimming events and won almost every time. Other competitions included horse shoes, tennis, table tennis, bowling and archery. In the evening we had a dance.

After church on Sunday morning, the basketball, softball throw, football throw and spin casting events were held. Again, LaRue County people were well represented.

Most of us finished on Sunday except for Fred and Alvis Shelton who stayed through Monday to compete in bowling, shuffle-board and billiards.

LaRue Countians won a total of 45 medals in the games and repeated as State Champions. Fred Shelton led the way with 13 medals. Other medal winners were: Donald Mather (12); Adrian Russell (9); Alvis Shelton (7); Mycia Bell (2); and James Pack (2).

All of the LaRue Countains came home with great expectations for the next *Kentucky State Games*, wherever they were held, and high hopes for the opportunity to qualify for the 1993 *National Senior Games* to be held in Baton Rouge, Louisiana, the Lord willing.

I have always enjoyed attending "big events" such as seeing Northern Dancer, Tim Tam, Tommy Lee and Carry Back win the

Kentucky Derby; the Kentucky Colonels win the professional basketball ABC Championship and so forth. My son must have inherited the tendency.

When the *Hands Across America* project began to be discussed, he told me he wanted me to take him to take part in it. He sent an offering and was given two locations where we could join the group; Wickliffe, Kentucky or Harrison, Ohio.

Donnie chose Harrison, Ohio. We left Hodgenville early on Sunday morning to drive to Harrison. We had been given a code to follow which helped us find our place to stand.

We were early, so we decided to go into town to get something to eat. While there we met a woman putting signs on posts. We talked to her and later met her daughter at the *Hands Across America* headquarters. They invited us to hold hands near them and we were happy to do so.

At 3:00 p.m. on May 25, 1986 we all took each other's hands.

Try to imagine 6 million people holding hands from Los Angeles to New York. There were some gaps, but there was enough electricity to make up for the gaps. Never had so many people come together in a common bond to something like this. We sang three songs while holding hands.

We were in level country so as far as we could see to the right and to the left, people were holding hands. As we sang "We are the World" goose bumps rose up all over me. It really made me proud to be an American.

The huge amount of money taken in by this was to go to the Africa Hunger Foundation. Bringing the people together like this was a big thing, but feeding the hungry was even greater.

In 1987 the Barren Run School had been closed nearly forty years. Bernice Upton and I decided it might be nice to hold a Barren Run School reunion. Bernice and I did most of the organizing at first, then Susan Cruse and Sarah Ellen Howard pitched in and helped us.

We had a pot luck supper and each of us brought our own lawn chairs. George Bertram loaned us a tent from the funeral home to set up in case it rained. It did drizzle a little, so the tent came in handy.

My old friend Parson Money had died the week before the reunion so I would be a pallbearer for his funeral on the afternoon of the reunion.

I went early to help set up tables for the reunion and greeted all the former school students. I never saw so much food in my life. LaHoma and I did get to eat before we left for the funeral. I changed clothes in the car.

Ruth Cruse, a prominent local artist, painted two pictures of the school. One is a front view of the school with the old well pump in front. The other is a back view of the school where she inserted two outdoor toilets below the school to make it look more natural. Both of the pictures look very much as the school looked in the thirties and forties when I attended there. I bought the rear view picture from her.

As I am finishing this book, I have been retired from the Post Office for two years and three months. I haven't had time to be bored yet.

I've made a few lifestyle adjustments. I'm having more time to spend with my grandchildren. I spend some time playing cards with my friends at the Senior Center in Hodgenville. I serve on every committee at church and in the community on which I'm asked to serve. LaHoma volunteers me to help on her committees from time to time. I'm active on the Board of Directors of *Kentucky's Senior Games* and I'm looking forward to the *Bluegrass Games* this summer. I'm writing this book and running for office.

Yes, I am running for office!

I have wanted to run for office most of my life. My mother told me, "Whatever you do, don't get into politics!"

I didn't promise her I wouldn't, but during the years I worked for the federal government, I was prohibited from running for any office.

Now that I'm retired, I am free and ready to serve my community and my state. I'm running for State Representative on the Democratic ticket in Kentucky's 26th district.

When I first started my race, I was mostly interested in programs for senior citizens. As I travel around my district and talk with voters, I find their concerns are becoming my concerns. Issues such as gun control and registration, health insurance for all, right to life, increasing Kentucky's tourism, increasing the appeal of LaRue County for tourism and many others are important and need to reflect the needs and desires of Kentucky's people.

I want to help raise interest in the Kentucky Senior Games and I want to help establish a LaRue County Lincoln Drama.

I am interested in helping to establish legislation to protect abused children and victims of spouse abuse. I want to see Kentucky take a firm stand against violence and abuse of the helpless.

I have been managing my campaign in about the same way I began building my skills as a runner twelve years ago - systematically, methodically and vigorously. I believe in what I'm doing. I believe, win, lose or draw, God is with me and I know my family and friends are behind me. Can anyone ask for more?

If I am elected, I am toying with the idea of getting back in running shape so I can run from LaRue County to Frankfort to my "swearing in" ceremony to demonstrate my enthusiasm and willingness to work hard for the people of my district.

It is about 75 miles from LaRue County's Lincoln Square in the center of Hodgenville to the state capitol in Frankfort. If I run ten miles a day, I can finish the run in a short run on the last day.

I haven't decided for certain if I'm going to attempt this, but I'm already eating a lot of fish, chicken and vegetables. I'm going easy on the sweet potatoes, however. I can already walk up the stairs without wheezing.

Come to think of it, it might be fun if some of my old running buddies wanted to run a mile or two to keep me company along the way. Of course, I have to win the first race to be able to start the second.

If the next sixty-two years are as eventful as the last, I have years of wonderful adventure ahead of me. I look forward to serving my Lord, my community and my state. I look forward to years of fellowship with the friends I have made over the years. I look forward to watching my children's children grow into healthy, committed Christian adults. I look forward to warm, happy years of shared experiences with my beloved wife, LaHoma.

Regardless of what the Lord has for me in my future years, you can rest assured I will give it the best I have to give and will run as hard as I can run.

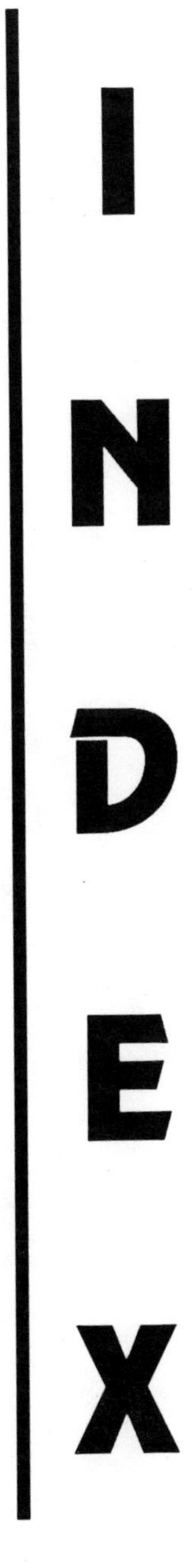
INDEX

Mather Family Records

1. 1944 Donald Mather LaRue Co. 4-H, stripped tobacco contest, 1st
2. 1947 Donald Mather Member, Magnolia basketball team, went to Sweet Sixteen quarterfinals
3. 1948 Donald Mather, All District basketball, Magnolia High School
4. 1955 Donald Mather, Airman of Month, Burtonwood AFB, England
5. 1958 Donald Mather, Ky. State Tobacco Show, 7th place
6. 1969 Sandra Mather, Ky. State Champions, LaRue Co. band
7. 1969 Sandra Mather, Ky. State Champions, majorettes
8. 1978 Donald Mather State Champion, saw-pulling contest
9. 1982 Jo Mather, Girls State, Morehead, Ky.
10. 1984 Donnie Mather, State Champion, 4-H speech contest
11. 1982 Jo Mather, State Girls Softball Tournament, with Charley's Angels
12. 1969 Sandra Mather, Represented Nolin RECC in state beauty pageant
13. 1984 Jo Mather, Represented Nolin RECC in state beauty pageant
14. 1984 Donnie Mather, State competition (Instrumental), 4-H Club
15. 1985 Donnie Mather, State competition (Instrumental), State Fair
16. 1986 Donnie Mather, State competition (Talent Contest), State Fair
17. 1985 Donald Mather, State record running across Kentucky
18. 1986 DonnieMather, State Champion, lip sync contest
19. 1987 DonnieMather, Semi-finals, national lip sync contest
20. 1986 Matt Shelton, State Champion, softball throw, Bluegrass Games
21. 1987 Matt Shelton, State Champion, softball throw, Bluegrass Games
22. 1987 Matt Shelton, State Champion, 100 meter dash, Bluegrass Games
23. 1987 Matt Shelton, State Champion, 200 meter dash, Bluegrass Games
24. 1988 Matt Shelton, State Champion, long jump, Bluegrass Games
25. 1986 Matt Shelton, State Runner-up, 50 meter dash, Bluegrass Games
26. 1986 Matt Shelton, State Runner-up, 100 meter dash, Bluegrass Games
27. 1986 Matt Shelton, State Runner-up, long jump, Bluegrass Games
28. 1986 Matt Shelton, Third place, 200 meter dash, Bluegrass Games
29. 1987 Donald Mather, State torch runner, Bluegrass Games
30. 1988 Donald Mather, State torch runner, Bluegrass Games
31. 1986 Donald Mather, State Runner-up, race walking, Bluegrass Games
32. 1987 Donald Mather, Third place, race walking, Bluegrass Games
33. 1988 Donald Mather, Third place, race walking, Bluegrass Games
34. 1988 Donnie Mather, Third place, Kentucky Speech Tournament
35. 1988 Donnie Mather, Sixth place, Ky. Catholic Forensic League
36. 1988 Donald Mather, Ky. Senior Games Quilt Show, 1st place
37. 1988 Donald Mather, Ky. Senior Games, 800 meter run, 1st place
38. 1988 Donald Mather, Ky. Senior Games, half mile race walk, 1st place
39. 1988 Donald Mather, Ky. Senior Games, one-and-one-half mile race walk, 1st place

40. 1988 Donald Mather, Ky. Senior Games, softball throw, 2nd place
41. 1988 Donald Mather, Ky. Bluegrass Games, 100 meter run, 2nd place
42. 1988 Donald Mather, Ky. Bluegrass Games, 200 meter run, 2nd place
43. 1988 Donald Mather, Ky. Bluegrass Games, high jump, 2nd place
44. 1988 LaHoma Mather, Ky. Health Department talent show, 1st place
45. 1989 Donald Mather, Ky. Senior Games Basketball Free Throw, 1st place
46. 1989 Donald Mather, Ky. Senior Games Basketball Floor shooting, 2nd place
47. 1989 Donnie Mather, Ky. Catholic Forensic Speech League, 1st place
48. 1989 Donnie Mather, Ky. High School Forensic League Speech, 2nd place
49. 1989 Donnie Mather, National Catholic Forensic Speech, lst place and National Philadelphia, PA Champion
50. 1989 Donnie Mather, Best Speech Student, LaRue County High School First Place Award Jr. and Sr. Year High School
51. 1989 Donnie Mather, Quarter - Final participant in National Forensic League Speech tournament - Golden, Colorado.
52. 1989 Matt Shelton, Voted by students as Mr. Magnolia in Magnolia Elementary School
53. 1989 Matt Shelton, Honor Roll Student - Magnolia Elementary School
54. 1989 Donald Mather, 11th place 1500 R/W National Sr. Games, St. Louis, MO
55. 1989 Donald Mather, 9th place 5000 R/W National Sr. Games, St. Louis, MO
56. 1989 Bryan Shelton, Best All Around Athlete, LaRue Co. Mini Olympics
57. 1989-1990 Donald Mather - Board of Directors Ky. Senior Olympic Games
58. 1989 Donald and Lahoma Mather and family 24 charter members of Lincoln Museum
59. 1959-1989 LaHoma Deane Mather Wife, mother, grandmother, mother - in - law, daughter, teacher, clerk - typist, help-mate and corner stone and supporter of all endeavors undertaken by the above, this is my legacy and my niche.
60. 1989 Donald Mather, 1st Place Javelin, Lincoln Trail Regional Games
61. 1989 Donald Mather, 1st Place Softball throw, Lincoln Trail Regional Games
62. 1989 Donald Mather, 1st Place 1 mile race walk, Lincoln Trail Regional Games
63. 1989 Donald Mather, 1st Place 50 meter Freestyle, Lincoln Trail Regional Games
64. 1989 Donald Mather, 1st Place 25 meter Freestyle, Lincoln Trail Regional Games
65. 1989 Donald Mather,1st Place 25 meter Breaststroke Lincoln Trail Regional Games

66. 1989 Donald Mather, 1st Place 25 meter Butterfly, Lincoln Trail Regional Games
67. 1989 Donald Mather, 1st Place 25 meter Butterfly, Kentucky Senior Games
68. 1989 Donald Mather, 1st place 25 meter Breaststroke, Kentucky Senior Games
69. 1989 Donald Mather, 1st Place 25 meter Freestyle, Kentucky Senior Games
70. 1989 Donald Mather, 1st Place - 50 meter Freestyle, Kentucky Senior Games
71. 1989 Donald Mather, 1st Place, Softball Throw, Kentucky Senior Games
72. 1989 Donald Mather, 1st Place, half-mile race walk, Kentucky Senior Games
73. 1989 Donald Mather, 1st Place, 1 mile race walk, Kentucky Senior Games
74. 1989 Donald Mather, 1st Place, Bowling Green Corvette 2 mile walk
75. 1989 Donald Mather, 2nd Place, Cincinnati, Thanksgiving Day Run/Walk
76. 1989 Donald Mather, 1st Place, St. Jude Run/Walk, Chattanooga
77. 1990 Donald Mather, 1st Place, Javelin Throw, Regional Senior Games
78. 1990 Donald Mather, 1st Place, Softball Throw, Regional Senior Games
79. 1990 Donald Mather, 1st Place, Discus Throw, Regional Senior Games
80. 1990 Donald Mather, 1st Place, 25 Meter Free, Style Swim, Regional Senior Games
81. 1990 Donald Mather, 1st Place, 25 Meter Butterfly Swim, Regional Senior Games
82. 1990 Donald Mather, 1st Place, 25 Meter Breast - Stroke, Regional Senior Games
83. 1990 Donald Mather, 1st Place, 50 Meter Free Style, Regional Senior Games
84. 1990 Donald Mather, 2nd Place, Free-Throw Shooting, Regional Senior Games
85. 1990 Donald Mather, 2nd Place, Floor Shooting, Regional Senior Games
86. 1990 Donald Mather, 1st Place, Shot-Put, Kentucky State Senior Games
87. 1990 Donald Mather, 1st Place, Discus, Kentucky State Senior Games
88. 1990 Donald Mather, 3rd Place, Basketball, Three-on-Three, Kentucky State Games
89. 1990 Donald Mather, 2nd Place, Softball Throw, Kentucky State Senior Games
90. 1990 Donald Mather, 2nd Place, 1500 Meter Race/Walk, Kentucky State Senior Games
91. 1990 Donald Mather, 2nd Place, 5000 Meter Race/Walk, Kentucky State Senior Games
92. 1990 Donald Mather, 2nd Place, Javelin Throw, Kentucky State Senior Games

93. 1990 Donald Mather, Elected Secretary of the Kentucky Senior Games Board of Directors
94. 1990 LaRue County Senior Citizens; won First Place in the competitions at the Kentucky State Summer Senior Games at Northern Kentucky University.
95. 1990 Donald Mather, 3rd place, 50 meter Breaststroke, Kentucky Bluegrass Games
96. 1990 Donald Mather, 2nd place, 50 meter Backstroke, Kentucky Bluegrass Games
97. 1990 Donald Mather, 3rd place, 50 meter Free-style, Kentucky Bluegrass Games
98. 1990 Donald Mather, 1st overall, "Walk with the Animals", U.K. campus
99. 1990 Donald Mather, 2nd place, 25 meter Free-style, Kentucky Senior Games
100. '90 Donald Mather, 1st place, 25 meter Backstroke, Kentucky Senior Games
101. '91 Donald Mather, 2nd place, Discus, Kentucky Bluegrass Games
102. '91 Donald Mather, 2nd place, Shot-Put, Kentucky Bluegrass Games
103. '91 Derek Shelton, 1st place, All-Star 10-11 year-old, District Champions
104. '91 Mike Shelton, 1st place, All-Stars District Champions Coach
105. '91 Courtney Decker, 1st place, Heartland Baby Show
106. '91 Donald Mather, 1st place, Discus, Lincoln Trail Senior Games
107. '91 Donald Mather, 1st place, Shot-Put, Lincoln Trail Senior Games
108. '91 Donald Mather, 1st place, 100 meter Run, Lincoln Trail Senior Games
109. '91 Donald Mather, 1st place, 1-mile Race/Walk, Lincoln Trail Senior Games
110. '91 Donald Mather, 2nd place, Shot-Put, Kentucky Senior State Games
111. '91 Donald Mather, 2nd place, Discus, Kentucky Senior State Games
112. '91 Donald Mather, 3rd place, Javelin, Kentucky Senior State Games
113. '91 Donald Mather, 3rd place, 200 meter Run, Kentucky Senior State Games
114. '91 Donald Mather, 3rd place, Softball Throw, Kentucky Senior State Games
115. '91 Donald Mather, 1st place, 25 meter Butterfly, Kentucky Senior State Games
116. '91 Donald Mather, 2nd place, 25 meter Breaststroke, Kentucky Senior State Games
117. '91 Donald Mather, 2nd place, 25 meter Backstroke, Kentucky Senior State Games
118. '91 Donald Mather, 1st place, 50 meter Backstroke, Kentucky Senior State Games
119. '91 Donald Mather, 1st place, 50 meter Flystroke, Kentucky Senior State Games

120. '91 Donald Mather, 2nd place, 50 meter Breaststroke,
Kentucky Senior State Games
121. '91 Donald Mather, 3rd place, 50 meter Freestyle,
Kentucky Senior State Games
122. '79 Donnie Mather, 8, youngest runner, lOK Railsplitter Run
123. '84 Derek Shelton, 3, youngest runner, 1 mile Railsplitter Run
124. '85 Bryan Shelton, 2, youngest runner, 1 mile Railsplitter Run
125. '86 Brett Decker, one-and-one-half, youngest runner,
1 mile Railsplitter Run
126. '87 Brett Decker, two-and-one-half, youngest runner,
1 mile Railsplitter Run
127. '91 Michelle Decker, 3, youngest runner, 1 mile Railsplitter Run
128. '91 Matt Shelton, 10-0 member, LaRue County High School
undefeated football team
129. '91 LaRue County Senior Citizens, 1st place,
Kentucky Senior Games, Henderson, KY
130. '92 Donnie Mather, The Russel H. Miller Theater Award
Western Kentucky University
131. '92 Matt Shelton, All-State, KY High School Athletic Academic
Association, L.C.H.C.
132. '92 Donald Mather, Democratic Candidate for State Representative,
26th District
133. '92 Donald Mather, Author, RUN KENTUCKY RUN
Invited to Kentucky Book Fair & KY Department for Libraries and
Archives, Frankfort, KY
134. 1972-73, Donald Mather, Chairman, Board of Deacons,
First Baptist Church
135. 1976, Donald Mather, President of PTA,
Hodgenville Elementary School
136. 1984, Jo Mather, President, Band of Hawks,
LaRue County High School
137. 1985-86, Donald Mather, Race Chairman, Railsplitter Run/Walk
138. 1984-86, Donald Mather, Board of Directors, Lincoln Days Festival
139. 1988, Donnie Mather, President, Band of Hawks,
LaRue County High School
140. 1988, Donnie Mather, Editor, School Annual,
LaRue County High School
141. 1989, Donald Mather, Chairman, Lincoln Museum Walkathon
142. 1989, Donald Mather, Royal Ambassador Director,
First Baptist Church
143. 1991-92, Donald Mather, Brotherhood Director, First Baptist Church
144. 1991-92, LaHoma Mather, Board of Directors, Lincoln Dayd Festival
145. 1989, Donald Mather, Co-Chairman, Barren Run School,
40 Year Reunion

10,000 METERS
RAILSPLITTER RUN WINNERS

	MALE		FEMALE
1979	Buddy Harpool	1979	Mary Crum Spalding
1980	Buddy Harpool	1980	Susan Leopold
1981	Bruce Hacker	1981	Pam Ruby
1982	Buddy Harpool	1982	Angela Murphy
1983	Buddy Harpool	1983	Rhonda Powell
1984	Buddy Harpool	1984	Tracy Gilliam
1985	Buddy Harpool	1985	Diane Tromley
1986	Buddy Harpool	1986	Carrie Tanner
1987	Swag Hartel*	1987	Mary Lou Feese
1988	Brian Hacker	1988	Joan Wilson
1989	Swag Hartel	1989	Kathi Blankenship
1990	Dennis Jessie	1990	Laura Hubbard*
1991	Alan Clinton	1991	Amy Viers

10,000 METERS - RECORD TIME

* Male: Swag Hartel, 1987 - :30:57
*Female: Laura Hubbard, 1990 - :39:20

Attending the 1989 Barren Run Elementary School Reunion, which closed in 1949, are as follows:

Ruby Rock; Oma Hornback Routt; Marlin Carroll; Susie Tucker Young; Ella Hornback Bell; Robert Hornback; Leroy & Ivy Routt; Clyde & Ivy Corum; Mildred & Otis Brooks; Mabel & Morrison Hubbard; Carl & Irene Routt; Maude Toohey; Chester Polly; Vernon & Bea Thurmon; R.J. & Sue Rock; Harold & Margie Routt; Walter & Joyce Rock; Dorothy Heath Cruse; Frankie Heath Bell; Eugenia Hornback; Mary Evelyn Milby; Alva Martin Tharp; Arvil Catlett; Robert & Barbara Routt; Doris Catlett; Hilda Walsh Edlin; Geneva Knight Walters; Maude Routt Lawless; Louise Tharp; Sara Ellen Howard; Maryann & Roger Edlin; Dora Lee Renfrow; Evelyn Corum Dunn; Ralph & Evelyn Catlett; Kaye Colette; Chester & Carrie Rock; Clavis & Lucille Bennett; Madison & Mary Mather; O'Dell & Opal Wells; Cecil & Voda Blankenship; Susan & Chet Cruse; Donald & LaHoma Mather; Leon Bryant; W.A. "Doc" Rock; Norman Rock; Webb Hazle; Theo, Jr. & Leona Terry & Brother Norman Douglas; Bernice Routt Upton; Raymond & Gladys Catlett; Clyde & Ann Catlett; Bernice Walters; George Grace; Cliff Bresh; Juanita Rock Bird; James B. & Eva Routt; James H. & Marie Catlett; Bud & Evelyn Catlett; Charles "Red" Hazle; George & Goldie Burba; Harold & Gladys Mairer; Jean & Bud Rock; Tony & Edna Oveson; Walter & Frankie Orrender; Edith Routt & Calvin West; Janie West; Harding & Mary Lois Catlett; Johnny Catlett; Francis Benningfield; Gibson & Josephine Heath Daugherty; Alice Fay Brown; George T. Burba, Jr.; Ollie J. Catlett, Jr.; Jesse & Sarah Massie; Gertrude Brackett; Marvin Routt; Lorena & Adrian Russell; Lee Ann Yarbrough; W.T. Hazle; Laverne Rock Willian; Anna Mae Tharpe; Emmett & Mae Alma Wright; Linda Daniels; Susie & Garnett Priddy; Calvin Thurman; J.W. & Mildred Routt; David Catlett; Hillary Tucker; Juanita Tucker; Sue Ann Tharp; and Sue Ann Breeze.

The oldest in attendance was Ella Hornback Bell, 87.

Edith Routt West travelled the longest distance - 600 miles from Metairie, LA.

Johnny Catlett served as Master of Ceremonies.

A Complete List of Events Donald Mather Competed In *After He Turned 50 Years of Age*

1. RAILSPLITTER RUN (8 times) - Hodgenville, KY
2. RUN ACROSS L.A. - Los Angeles, CA
3. NATIONAL SENIOR OLYMPICS - St. Louis, MO
4. KENTUCKY BLUEGRASS GAMES (7 times) - Lexington, KY
5. KENTUCKY DERBY MINI-MARATHON (5 times) - LOUISVILLE, KY
6. WENDY'S CLASSIC (5 times) - Bowling Green, KY
7. METRO-MARATHON (2 times) - Louisville, KY
8. LEXINGTON MARATHON
9. BLUEGRASS 10,000 METER - Lexington, KY
10. THANKSGIVING DAY RUN (2 times) - Covington - Cincinnati
11. HOBART BEECH VFW RUN (3 times) - New Albany, IN
12. STEAMBOAT DAYS (3 times) - Jeffersonville, IN
13. KENTUCKY SENIOR GAMES - Bowling Green, KY
14. KENTUCKY SENIOR GAMES - Northern Kentucky University
15. KENTUCKY SENIOR GAMES - Henderson, KY
16. KENTUCKY SENIOR GAMES (3 times) - Lexington, KY
17. KENTUCKY SENIOR GAMES - Owensboro, KY
18. GOLDEN ARMOR (6 times) - Radcliff, KY
19. LIONS CLUB - North Hardin High School
20. MAGNOLIA DAYS - Magnolia, KY
21. MAYFEST - Hardinsburg, KY
22. CANNED GOODS RUN - Louisville, KY
23. LEPERCHAUN RUN - Louisville, KY
24. CHEROKEE CLUB - Louisville, KY
25. RIVER BANK RUN (3 times) - Louisville, KY
26. OLD LOUISVILLE RUN
27. FORD RANGER RUN (2 times) - Louisville, KY
28. MIDNIGHT CHASE - Louisville, KY
30. CANDLELIGHT RUN (2 times) - Louisville, KY
31. MARENGO CLASSIC - IN
32. DICK LUGAR RUN - New Albany, IN
33. GREEN RIVER CLASSIC - Campbellsville, KY
34. COW DAYS (6 times) - Greensburg, KY
35. STAN COTTRILL RUN (2 times) - Munfordville, KY
36. TOBACCO FESTIVAL - Shelbyville, KY
37. LIFE BEGINS AT 40 (5 times) - Louisville, KY
38. BELVEDERE to SOUTH RADCLIFF (1 time)
39. SENECA SUNRISE - Louisville, KY
40. OLD KENTUCKY HOME (5 times) - Bardstown, KY

41. NIBROC RUN (5 times) - Corbin, KY
42. WILDERNESS ROAD - London, KY
43. SPRING FLING (2 times) - St. Catherine College
44. MOONSHINER 15K - Springfield, KY
45. YMCA RUN (8 times) - Glasgow, KY
46. TUMBLEWEED CHASE (3 times) - Louisville, KY
47. CITY RUN - Louisville, KY
48. RUN FOR THE ARTS - Louisville, KY
49. TANK TRAIL (5 times) - Fort Knox, KY
50. SALEM ROAD RACE (2 times) - Salem, IN
51. WHITE MILLS DAY (4 times) - White Mills, KY
52. DOWN HOME DAYS (2 times) - Big Springs, KY
53. RURITAN RUN (4 times) - Upton, KY
54. SONORA DAYS - Sonora, KY
55. JEFFERSONVILLE 5K - IN
56. BANANA FESTIVAL - Fulton, KY
57. PIONEER DAYS (4 times) - Harrodsburg, KY
58. MILITARY CHALLENGE - Louisville, KY
59. SPENCER COUNTY DAYS - Taylorsville, KY
60. BANKER'S RUN - Munfordville, KY
61. HANGOVER CLASSIC - Louisville, KY
62. GOLD RUSH (5 times) - Fort Knox, KY
63. BULLION BURT - Fort Knox, KY
64. SCOTTSBURG CHASE - IN
65. SCOTT-BOURBON CLASSIC (2 times) - Paris to Georgetown, KY
66. SOUTH INDIANA CLASSIC (2 times) - Floyd Knobs, IN
67. GREENTREE MALL CLASSIC - Clarksville, IN
68. ONE MILLION DOLLAR RUN - Bowling Green, KY
69. BIG RED RUN - Bowling Green, KY
70. RUN FOR YOUR HEALTH - Bowling Green, KY
71. CATFISH RUN - Morgantown, KY
72. OLDHAM COUNTY DAYS - Oldham County High School
73. TOBACCO FESTIVAL - Lancaster, KY
74. BELL PEPPER RUN - Columbia, KY
75. BIG MAN RUN - Louisville, KY
76. G.A.P. RUN - Louisville, KY
77. WHAS CRUSADE RUN - Louisville, KY
78. RUN FOR SIGHT (2 times) - Brandenburg, KY
79. QUEEN CITY RUN - Clarksville, TN
80. HERALD NEWS RUN - Lincoln Park
81. LITTLE RIVER RUN - Hopkinsville, KY
82. PENNYRILE SENIOR GAMES - Hopkinsville, KY
83. HEARTLAND RUN (3 times) - Elizabethtown, KY

84. DANIEL BOONE RUN (2 times) - Winchester, KY
85. RUN WITH THE STARS (2 times) - Bowling Green, KY
86. BURGIN BEGINNING - Burgin, KY
87. DOG DAYS - Elizabethtown, KY
88. FIDDLERS RUN - Leitchfield, KY
89. BLUEGRASS RUN - Rosine, KY
90. STATE PARK RUN (2 times) - Barren River Lodge, KY
91. HARDYVILLE DAYS - Hardyville, KY
92. APPLE FESTIVAL - Liberty, KY
93. GREAT PUMPKIN RUN - Paducah, KY
94. M.A.D.D. RUN - Radcliff, KY
95. MUDD RUN - Shepherdsville, KY
96. WAVE 970 RUN - Louisville, KY
97. UK/UL RUN/WALK - Louisville, KY
98. GALLATIN DAYS - Gallatin, TN
99. HILLBILLY DAYS - Pikeville, KY
100. EARTH RUN (2 times) - Mammoth Cave, KY
101. JACKSONIAN RUN - Scottsville, KY
102. RUN WITH CHRIST (2 times) - Scottsville, KY
103. POKE SALLET RUN - Harlan, KY
104. FIRECRACKER RUN - Sebree, KY
105. RIVER RUN - Maysville, KY
106. GREEN COUNTY TRIATHALON - Greensburg, KY
107. HONEYBEE RUN - Jackson, KY
108. HARDWOOD FESTIVAL - Morehead, KY
109. TOBACCO FESTIVAL - Carrollton, KY
110. APPLE FESTIVAL - Paintsville, KY
111. OLD FASHION DAYS - Greenup, KY
112. VALENTINE RUN - Lexington, KY
113. WALK FOR CHRIST (3 times) - Glasgow, KY
114. BUD'S LAKE - Hodgenville, KY
115. SCOTTISH HIGHLAND GAMES - Glasgow, KY
116. CAPITAL EXPO - Frankfort, KY
117. TORCH RUN (2 times) - Frankfort to Lexington
118. CHARLESTOWN CHALLENGE - Charlestown, IN
119. GASLIGHT RUN - Louisville, KY
120. FAIRDALE WALK - Fairdale, KY
121. RAMBLE FOR THE ROSES - Louisville, KY
122. STRAWBERRY FESTIVAL - Starlight, IN
123. CHAMPIONS ON THE MOVE - Bellarmine College
124. WALK FOR TOTS - Columbia, KY
125. WALK AMERICA - Elizabethtown, KY
126. HANDS ACROSS AMERICA - Harrison, OH

127. HILL RUN - Corydon, IN
128. CORVETTE RUN - Bowling Green, KY
129. APRIL SHOWERS - Bowling Green, KY
130. RUN WITH ANIMALS - Lexington, KY
131. FROGTOWN HOP - Louisville, KY
132. GARDEN SPOT TROT - Franklin, KY
133. KAREN LAWRENCE RUN - Chattanooga, TN
134. LINCOLN TRAIL SENIOR GAMES (3 times) - Hodgenville, KY
135. SUPER CITY WALK - Churchill Downs
136. LINCOLN MUSEUM WALKATHON - Hodgenville, KY
137. LAKE FESTIVAL - Kentucky Lake State Park
138. FEELING GOOD RUN - Campbellsville, KY
139. TURKEY TROT (5 times) - Glasgow, KY
140. IROQUOIS HILL CLIMB - Louisville, KY
141. RUN WITH THE HOGS - Louisville, KY
142. FOOTHILLS RUN - Albany, KY
143. ICECYCLE RUN - Fort Knox, KY
144. JINGLEBELL CLASSIC - Louisville, KY
145. POWDER KEG - Clarksville, IN
146. SPRING RUN - Mount Washington, KY

Mail orders with checks payable to:

DONALD MATHER
379 McDowell Road
Hodgenville, KY 42748
502-358-4210

Please mail

Run Kentucky Run

to:

Name: ______________________________

Address: ______________________________

City: ______________________________

State: ______________________________

Zip: ______________________________

Phone: ______________________________

PRICE PER BOOK: $15.95

Times (x) number of books: ______________

Plus Sales Tax *(KY residents add .96 per book)*: ______________

Plus $3.00 S & H (x) number of books: ______________

TOTAL PRICE: $ ______________

- ***Cashier's Checks & Money Orders are mailed within ONE week.***
- ***Allow 4 to 5 weeks for clearance of personal checks.***